CONSTRUCTING CHARISMA

Constructing Charisma

Celebrity, Fame, and Power
in Nineteenth-Century Europe

Edited by

EDWARD BERENSON and EVA GILOI

Berghahn Books
New York • Oxford

First published in 2010 by

Berghahn Books

www.berghahnbooks.com

©2010, 2013 Edward Berenson and Eva Giloi
First paperback edition published in 2013

Library of Congress Cataloging-in-Publication Data

Constructing charisma : celebrity, fame, and power in nineteenth-century Europe / edited
by Edward Berenson and Eva Giloi.
  p. cm.
  Includes bibliographical references and index.
  ISBN 978-1-84545-694-8 (hbk.)--ISBN 978-0-85745-815-5 (pbk.)
  1. Mass media—History—19th century. 2. Europe—History—1789–1900.
I. Berenson, Edward, 1949– II. Giloi, Eva.
  P90.C66 2010
  302.2'34—dc22

                                                                    2010010760

British Library Cataloguing in Publication Data

A catalogue record for this book is available from the British Library

Printed in the United States on acid-free paper.

ISBN: 978-0-85745-815-5 Paperback   ISBN: 978-0-85745-839-1 Retail eBook

∿: CONTENTS :∿

❖ ILLUSTRATIONS ❖

~:~

Introduction

EDWARD BERENSON AND EVA GILOI

Fame, charisma, celebrity—we use these three words commonly nowadays and often interchangeably. We grant celebrity status to prominent actors and actresses, sports figures, television personalities, and political leaders, some of whom we call famous and charismatic as well. As a former president of the United States, Bill Clinton is famous. He also enjoys celebrity status thanks to myriad magazine covers sporting his easily recognized face. And those with fond memories of his presidency tend to consider him charismatic as well. Princess Diana shared these attributes, only much more so, her apparent charisma enhanced by the whiff of royalty, the movie-star glamour, her millions of adoring fans.[1]

So, are celebrity, fame, and charisma one and the same? If they are, why the three different terms? If not, how do they differ?

Such questions first surfaced not in the twentieth century, as we often think, but in the nineteenth century, that great age of hero-worship when it became common to worry that individuals could be celebrated for no good reason.[2] Though fame, and to a lesser extent charisma, existed in ancient and medieval times, the primitive state of communications kept the number and reach of those who enjoyed them within narrow bounds. Not until the invention of printing was fame untethered from its characteristically short leash. And even then, widespread illiteracy limited the number of famous people and the size of their audience. In the 1790s, Edmund Burke thought the reading public no more than 5 percent of the population.[3]

At about this time, copper engravings and lithographs expanded the audience for famous people, making certain faces widely recognizable across Britain, the US, and the Continent: Napoleon Bonaparte, Benjamin Franklin, Thomas Paine, Maximilien Robespierre. Still, communication remained slow, circulation low, and illiteracy high. The famous and celebrated constituted a tiny elite.

Their numbers began to grow during the first half of the nineteenth century, when newspaper readership, popular lithography, photography, and other media gradually but steadily expanded, as did a general democratization of culture and politics in the post-French revolutionary era. But only after 1850, with the emergence of the first mass media, did charisma, celebrity, and fame explode into the kind of phenomena we know today. Most prominent among the new media stood the cheap, industrially produced newspapers, epitomized by France's *Petit journal*, founded in 1863. The four-page paper sold for one penny a copy and appealed to newly literate and relatively unsophisticated readers. By the early 1870s, its circulation reached a half-million copies a day.

With the advent of mass newspapers, the "celebrity" became a common cultural type, constituting a new and powerful social force. Thanks to ever more complex technologies—steam-powered rotary presses, automatic paper folders, linotype machines, railroads, telegraphs, and soon telephones, and innovative photographic techniques—ordinary people could identify with the famous; feel that they knew the hero, leader, or "star"; and imagine that public figures belonged to their private lives. In turn, cultural figures, political outsiders, and imperial adventurers gained influence over followers who sought new agents of authority to orient them in an uncertain world. Increasingly, established leaders—kings, presidents, clergymen—had to operate within the new culture of celebrity, which forced them to compete for the recognition they had long taken for granted.

In the essays that follow, we trace these developments, all too familiar in our own celebrity-obsessed present, back to the nineteenth century. Our contributors show the extent to which the celebrity culture owed its origins to Europe and not just the United States. In the process, we examine how fame, celebrity, and charisma functioned, what cultural needs they fulfilled, how they were produced—even self-consciously constructed—and what kinds of political and social authority they conferred.

Charisma, Fame, Celebrity

Our first task is to untangle the three terms—to outline how celebrity, fame, and charisma differ and how they overlap. Perhaps some contemporary examples will help. Barbara Walters is certainly a celebrity and one of the most famous women in the United States. But does she count as charismatic? Or take Angela Merkel, the German Chancellor. She is famous, even a celebrity, and Germans found her competent and believable enough to elect her as their head of state. But it is unlikely that the bulk of her voters supported her because she possesses a certain something, an extraordinariness, as Max Weber would have put it, known as charisma. We might say the same of Britain's Gordon Brown or Spain's José Luis Rodríguez Zapatero.

As these examples suggest, charisma and fame are not equivalent terms. Charisma points to a quality that Merkel lacks, but that belongs, for example, to Hugo Chavez and Nelson Mandela. All three of these political figures possess (or possessed) power, but for Merkel, that power derives almost entirely from institutions and the law. It is a largely rational, identifiable power whose origins and nature can be readily explained. Chavez and Mandela enjoy[ed] legal, institutional power, but a significant part of their authority comes from another realm. It is, as Weber termed it, a "residual" form of authority whose origins lie outside tradition, on the one hand, and institutions and law, on the other. This residual authority seems a kind of gift, an inexplicable, indefinable force that makes those who possess it different from other people, magical in a way, and all the more powerful for the impossibility of putting one's finger on its source.

This third form of authority, or charisma, has ancient roots. As Stephen Minta shows (chapter 7 below), the term *ka-ri-si-jo* first appeared in the second millennium BCE. It evoked the notion of "grace" or "favor" that foreshadowed its appearance in Homer as *Kharis*, a gift from the gods, and in the Apostle Paul as *kharisma*, God's gift of eternal life. The word thus entered the Greco-Roman vocabulary as a religious term and retained its association with the divine until the early twentieth century, when Max Weber pressed it into secular, sociological use.[4] But even for Weber, charisma did not entirely lose its religious connotations. "The term 'charisma,'" Weber wrote, refers "to a certain quality of an individual personality by virtue of which he is considered extraordinary and treated as endowed with supernatural, superhuman, or at least specifically exceptional powers or qualities. These are ... not accessible to the ordinary person, but are regarded as of divine origin or as exemplary, and on the basis of them the individual concerned is treated as a leader."[5]

The last part of the quotation is key—the extraordinary person's treatment "as a leader." Because charisma resides in certain extraordinary individuals, Weber's commentators have often thought it to be mainly a psychological phenomenon, a secularized version of its original biblical usage as a gift of private grace from God. But for Weber, charisma required a relationship between the leader and his flock,[6] and the best analysts have rightly understood Weberian charisma as at once psychological and sociological, as being both a personal quality and a social phenomenon.[7]

On the personal level, the charismatic leader is endowed with a sense of mission; he believes in his divine vocation earlier and more fervently than anyone else. This sense of mission can be revolutionary or stabilizing, depending on the social circumstances. In his earliest writings on the subject, Weber maintained that charismatic figures could be insiders or outsiders; they could be either established figures who give society legitimacy and strength or emergent idols who transform it into something new.[8] His *Sociology of Religion* argues that in primitive societies, both magicians and prophets could have charisma. The former shored up the existing order by solving problems that appeared to threaten it, while the latter pointed to new forms of existence by championing alternative systems of belief. Both magicians and prophets could be charismatic because they embodied extraordinary powers and a supernatural ability to satisfy the needs of those they influenced and led.[9]

If, in primitive societies, charisma could guarantee order and stability, in more complex ones with established legal systems, Weber found charisma to be a revolutionary force. Without charisma, it would be difficult, the sociologist said, to explain any dramatic or revolutionary change and impossible to account for the emergence of leaders or exemplars from outside traditional or bureaucratic circles of rule. Above all, charismatic individuals and the devotion they evoke "revolutionize men from within." They "effect a subjective or *internal* reorientation born out of suffering, conflicts, or enthusiasm." By changing the people who grant him authority, the charismatic leader "shapes material and social conditions according to [his] revolutionary will."[10]

Crucial as charismatic leaders are, their followers also have a defining role to play; charisma is both a social and an individual trait. People with charisma possess extraordinary personal qualities, but Weber insisted that those qualities had to be validated by a group or community and that validation would come only if the charismatic individual regularly provided evidence of his attributes. To do so, he had to pass tests, endure trials, or show success, however success was defined. "Recognition on the part of those subject to authority," Weber wrote, "is decisive for the validity of charisma… If proof and success elude the leader for long … it is likely that his charismatic authority will disappear."[11]

Even if charisma evaporates, celebrity or fame can persist, thus highlighting the difference between these terms. As Edward Berenson shows in the case of Henry Morton Stanley, the excess violence associated with the explorer's expeditions deprived him of charismatic authority—his ability to inspire people to imitation and action—but not his celebrity status. And in the long run, his fame has endured. It has lasted not just because everyone remembers the greeting, "Dr. Livingstone, I presume?" but because an endless stream of biographies and other writings have kept his memory—and thus his fame—alive.[12]

Like charisma, fame has ancient roots. It comes, as Minta shows, from the Greek and Latin, "to speak." Fame applied to those "much talked about." The voices in question could be those of the gods, but for the most part, it was human beings who talked the talk of fame. If charisma was a gift from God, fame had its feet on the ground. As our contributor Leo Braudy suggests in his seminal book, *The Frenzy of Renown*, fame is a worldly phenomenon. Alexander (the Great), whom Braudy dubs the world's first famous person, achieved this distinction by creating a mythical version of himself, an image that would make people talk. He did so by comparing his own exploits to the heroic adventures of Greek legend, those of Achilles, Dionysus, Perseus, and Hercules.[13] Alexander took supernatural beings as his models, but his fame originated in the reputation created in the here and now.

Later, in Roman times, fame "was defined by action in public for the good or ostensible good of the state."[14] Those seen as taking such action, as contributing to Rome's historical mission, could achieve renown. The individuals in question took steps to identify themselves with the good of the state, but to a large extent, it was poets and historians who endowed public men with fame. The pivotal role these writers played made them potentially as important as those they wrote about. "Horace praises Augustus," says Braudy, "but also writes that his own poetry will last longer than even the Pyramids. Ultimately, he implies, the fame of Augustus depends on the quality of Horace's verse."[15] It depends, that is, on Horace's ability to inspire awe and reverence for the emperor, on his success in making Augustus a man "much talked about." Once that talk fades away, the poet's artful words remain. The poet's fame, a "literary fame," might not get lost in time. Renown was defined "not by the things of the world but by its intangible ability to transcend them."[16] In this sense, fame could shade into charisma, as the writer's timeless words seemed to enjoy the gift of eternal life.

Despite this apparent blurring of the two terms, charisma and fame remain distinct. If timeless texts can possess a certain charisma, it is of a secondary kind, not unlike the traces of extraordinariness that endure after the charismatic individual is gone. Weber speaks of the "depersonalization of charisma," in which a political office or bureaucratic structure retains something of the great man's aura even as the original charismatic authority fades away.[17] With the creation of hereditary nobilities and inherited kingship, heirs and disciples seek to keep charisma's memory alive, to preserve the original extraordinary acts of the charismatic forefather by institutionalizing them in orders, castes, and offices. These institutions confer legitimacy on those who hold them, as do certain sacred or iconic texts and symbols said to embody the original charismatic deeds. Such "charismatic legitimation," as Weber calls it, bolsters a privileged elite and justifies its economic privileges. But by serving this elite, the institutionalization of charisma is "radically opposed" to "genuine charisma," a form of "legitimation [based on] heroism and revelation" rather than "enacted or traditional order [and] acquired rights."[18] For this reason, Weber writes, "It is the fate of charisma to recede before the powers of tradition or of rational association after it has entered the permanent structure of social action."[19]

Genuine charismatic authority, Weber's "residual" form of *Herrschaft* derived neither from law nor tradition, seems to require the presence, or the illusion of presence, of the extraordinary individual. Without such presence, the emotional bond between leader and followers lying at the heart of charisma cannot take shape. That presence can be illusory, the result of an artificial intimacy created by mass media. But followers must believe the leader is available to them; they must think they know him and he potentially knows them.[20] Fame, by contrast, can exist and persist without such a presence. To be famous, one must be the object of discussion, but there need be no relationship between the famous person and his or her audience. In fact, as Braudy makes clear, absence and inaccessibility can enhance the fame of an individual who appears so sure of himself as to be uninterested in public acclaim.[21]

If charisma and fame have ancient roots, celebrity is largely new. It is surely no coincidence that "celebrity," an ephemeral version of fame, is tightly connected to the mass press born in the 1860s, a medium whose raison d'etre was to bury yesterday's events under those of today. Thanks to the unprecedented speed of steam-driven presses and the news gathering prowess of telegraphs, railroads, and steamships, journalists could quickly compose and transmit their stories. Materials written in the evening could be reproduced hundreds of thousands, even millions, of times by early the following day. As newsprint dropped in price and print-runs accelerated, editors became insatiable for fresh material, for copy that would appeal to a huge variety of people. After the mid nineteenth century, readers who had once saved newspapers for future reference now found themselves inundated by penny papers as ephemeral as the stories they published. If the "news" made yesterday old, so too would it shrink the lifespan of fame. Individuals, like events, found themselves celebrated and then discarded along with the papers in which they appeared.

Such was not, of course, inevitably the case, since some events and people commanded longstanding and regular attention. This is why celebrity did not replace fame, but coexisted with it—sometimes in the same person. Sarah Bernhardt was a celebrity because the newspapers focused excessively on her when she opened a new play, or as Mary Louise Roberts shows, when she did something eccentric and made a spectacle of herself. She also enjoyed fame as France's most successful actress of the *fin de siècle*, a star whose accomplishments in the theater overshadowed those of almost everyone else. And as both Kenneth Silver and Venita Datta suggest, Bernhardt at times achieved charismatic status as well. Though no revolutionary figure, Bernhardt helped shape French society at two crucial historical points. After the Dreyfus Affair (1894–99), an event so divisive as to create an incipient civil war, the actress assumed roles both on stage and in her public persona that helped calm political passions and bring the French people together. She produced a similar charismatic effect during the First World War by visiting the front and shoring up the nation's wounded morale through a series of dramatic public interventions. Here we find a reassessment of Weber's stricter views, which denied that purely cultural performers—musicians, actors, artists—could move followers to political action. Instead, Weber's charismatic "ideal types" were Bolshevik revolutionaries and populist demagogues such as Karl Lueger, the anti-Semitic mayor of *fin-de-siècle* Vienna.[22]

Unlike Lenin and Lueger, who divided their compatriots, often deliberately, and operated in overtly political realms, Bernhardt, perhaps inadvertently, helped bring a polarized French nation together. She did so on the basis of staged performances rather than direct political acts. Her large following, whose members hailed both from the right and the left, projected political significance onto her, whether she sought it or not. In her roles as Joan of Arc (1890, 1909) and the Duke of Reichstadt, Napoleon's Austrian-reared son, the actress appeared to merge into the figures of national legend she played. In the process, she became a national legend herself.[23] Bernhardt starred as Reichstadt in Edmond Rostand's *L'Aiglon* (1900), produced just three years after the playwright's wildly successful *Cyrano de Bergerac*, whose opening had nearly coincided with the publication of Émile Zola's *J'Accuse* in January 1898. In that highly fraught moment, when Zola's famous polemic made the Dreyfus case an *affaire*, Rostand's piece brought the country's warring Dreyfusard and anti-Dreyfusard camps into the same theater at the same time, rallying them together, as least momentarily, around the national legend of Cyrano. As integrating figures, Bernhardt and Rostand demobilized the French public at a moment of crisis, fostering, as it were, a politics of de-politicization. Reformulating Weber's assertion that charismatic leaders move their followers to political action in dramatic ways, we might say that Bernhardt and Rostand moved their fans to *inaction*; they soothed political passions, but to equally dramatic effect.

If the case of Bernhardt makes it difficult to distinguish celebrity from charisma, star power from genuine power, it is because since the mid nineteenth century, and perhaps before, it became increasingly common to possess both celebrity status and charisma, sometimes simultaneously. As Berenson shows, Stanley and his fellow explorer Pierre Savorgnan de Brazza became celebrities thanks to extensive, even obsessive, coverage of their African journeys and their "triumphal" homecomings once safely returned to their native lands. That coverage drew enormous crowds, which themselves became the subjects of journalistic reports. Individuals fascinated by Stanley and Brazza learned that many of their countrymen and women shared their interest, and that knowledge helped turn those crowds into a loyal following whose members invested the two explorers with charisma. Their devoted, emotionally engaged flocks gave them substantial political clout and validated their charisma, both in the eyes of elected leaders and ordinary citizens, who longed for people in whom they could have faith. As a result, both men gained the power to reshape their countries' political debate over empire and influence foreign policy in significant ways. They achieved such power despite their status as political outsiders and often against the wishes of the legitimate leaders they supposedly served.

If Stanley's charisma ultimately faded into celebrity, Bernhardt followed the opposite path: her celebrity status turned into genuine charismatic appeal. Did other cultural figures do the same? As Minta's chapter shows, Lord Byron always envisioned himself as a famous political orator or statesman, and not primarily a poet. He worried that his reputation as a dangerous, rogue writer might harm a potential political career, though such apprehensions did nothing to divert him from the Greek War of Independence and a directly political course. Rather than dilute his political effect, his great celebrity as poet and renegade Romantic drew a broad European following to his chosen cause, turning literary fame into political clout—at least in Greece.

Given Byron's status as both a cultural and a political figure, it is unclear whether Weber would have considered him charismatic. Minta clearly does, but for reasons at odds with the sociologist's views. If Weber defined charisma as the (successful) ability to lead men in a transformative way, Minta locates the source of Byron's charisma in the perceived failures of his personal life, in the sexual transgressions that made him seem dangerous and magnetic. Repelling some compatriots, attracting others, Byron's transgressions left few who followed his career emotionally uninvolved. The poet may have found fame in Greece for his political stance, but in Britain, his tumultuous personal life overshadowed any political influence he might have enjoyed. Minta thus leaves Byron's charisma with the power to seduce, but not necessarily to produce concrete political change, at least for his fellow countrymen.

Like Byron, the great pianist Franz Liszt deeply moved his audiences, although for different reasons and in different ways. His fans, Braudy writes, "Collected his green silk gloves and his cigar butts as avidly as any religious devotee saved the relics of martyrdom," and thanks in part to newspaper coverage, people became emotionally invested in his private life. A "Lisztomania," as Heinrich Heine termed it, made the performer seem to transcend ordinary life. But did Liszt, the musical performer, possess charisma? In terms of our own contemporary discourse, he certainly did. Liszt exuded that "certain something," the "it" we associate with Bruce Springsteen, Madonna, and Mick Jagger. But in attributing charisma to performers such as these, individuals with genuine talent, albeit magnified by increasingly sophisticated publicity machines, we risk using the term too promiscuously, stripping it of the analytical utility Weber intended. As Dana Gooley writes: "A performer like Liszt, no matter how popular, does not wield the kind of authority Max Weber described."

Elsewhere, Gooley notes that Hungarian nationalists of the 1840s tried to identify Liszt with their cause, briefly endowing him with the charismatic authority of national exemplars like Giuseppe Garibaldi and Lajos Kossuth.[24] But Liszt made an unlikely nationalist icon. He spoke hardly a word of the Magyar language and mostly presented himself—and was widely seen—as a "cosmopolitan" Parisian, a brilliant performer whose aristocratic airs and international appeal made him a man of the world. Though Liszt paid lip service—albeit in French—to Romantic Magyar nationalism, his Hungarian admirers could not convincingly claim him as one of their own.[25] Liszt never succeeded in wielding charismatic authority as an embodiment of Hungary's nascent national cause.

It may well be that Bernhardt and Byron stand as exceptions that prove a rule exemplified by Liszt. For the most part, cultural figures have possessed little authority in the Weberian sense—as popular and emotionally potent as they can be. In the nineteenth century, musicians, artists, and actors only rarely developed political clout. And even today, audiences are wary of celebrities' involvement in political movements, often seeing it as an example of self-promotion rather than genuine belief. When movement leaders enlist a celebrity for their cause, the famous person can divert attention from the cause to him or herself, thus diluting much of his or her political effect.[26] The "charismatic" artist turns politics into just another performance. For this reason, and Bernhardt's example aside, celebrity appeal infrequently translates into charisma, into residual political authority in the Weberian sense. There are good grounds for being parsimonious in the use of the sociologist's famous term.

One explanation for our too-ready attribution of charisma to actors, actresses, musicians, and sports heroes turns on the deceptive similarities between celebrity and charisma. Both require presence, whether mediated or direct, and both evoke emotional responses and attachments on the part of followers and fans. The latter seek out the celebrated and charismatic as much for who they are as for what they have done. Fans and followers endeavor to understand themselves in relation to the distinctive individuals in question, and in doing so, help shape the meanings they convey. "Instead of passively responding to its idols," Braudy writes, the audience "takes an active role in defining them." Followers are "willing to be manipulated but eager to convey how that ought to be done more expertly."[27]

In this sense, celebrity and charisma resemble each other more than they resemble fame, which, as we have seen, requires no immediacy of presence and no emotional response. If charisma and celebrity are "hot," fame is "cool."[28] In the late eighteenth century, Benjamin Franklin stood as one of the most famous men on earth, though he attracted no great following nor evoked a widespread emotional response. Jean-Jacques Rousseau, by contrast, did just that. For this reason, Braudy describes him as perhaps Europe's first great celebrity.[29] People flocked to him not for what he had written, but for what his personality seemed to represent, underlining, once again, the pivotal role followers play in "constructing" charisma, a recurrent theme of this book. Here again, celebrity shades into charisma, as Rousseau's apparent independence and freedom lent him a certain authority, causing established leaders to fear him as dangerous to the status quo.[30] Still, since Rousseau rejected any such authority, it is unclear whether he should be called charismatic. His example highlights the ambiguous, complex relationship between celebrity and charisma and the ability of fame to coexist with one or both.

Braudy attempts to navigate these ambiguities by positing two different kinds of charisma, one political ("instrumental charisma") and one cultural ("intrinsic charisma"). The former applies to political figures like the demagogues of the late nineteenth and early twentieth centuries, individuals who wanted to use their charisma to alter the status quo. The latter refers to an ahistorical authority detached from any specific political context. It manifested itself in "international wise men," like Rousseau, Voltaire, Franklin, and Johann Wolfgang von Goethe, whose cultural works inspired followers to pursue idealistic goals—humanism, in this case—rather than immediate political aims. Braudy adds that intrinsic charisma can shade into instrumental charisma, as when US and French revolutionaries drew on the ideals of enlightened humanism to formulate concrete political demands. In cases such as these, Braudy reclaims the influence of poets and authors in moving followers to act, even if that influence is posthumous and indirect.

The question of whether, or how, cultural figures could develop charismatic authority thus represents a major reevaluation of Weber's seminal work. Our authors suggest other revisions as well. Even though most contributors to this volume echo the German sociologist in linking charisma to political authority and to extraordinary, often heroic, individuals, no one remains within the limits of Weber's founding views. While Weber relegated supporters and audiences to a largely passive role,[31] several of our authors argue that followers can "construct charisma from below," creating—not just validating—the charisma of their leaders. Although Weber ignored the penny press, our contributors reveal the extent to which mass media amplified and expanded charismatic experience, often entangling charisma, celebrity, and fame. If Weber limited charisma mainly to singular, heroic men, Peter Fritzsche suggests that even the "common man" could enjoy a certain charisma, or at least celebrity. And though the sociologist allowed "legitimate" leaders no more than faint charismatic remains, Martin Kohlrausch demonstrates the extent to which traditional elites devised new forms of "charisma from above." Finally, in a crucial revision to Weber, Roberts and others make gender a central concern, revealing among other things how charisma could apply to women as well as men. We examine these revisions of Weber's original definition of charisma in three sections below.

Constructing Charisma from Below

The nineteenth century saw an explosion in the number of charismatic figures, largely because the audience for them grew so significantly. Increased literacy and expanding media outlets allowed political figures to broadcast their ideas widely. Rapid urbanization created the crowds that formed the basis of charismatic movements. Berlin, for instance, doubled in size from one million people in 1875 to two million in 1905, while by 1914, Paris boasted a population of three million inhabitants, and London seven million people. These urban populations were composed mostly of an industrial working class and a lower middle class of craftsmen and tradesmen, hard-pressed by economic worries but with high expectations of political participation. The "common man" thus became a prime target for late nineteenth-century political demagogues, who exploited popular discontents to bolster their own cults of personality. Rabble-rousers like Adolf Stoecker in Berlin and Karl Lueger in Vienna anticipated the fascist politics of the twentieth century. Already at the *fin de siècle*, Lueger built on his charismatic authority as a political outsider to achieve legitimacy in the electoral realm—just as Hitler would do three decades later.[32]

But was the "common man" simply a target for charismatic demagogues and little more? Could the anonymous and unknown have a connection to the limelight beyond a potential fifteen minutes of fame? Fritzsche shows how individuals with no direct access to the levers of power could participate in extraordinary events; how ordinary people developed a kind of celebrity in the revolutionary events of 1789–1815. Taking as his touchstone the letters collected from the battlefield at Waterloo, Fritzsche asks why such intimate scraps, written by common soldiers, suddenly became collectors' items, valued for the unique personal observations they revealed. As the revolution destabilized authority in general, Fritzsche argues, the concept of a definitive canon of interpretation lost its legitimacy. Instead, voices of ordinary individuals present at earth-shattering events became alternative sources of authority, turning once hidden, mute subjects into minor celebrities. Stepping onto the stage of history—as soldiers, émigrés displaced by the revolution, or eyewitnesses to occupation—unknown observers developed unique, and uniquely important, perspectives on a shared, mass historical experience. Even after the events in question had ended, ordinary people kept their attachment to them alive by consuming them as tourists, visiting battlefields, wax displays, and revolutionary Parisian sites. In doing so, they solidified memories and interpretations by purchasing souvenirs and war relics sold for that purpose.

Fritzsche's contribution is one of numerous essays in this volume highlighting how everyday objects and practices affected the relationship between ordinary people and individuals of note. The consumption and manipulation of material culture was especially vital in allowing fans to live out their celebrity identifications. In France, consumers indulged in Brazza and Bernhardt writing paper and pens, teacups and dessert plates, buttons and cufflinks. As Kohlrausch demonstrates, even monarchs like Wilhelm II were "sold" to a mass of consumers, who saw his bizarre visage in everything from films and photographs to chocolates and cigarettes. The Kaiser, like Bernhardt, now represented a distinctive "brand," an industry in his own right.

The ubiquity of Bernhardt's memorabilia created an aura of replication far more important to the production and maintenance of her fame than her unique, authentic stage performances. Similarly, Liszt's fame persisted long after the memory of his talents as composer and pianist faded, thanks to the journals, lithographs, and souvenirs that endlessly reproduced his image. The material investment made by followers as consumers and media audiences thus contributed to the development of a celebrity's fame, and even became, to some extent, a self-fulfilling prophecy: with so many fans willing to invest in a given celebrity, he or she must have a special link to the important, sublime elements of life.[33]

Potent as material culture was in creating celebrity and charisma, it could also undercut them. As Eva Giloi demonstrates for Wilhelm I's photographic portraits, it was not the mere existence of such objects, but the social practices involved in their consumption that proved decisive in shaping the emperor's public appeal. While the widespread sale of the emperor's image undermined his regal aura, he could reverse the process by autographing the photographs, as if to give these objects his royal touch. Even so, what people did with the autographed photographs once they received them, let alone the lengths to which they went to obtain them, counteracted that aura again. By stalking the monarch to gain his signature, or bidding on signed photographs at public auctions and incorporating them into their family albums, subjects engaged in private practices that diminished the unattainability traditionally enjoyed by the monarchy.

Berenson similarly uncovers the dualistic, even treacherous, nature of fan mail sent to imperial adventurers in France and Britain. To the admirers of Stanley and Brazza, letters became a way of experiencing a "non-reciprocal intimacy at a distance," through which they could connect themselves emotionally to the famous individual without his direct involvement.[34] This identification often turned into a sense of entitlement, as some letter writers resented the one-sided nature of the exchange and complained when they failed to receive a letter from the celebrity in return. Again, letter-writing practices enabled followers to participate in—but also to define the limits of—the celebrated or charismatic figure's appeal.

To prevent followers and audiences from slipping outside their control, celebrities and charismatic leaders adopted new procedures and technologies to construct attractive, mesmerizing images of themselves. Braudy notes how certain nineteenth-century political and cultural performers—from Napoleon to Liszt and beyond—alternated between the grand public performance and a stance of inspired separateness, enhancing their stature by making themselves scarce. The French symbolist writer Stéphane Mallarmé made the latter approach into a high form of art. As Emily Apter argues, Mallarmé represented the "I am not there" model of celebrity; he was known not for his "well-known-ness," but for his carefully constructed obscurity. Mallarmé attached his name to the names of other apparently more famous people—Edouard Manet, Paul Gauguin, Edgar Allen Poe—in ways that cast the light of celebrity on him without pushing the shadows all the way back. Mallarmé accomplished this feat through what Apter calls "celebrity gifting," subtly valorizing oneself by paying homage to another.

Mallarmé hardly stood alone in being preoccupied with his audience. Many cultural actors obsessed over their effect on spectators, though the methods they used to engage their audiences varied a great deal. Some employed new technologies, as theater directors did beginning in the late 1700s, when the introduction of oil lamps gave actors a luminous, awe-inspiring presence. Forty years later, Liszt took advantage of new piano-making techniques to show off his virtuosity in ways still inaccessible to Haydn or Mozart. Meanwhile, others altered the form and shape of their work. In the early nineteenth century, John Constable began producing monumental landscape paintings both to drama-tize himself and, more important, to guarantee his pictures' placement in the center of the Royal Academy's walls. (Smaller paintings were often hung near the ceiling, where they faded into oblivion.) In each case, celebrity status de-pended in part on innovative ways to draw audiences in.

Charisma from Above: Traditional Elites

If the pressures of media, performance, and audience shaped the lives of cul-tural figures, and even ordinary people, our authors show that they also af-fected traditional elites, who now had to take charisma into account. In making this case, Kohlrausch, in particular, demonstrates the limits of Weber's views. For the sociologist, traditional monarchs possessed a diffused "hereditary cha-risma" (*Erbcharisma*), which inhered in dynasties, as well as a certain "charisma of office" (*Amtscharisma*), which resided in institutions. Official in nature and independent of any individual prince's talents and personality, charisma of birth and office lacked the special, near magical qualities of charisma in its pur-est form.

Kohlrausch convincingly disputes such ideas by showing the extent to which Germany's Wilhelm II contended with the power and authority of charismatic outsiders by developing a media-related "genuine" charisma of his own. For the Kaiser, neither hereditary nor office charisma could suffice in the modern, mediated world. To create a new charismatic persona—a "charismatized" mon-archy—Wilhelm used the mass press, photography, and film to present himself as a transcendent figure, always larger than life. At the same time, he "personalized" the monarchy, styling himself as a man of flesh and blood, rather than a distant figure of royal authority. The mass press, which depended on emotional, sensationalized reporting to increase its sales, highlighted the Kaiser's distinctive appearance and dramatic pronouncements, but also accentuated the idea that he was a real human being with emotions that the average newspaper reader could grasp. When the emperor became embroiled in scandals uncovering his personal failings, the two elements of his public persona—his charismatization as an extraordinary leader and his "personalization" as a normal human being—came into fatal conflict. Kohlrausch's essay shows that charisma, when harnessed by existing elites, did not always work to renew their legitimacy or to stabilize the status quo.

As for democratically elected leaders, by the late nineteenth century, they too had to compete with individuals made powerful by mass media and widespread public support. Such leaders did so both by developing publicity machines designed to make them appear "charismatic" in new ways and by acquiescing to highly popular demands advanced by charismatic outsiders, demands no government, however firmly established, could afford to ignore. Berenson shows that French imperial heroes developed so much charismatic appeal in the late nineteenth century that republican officials found themselves forced to pursue dubious, even disastrous, imperialist policies. Against their will, elected leaders became followers obliged to conform to the public passions certain adventurers had aroused.

Gooley's chapter on Liszt twists these themes in interesting ways. Unlike the Kaiser, who sought to bolster traditional authority using the most modern media techniques, the newcomer Liszt boosted his untraditional, mediated stature by enlisting old-fashioned, aristocratic forms of display. The pianist's strategy of situating high-ranking aristocrats around his piano while performing on stage neatly illuminates the dual, traditional-modern, nature of his fame. During the performance, aristocrats cordoned him off from the rest of the audience, as if he were playing in a nobleman's salon. But afterwards, Liszt could advertise his prestigious devotees in press appeals destined for the public at large. Like the Kaiser, he tacked back and forth between separation and accessibility, between aristocratic exclusivity and an apparent availability to one and all. Rather than draw a sharp line between the outsider and insider, modernizer and traditionalist, Gooley demonstrates Liszt's ability to combine the two stances in the most advantageous ways.

Gender and Charisma

Readers will have noticed that most of the figures mentioned thus far are male; with some notable exceptions, the overrepresentation of men characterizes the book as a whole. What does this emphasis on men say about the relationship during the long nineteenth century between gender, on the one hand, and fame, celebrity, and charisma, on the other? Certainly, there was no shortage of famous women during this period; several immediately come to mind: Bernhardt, Jenny Lind, Lola Montez, George Sand, Jane Austen, George Eliot, not to mention Queen Victoria, the woman who gave much of the century its cultural name, at least in the English-speaking world. Some of these women became celebrities as well, but how many appeared to possess charisma? Not Victoria, who shunned the limelight and took pains to avoid the kind of publicity that gave Wilhelm II new forms of authority, however short-lived they were. If Victoria stood out as the world's most famous woman, she owed her status mostly to tradition and to a deep reverence in Britain for the monarchy. It is true that Benjamin Disraeli and others invented new traditions for the Queen, but their ability to do so only emphasizes the extent to which her authority stemmed from the forms and rituals of monarchy, even if certain of them had existed for only a short time.[35]

Though women could be famous in the nineteenth century, it was difficult for them to enjoy celebrity. This was, after all, the era of separate spheres, the time when the prevailing gender order frowned on women in public life. The ideal (bourgeois) woman married young, had many children, and remained at home. She created a haven of comfort and solace for her husband, who needed a place of respite from the rigors of the marketplace.[36] In reality, plenty of women worked outside of the home, but those who did so had to take special care to avoid the public eye.

The few women celebrities who emerged during the period mainly came from the theater. As Roberts makes clear, they raised hackles in the public arena. Actresses' ability to take on different roles, even roles as men, threatened to blur the boundaries between the genders and give other women the idea that their identities were anything but fixed. For these reasons, male writers and journalists tended to denigrate actresses, questioning their morals and placing them outside of polite society.[37]

To escape such a fate, writes Roberts, Bernhardt and the painter Rosa Bonheur adopted the pose of eccentricity. They lived with wild animals, slept in coffins, wore bizarre clothes, chain-smoked, and shunned marriage, among other strange and unusual things. Though Bernhardt and Bonheur deliberately adopted the eccentric's role, the public understood their bizarre habits as natural, as whims and excesses stemming from their unique artistic personalities. As eccentrics, the two women resembled no one else and, for that reason, could not be judged by the standards that applied to ordinary human beings. Hence their ability to defy virtually every convention of nineteenth-century femininity while being celebrated both by the public at large and by those male writers normally vigilant against any violation of prescribed female roles.

Eccentricity thus made Bernhardt and Bonheur's celebrity possible, but as Roberts argues, it prevented them from subverting rigid gender expectations and from exercising authority as models of what women could be. As innately strange beings dancing to a tune of their own, the two women appeared to exist in a realm closed to everyone else. Eccentricity kept them from being charismatic, at least for a following eager to loosen gender norms. But even though the two women's unique status did little to change gender relations in the short term, Roberts' interpretation raises the question of whether, in the long run, their antics broadened the definition of acceptable behavior for women.[38]

If Bernhardt enjoyed fame and celebrity more than charisma, were there other nineteenth-century women more charismatic than she? One candidate might be the socialist theorist and organizer Flora Tristan, a single woman who toured France in the 1840s to organize working men. At a time when middle-class women rarely went out alone, Tristan traveled from city to city with a message of working class solidarity and alliances between male and female workers.[39] She appeared to possess extraordinary personal magnetism, earning the endorsement of men unaccustomed to women lecturers, let alone those who spoke in the name of laborers as a whole. Still, as a political radical, her influence remained small and the publicity surrounding her relatively slight. If she created an unlikely emotional connection with men utterly different from herself, it was a connection whose impact on the country at large barely registered at all.

Not until the end of our period can we find truly charismatic women. By then, suffrage movements and the loosening gender order allowed women to emerge from the margins of political life. Key feminist heroines seized authority and power thanks to a following that validated their charismatic rank. The best examples are doubtless Emmeline and Christabel Pankhurst, leaders of the British women's suffrage movement. Their skillful oratory and personal presence earned them a huge number of supporters and placed women's rights at the center of Britain's early twentieth-century debates. In organizing demonstrations, jousting with opponents, and especially advocating militant, even violent action, they adopted a classically "male" political mode. To that, the Pankhursts added a more "feminine" role as martyrs, sacrificing themselves for the benefit of others. In jail, their hunger strikes and the graphic images of force-feedings through thick rubber tubes turned them into living saints suffering on behalf of an increasingly popular cause.

In this sense, the Pankhursts resembled certain charismatic male outsiders, individuals with neither traditional nor legal authority, but who attracted a great many followers and changed the political landscapes of their countries. The explorer Brazza played such a role, earning his charismatic stature in part by appearing, like the Pankhursts, to suffer on behalf of his compatriots. If the Pankhursts' militance and martyrdom helped create a new image of women, one that combined strength and suffering, Brazza exemplified new or renewed forms of masculinity. His apparent fearlessness in confronting the African unknown made him appear the quintessential male, while the extraordinary hardship, deprivation, and disease he suffered gave him a martyred, feminine persona, one enhanced by his oft-stated desire to nurture African peoples supposedly in need of European help. As a manly but gentle explorer, Brazza fashioned himself as a conqueror who seized territory without violence and an adventurer equally devoted to the pursuit of knowledge and the betterment of humankind. His persona offered one potential solution to the "crisis of masculinity," the sense of male weakness and gender confusion widely perceived in *fin-de-siècle* Britain and France.[40]

As outsiders who took center stage, Brazza, the Pankhursts, and many other nineteenth-century figures developed charisma in a Weberian sense. Still others became celebrities, their "well-knownness" sometimes enduring as fame.[41] As several of our contributors make clear, these developments could not have happened without what Braudy calls the great media expansion of the nineteenth century. Mass journalism, photography, and new, rapid means of communication helped create cultures of charisma, celebrity, and fame; cultures that divided societies into leaders and followers, stars and fans, even as it narrowed the distance between them.

PART I

Constructing Charisma

CHAPTER 1

Charisma and the Making of Imperial Heroes in Britain and France, 1880–1914

EDWARD BERENSON

In 1874, an unknown French naval ensign, Pierre Savorgnan de Brazza, went to Africa to seek a water route from the Atlantic Ocean to the smooth lake-like reaches of the Upper Congo River. He hoped to bypass the 32 cataracts that forbid all navigation on the lower Congo up to what became known as Stanley Pool. In exploring the banks of the Congo, Brazza claimed a huge swathe of Equatorial Africa for France. It mattered little that this territory lacked economic or strategic value. Brazza's extraordinary bravery, his apparent willingness to suffer to achieve a nearly impossible goal, made him one of France's greatest national heroes and its champion of escalating imperial growth.

A dozen years later Brazza's rival, Henry Morton Stanley, world-famous for having "found" David Livingstone, set out in quest of yet another lost European, Emin Pasha. Originally known as Eduard Schnitzer, the Prussian-born Emin served as governor of Equatoria, the Sudan's southern-most province. Stanley's new trip failed to realize its goal: Emin refused to be rescued and returned to "civilization." En route, Stanley lost half of his European lieutenants and three-quarters of his 700-man African troop. The expedition resulted in the deaths of hundreds of other Africans. But these horrors troubled the explorer's compatriots very little, at least at first. Stanley's courage, drive, perseverance, and initiative struck a chord with British journalists and many of their readers, as did his narrative gifts as a writer. He emerged from Africa a conquering hero, feted by Queen Victoria and lionized by the crowd. His fame enabled him to goad Prime Minister Salisbury into a more forward policy in East Africa than the cautious British leader had intended to pursue.

After the turn of the century, General Hubert Lyautey spearheaded France's effort to seize Morocco, a Muslim country fiercely protective of its independence. The material advantages of this colonial project were slim and the risks large, as France's quest for Morocco brought it to the verge of war with Germany in 1911 and helped precipitate the Great War three years later. Nonetheless, Lyautey, a famous soldier also renowned as a man of letters, became a towering French hero and celebrity, a rare military man elected to the prestigious *Académie Française*. He would end his career a Maréchal de France, the highest rank a French officer can attain.

Why did these three men earn many of their countries' highest honors and create huge public enthusiasm despite the futility and even the failure of much of what they undertook? Why did they become heroes and celebrities in their respective homelands, individuals capable of influencing public policy and even of altering the course of events? They did, of course, achieve some recognizable successes, especially Stanley, who made important geographical discoveries and who became the first European to navigate the entire length of the Congo. But his final expedition, the one that made him a charismatic hero, accomplished none of its goals and achieved no material gains. Likewise, Brazza won a large colony for France, but what became French Equatorial Africa drained the mother country economically and created a moral burden similar in kind, if not in degree, to the one associated with King Leopold's ghost.[1] As for Lyautey, he succeeded in imposing a French protectorate on Morocco, but the conquest of that country required almost constant fighting there from 1904 to 1925. The losses greatly outweighed the gains.

As we examine the surprising, and in some cases, enduring stature of these men, we can find guidance in the concept of charisma elaborated early in the twentieth century by the canonical German sociologist Max Weber. The actions and perceived accomplishments of the three men studied here endowed them with charisma as Weber and certain of his commentators have understood the term. We are concerned with Weber's original writings, not with the superficial, pop culture renderings common nowadays.[2] In taking up the phenomenon of charisma, a religious concept Weber borrowed from the Protestant legal scholar Rudolf Sohm, the German sociologist had much more in mind than the personal magnetism and star-power we associate with certain movie idols, politicians, and business tycoons.[3] To view someone as charismatic is to develop a significant emotional connection with him or her, to devote, even subordinate, oneself to the individual in question.

In the late nineteenth century, when most political leaders in France and Britain possessed little emotional appeal, a small group of explorers and adventurers, their exploits narrated and amplified by a new mass press, came to be seen as heroic, exemplary men. If government officials often shied away from new imperial commitments, stymied in many cases by public indifference, even hostility, the charismatic authority that enveloped colonial heroes did much to change public attitudes toward imperialism in both countries. Thanks to the aura surrounding these men, many people once opposed to empire came to lend it their support, especially during the years when imperial heroes dominated the news. At times, their untraditional authority pushed governments in the two countries further than they wanted to go, and in many cases led them into dead ends or foreign policy disasters inexplicable but for the charismatic sway these heroes held over ordinary people and political leaders alike. There was nothing rational about sending General Charles Gordon to Khartoum in 1884 or Stanley to rescue Emin Pasha three years later or Jean-Baptiste Marchand to Fashoda or even Lyautey to Morocco. The explanation for these ventures turns on the irrational enthusiasm they generated and the charismatic confidence they wrought.

We have analyzed Weber's understanding of charisma in the introduction to this volume; it will suffice, here, to recall that for the sociologist, "charisma" was first and foremost a way of understanding forms of authority, command, power, or influence (*Herrschaft* in German) that came neither from tradition nor from law. Throughout history, Weber wrote, most authority derived from one of two sources: political elders who traced their power back into the deep mists of time; or bureaucracies designed to administer and enforce laws developed through rational processes of deliberation and debate. Both forms of authority rested on a structure of rules, whether in the form of "precedents handed down from the past," or, as in the case of bureaucracy, on "intellectually analyzable" statutes and procedures. But there was a third form of authority opposite to the others in being "foreign to all rules."[4] This third, or residual form, harked back to the "gifts of grace" (charismata) that God originally gave to Christ and later came to inhere in certain extraordinary individuals.

As suggestive as Weber's discussion of charisma is for understanding hero worship in general, the sociologist never adequately explained why an individual's extraordinariness inspires people to devote themselves to him or her, to grant authority and to feel "absolute trust in the leader." He failed to make clear, in other words, why a relationship, an emotional connection, develops between the extraordinary person and those who see him as such.

A variety of theorists have attempted to understand the psychological processes underlying attributions of charisma.[5] In the early 1980s, Charles Camic turned to Freud and psychoanalytic theory for help in uncovering the prerequisites or sources of charisma. If, as Weber suggested in *The Sociology of Religion*, the "preconditions for attributions of specialness" or charisma lie in "extraordinary human needs," Freud's understanding of those requirements, Camic maintained, help us determine when those preconditions exist and what forms they take.

According to Freud, all people have four basic needs: sexuality and aggression (id); the need to rein in sexuality and aggression by conforming to moral standards and restrictions (superego); the need for protection, certainty, and physical security (ego); and the need for achievement and attainment, mastery, and self-regard (ego-ideal). In *The Sociology of Religion*, Weber had identified "dependency needs" (ego in Freudian terms) as preconditions for the emergence of charismatic figures, namely the magicians and prophets who could satisfy these needs. But, in Camic's view, individuals who could fulfill the other Freudian needs—aggression, morality, self-regard—might also be seen as charismatic. Whether charismatic individuals emerge depends, in this view, on whether the needs in question are ordinary or extraordinary. At first glance, it might seem as though the needs of the id, superego, and ego are ordinary by definition, since everyone is said to have them. But ego psychologists have considered these needs extraordinary when individuals are helpless to fulfill them on their own, when, that is, they depend on others to satisfy them. Those with the ability to do so may be seen as charismatic.[6] People can become helpless or dependent either as a result of a socialization process that prevents them from acting on aggressive or sexual needs or as the result of the feelings of loss and disorientation that arise in situations of rapid change.

In this Weberian-Freudian view, four different kinds of charismatic figures emerge: those attributed with omnipotence, excellence, sacredness, and uncanniness. Since these categories include a potentially vast array of possibilities, from military leaders to science geniuses, clergymen to movie stars, Camic allows too many different kinds of people, in far too many different situations, to count as charismatic. He fails as well to distinguish clearly enough charismatic individuals from merely celebrated ones.

If psychoanalysis plays too loosely with the term charisma, perhaps there is a more precise way to understand the charismatic bond? According to the philosopher Stephen Turner, what makes someone a hero in the eyes of his potential following, a person who in Machiavelli's terms possesses audacity, prowess, and luck (*Fortuna*), is the capacity to change people's expectations.[7] Charisma, Turner writes, is the ability to open up new possibilities, to make people believe in the realization of crucial things they had always thought impossible. One way heroes do this is by serving as exemplars and pioneers, by showing through their actions that something thought prohibitively dangerous can, in fact, be done without grievous harm. In the 1960s, civil rights leaders, for example, took risky steps by unilaterally integrating segregated facilities, organizing and leading marches, and enduring prison and beatings before ultimately gaining a victorious release. Their victories encouraged others by showing that undertakings, once thought futile, could now produce success. The heroes' actions thus changed the perceptions of others, broadening their horizons and improving their lives.

Even when the trails heroes blaze are too difficult for others to follow, charismatic figures nonetheless open up new possibilities. They do so by demonstrating what can be done and allowing large numbers of people to associate themselves, however indirectly and vicariously, with what they have achieved.[8]

When an explorer travels, for example, to uncharted regions, he, and occasionally she, does things essentially no one else can repeat. He braves harsh climates, tropical diseases, and potentially lethal attacks, while solving long-standing geographical puzzles and interacting with previously unknown peoples, whose primitiveness appears to highlight European superiority, including the superiority of those in thrall to the heroic adventurer. By accomplishing such feats, the explorer seems to expand the limits of human possibility and broaden everyone's horizons. And when travelers claim new territories for their home countries, they appear to magnify the country's importance, giving it added prestige and standing in the world. That standing rubs off on those following the explorer's adventures, making them feel more significant by virtue of their connection, however imaginary and vicarious, with the hero.

In sum, the charismatic hero, as opposed to the mere celebrity, blazes new paths and opens new possibilities.[9] He offers inspiration and the ability to participate indirectly in what he has done. He can offer protection and a feeling of strength, instead of the weakness and vulnerability that may have existed before. In doing these things, the hero fulfills what for Weber lay at the very heart of charisma, the ability to produce changes within other people.[10]

If Turner's cognitive psychology, like Camic's psychoanalytic one, provides important clues as to why great explorers of the nineteenth century might have developed charismatic authority and bonded emotionally with a large number of followers, there is perhaps yet another, newer kind of psychology to consider. The latter comes from the neuroscientific revolution of the past few decades and especially the recent findings of "affective neuroscience," the study of emotions and the brain. According to Jaak Panksepp, author of the key synthesis in the field, there are four basic "command systems for emotionality" common to all mammals, including human beings: seeking, rage, fear, and panic.[11]

In terms of charisma, the most important of the basic four "command systems" is seeking, the vital emotional substructure that "makes animals intensely interested in exploring their world and leads them to become excited when they are about to get what they desire."[12] This system enables animals to find what they need to survive and eagerly to anticipate those essential things: food, water, warmth, and sex. In humans, the seeking system lies at the root of curiosity and all intellectual pursuits and produces feelings of interest, curiosity, excitement, and eager anticipation. One hypothesis, unprovable but worth considering, is that the actions of certain exciting individuals, people who, for example, undertake daring forays into the unknown, stimulate seeking circuits in the brains of those aware of their exploits. Such might especially be true of newspaper readers who already felt a need for protection, reassurance, and solace, and for that reason had begun to follow the doings of exceptional people in the news. In fact, Panksepp has found neurological evidence that seeking inhibits fear, thus suggesting why those worried about their own prospects or about the future of their country might be drawn emotionally to charismatic figures who seem immune from fear.[13] In any case, the stimulation they provide could help account for the emotional connection that ordinary people feel toward them and why daring seekers held particular appeal in the late nineteenth century. This was a time when European societies appeared increasingly mundane and bureaucratic, when manliness seemed under assault, and when British and French newspapers brimmed with reports of threats to their countries' safety and well-being.

As for the explorers and adventurers themselves, they appear to be paradigmatic cases of the kinds of people Panksepp would describe as having overactive seeking drives. Such individuals found themselves so moved by what the neuroscientist calls the "foraging/exploration/investigation/curiosity/expectancy/seeking" system that they showed themselves willing, even compelled, to place themselves in situations of unimaginable danger and brave what for most others would be unendurable pain. Individuals such as Stanley, Brazza, and Lyautey seemed motivated more by the quest than the goal—itself often ill-defined; more by the desire to plunge into the unknown than by the need to master it. In the late nineteenth century, the charisma of such individuals depended little on whether or not their missions achieved their purported goals, or whether they returned home with measurable gains. The aura inhered in the quest itself.

Ordinary people, those endowed with normal impulses to seek, may have derived vicarious excitement from the plethora of front-page columns narrating the exploits of those who risked life and limb in the heart of Africa, the deserts of Sudan, the Moroccan mountains and plain. Newspaper readers, who felt their lives constrained by everyday routines, overshadowed by a dangerous present and uncertain future, could look to fearless others for the vicarious thrill of the hunt, for an emotionally liberating quest for new knowledge, new trials, and new acquisitions abroad.

Between 1880 and 1914, Stanley, Brazza, and Lyautey played such an emotionally liberating role. In their dauntless embrace of the African unknown, these three men inspired their countrymen and women to seek new and better things, while making the world seem less uncertain and less vulnerable to forces beyond their control. All three came to possess the two forms of charisma Weber identified in the *Sociology of Religion*, the charisma of both magicians and prophets. As latter-day magicians, the three men appeared to embody something essential to their existing orders; as prophets, they became exemplars of efforts to cure their societies' ills. As we shall see, they also embodied the manliness viewed as a central quality of the two societies, a manliness widely deemed at risk.

If Weber neglected the emotional underpinnings of the charismatic relationship, he also failed to take up the crucial question of mediation, the pivotal role outlets of communication played in attributions of charisma. This lacuna explains in part why he predicted that charisma could not but wither away and why he failed to notice the eruption of charisma in the latter decades of the nineteenth century. During the three decades before Weber formulated his ideas about charisma, the largest newspapers and magazines had freed themselves from the financial and ideological control of both political parties and the state.[14] Though parties maintained their own newspapers, these outlets shrunk in size and influence relative to the mass-circulation dailies newly dominant in the last third of the nineteenth century. For this reason, among others, party bureaucracies could not maintain the kind of control over the political process that Weber believed would contain the charisma of individual politicians and eventually all but snuff it out.

The Victorian-era eruption of charisma resulted in large part from a revolution in communication, in which near-universal literacy and an industrialized penny press created a mass market for print.[15] The development of the press as a mass medium gave journalists and editors the power not just to make certain people famous, but also to spread that fame to the farthest corners of a country. Individuals who remain largely unknown, whatever their personal qualities, cannot appear charismatic in socially and politically significant ways. Only when the media paid considerable attention to a particular person, covering his or her deeds and accomplishments, lauding her in editorials, interviewing him, inviting her to contribute articles, did the public gain enough information to endow this individual with the potential for charisma.

Crucial as well were new journalistic techniques, especially the interview, which became widespread in the 1880s.[16] The interview focused the journalistic spotlight on individuals and personalities and placed particular people at the center of journalists' reports. Such personalization and attention to individuals also found encouragement in the rapid democratization of literacy after mid century. Writers now needed to appeal to newly literate but unlettered readers often unmoved by argument and analysis. This audience wanted colorful narratives and engaging personalities, heroes and villains like the ones featured in the popular literature and melodramatic theater of the time.[17]

The bulk of those who figured prominently in newspaper narratives became, at most, celebrities—individuals who developed a certain reputation, even fame, for who they were or what they had done. It mattered little, then as now, whether they had made genuine accomplishments or whether they were "known for [their] well-knownness," in Daniel Boorstein's oft-quoted phrase.[18] Usually, the press attended to them for a short time, before dropping them for good. There were some figures, however, who stood out from this pack, who possessed considerably more political, moral, and cultural weight. Such rare individuals distinguished themselves not just as celebrities, though they often became that as well, but as heroes, people whose "charisma," Weber wrote, "rests upon 'heroism.'"[19] At the end of the nineteenth century, a time when a great many British and French people longed for heroes and put their faith in scientific and personal quests, Stanley, Brazza, and Lyautey, all seekers par excellence, appeared to satisfy a great many individual and social needs.

Two of these three charismatic men, Stanley and Lyautey, published their own accounts of daring colonial exploits, but neither would have had the resonance they enjoyed without the great echo chamber of newspapers and magazines.[20] Stanley, in particular, sold a great many copies of his books. But sales numbered in the hundreds of thousands, while his renown spread to tens of millions. Book reviews, illustrated weeklies, boys' magazines, and journalistic coverage of his triumphal homecomings, society receptions, and lecture tours—all repeated and amplified the heroic narratives recounted in his bestselling books.

Like Stanley, Brazza and Lyautey possessed friends and allies who straddled the worlds of journalism, geography, and politics, and who deliberately turned the media spotlight toward them. In each instance, journalistic coverage gave the hero a certain renown, and that renown drew crowds to his side. The crowds then became part of the story, a story almost guaranteed to attract ever larger numbers of people eager to see first-hand what the hullabaloo was all about.[21] Reporters now offered the size of the crowds as proof of what a great, popular hero the individual in question had become. In diaries and personal correspondence, a large number of people, unknown to the hero, wrote of their efforts to catch a glimpse of the man and of their often-worshipful admiration for him. Given such public endorsement, political officials had no choice but to take these individuals, along with their ideas and demands, into account. They did so, often as not, against their better judgment and not infrequently suffered as a result. In some cases, however, political leaders managed to harness the heroes' charisma to their advantage, enhancing their own standing by associating with the charismatic authority the hero had earned.[22]

One key theme of the journalistic treatment of our three men was the manliness and virility they were all said to exude. Manliness became a central public concern in both Britain and France, where a plethora of influential commentators spoke in worried, even frantic, tones about a "crisis of masculinity" afflicting their countries in the closing decades of the nineteenth century. The apparent feminization of family life, the growth of unphysical office work, the new emphasis on consumption rather than production, the mounting fears of "degeneration," and the advent of emancipated women—all these phenomena appeared to threaten male power, independence, initiative, and even sexual potency. Virility itself seemed at risk, and with it, the strength and international standing of the countries for which weakened men would someday have to fight.[23] Like many cultural phenomena, the "crisis of masculinity" lived in the "imaginary," in a discourse-world neither true nor false but fully belonging to the reality it partially described.[24]

Commentators of the late nineteenth century considered it imperative to reverse this masculine decline. One way to do so was to put forward images of manly men—soldiers, adventurers, explorers—who would inspire their male counterparts at home. Many of these images emerged from a new and highly popular literature of adventure produced in France by writers such as Jules Verne and Paul d'Ivoi, and in Britain by Robert Louis Stevenson, Henry Rider Haggard, and Rudyard Kipling.[25] But even more important were images of real adventurers, men whose exploits took them to lands marked for imperial conquest. The first of these popular imperial heroes tended to be explorers, while later, military figures came into play.

Given the absence of war in Western Europe between 1871 and 1914, these figures operated in colorful, seemingly exotic locales abroad. They saw themselves compared to the heroes of ancient and medieval myth, heroes who left Europe for the dangerous, unknown heart of Africa, into which they disappeared. The references to mythical heroes resonated widely in countries like Britain and France, where educated people knew a great deal about ancient times, and others had been imbued with folktales and religious narratives centered on extraordinary, often supernatural individuals, known as saviors and saints.[26] The association of ancient myth and modern publicity thus enhanced the ability of colonial figures to capture the public imagination, making proto-imperial exploration and conquest into phenomena a great many people could support.

Still, despite the similarities among our three mythic seekers, the different national contexts shaped in particular ways the nature of their charismatic appeal and the lure their individual styles of manliness achieved. Take the case of Henry Morton Stanley. The latter's editor at the *New York Herald*, James Gordon Bennett, understood the resonance of myths in which great heroes appeared to cross a threshold into the unknown. He announced to the world that the great Doctor Livingstone was lost and that Stanley would find him. In one of the world's first "media events," Stanley made his way to a small town on Lake Tanganyika, where he encountered the aging explorer. The journalist's bizarrely understated greeting, "Dr. Livingstone, I presume?," ultimately echoed around the world. A telegram from Bennett declared, "You are now [as] famous as Livingstone, having discovered the discoverer."[27] Stanley's book, *How I Found Livingstone* (1872), became a huge bestseller and turned the journalist/explorer into an international celebrity and lecturer in demand.

The height of Stanley's fame came in 1890, when the explorer returned triumphantly to Britain from the Emin Pasha Relief Expedition (an East African wild goose chase at once epic, tragic, and grotesque). A "Stanley craze" set in, as huge numbers fell under his charismatic sway. Crowds greeted his ship in Dover and then his train in London.[28] When the Royal Geographical Society held

Illustration 1.1. Mr H.M. Stanley is greeted by crowds of well-wishers on his return to Victoria Station in London after the Emin Pasha Relief Exhibition. (*Source:* Illustrated London News)

a meeting in Stanley's honor at Royal Albert Hall, 7,000 people, including the Prince and Princess of Wales, packed the room. As Stanley rose to speak, he was "hailed with prolonged cheering," cheering so loud that it nearly drowned out the marching song, "See the Conquering Hero Comes," vibrating on the organ.[29] The following day, Queen Victoria invited Stanley to Windsor Palace for a private audience, and she commissioned an official painting of the "intrepid" British hero. On this, the Queen was behind the times, as Stanley's image had

Illustration 1.2. Stanley speaks at a packed Albert Hall. (*Source:* The Graphic)

appeared on so many magazine covers and advertisements that he had long been one of Britain's best recognized men. It goes without saying that Madame Tussaud's featured his replica in wax and that visitors thronged the part of the exhibit devoted to him.[30] Stanley's 900-page *In Darkest Africa*, which he wrote in 50 days at the rate of 8,000 words a day, immediately sold 150,000 copies in hardback. This uneducated Welshman, who grew up in a workhouse, received an honorary law degree from the University of Edinburgh and an honorary doctorate from Oxford.[31] Queen Victoria knighted him in 1898.

Like Hollywood stars of later times, Stanley found himself surrounded by fans everywhere he went. People tried to see him, touch him, shake his hand, obtain his autograph and pieces of his clothing. He was deluged with mail, as a great many people participated vicariously, and often emotionally, in Stanley's life. They thought about him, worried about him, prayed for him, and exalted in his manly fame. "Not once," wrote one G. Momt, "but a thousand times we spoke of you, and prayed for you, when countless hearts throbbed with fear at your possible fate … but we are glad and rejoice again at your triumphal return and glorious success, proving yourself as always a Man, a Christian, and a hero."[32]

In letter after letter, Stanley's fans told him how much he meant to them. "We are personally unknown to you," wrote one H.S. Burcombe. "Still, we take—and have taken—a very very deep interest in your welfare and career past, present, and future … May the Almighty Guardian whose guidance and protection you so signally experienced in your African travels *ever* watch over, guard and guide you" (emphasis in original).[33] Even young children joined in the celebration. An eleven-year-old girl told him, "It was very kind of you to go through such perils to rescue Emin Pasha."[34]

There is strong evidence that Stanley's fame directly affected British colonial policy. After the Emin Pasha expedition, the explorer enjoyed such public support that Prime Minister Salisbury found himself forced to confront Germany over African lands the Tory leader considered of little interest.[35] More than perhaps any British political figure or intellectual proponent of empire, Stanley turned his compatriots toward Africa and the prospect of further expansion there.

He also popularized a tough, fierce version of masculinity at odds with the image of male domesticity typical of British middle-class men during the early and mid-Victorian periods.[36] Throughout the first half of the nineteenth century, legions of bourgeois men, their values shaped by Evangelical Protestantism, had seen the family as a "haven in a heartless world," a place of nurture and comfort to which they could retreat from the competitive, amoral marketplace of capitalist life.[37] Their wives, dubbed angels of the home, helped them restore the moral values that the world of business had undermined. Women were thus central to that private domestic sphere, but men remained in charge. Their manliness came from their power in the home, and from the seriousness, self-denial, and rectitude with which they maintained their dominant place.

In the second half of the century, male domesticity and the values that sustained it gradually evaporated as post-Napoleonic peace and Britain's international supremacy, both military and economic, appeared to give way. The Crimean War and Indian Rebellion of the late 1850s revealed the potential vulnerability of the empire and the mounting economic and diplomatic challenges from rival European powers. By the 1880s, the apparent peacefulness and prosperity of mid-century Britain, wrote the Cambridge law professor Henry Maine, seemed little more than a "bitter deception." Meanwhile, Otto von Bismarck's successful wars against Denmark, Austria, and France, combined with Germany's new industrial prowess, made the Iron Chancellor's empire appear a dangerous threat. So did a wounded France looking for revenge on the continent and compensation against Britain's colonial and proto-colonial domains.[38]

These developments produced a cascade of pessimistic late-century commentary about Britain's future and its ability to withstand the supposedly imminent European wars. "We cannot turn to the newspapers of the day," wrote Francis de Labillière in 1885, "without reflecting and feeling that within a short period we may find ourselves at war with one, if not two of the great powers of Europe."[39] In terms of masculinity, the increasingly dangerous world of the late century seemed to require not the domesticated male of the first half of the century, but one endowed with the robustness, perseverance, and stoicism needed to face up to these growing threats. Britain required a man no longer defined by gentle family life, but by a fierce engagement with the world.[40]

No one seemed to embody these traits more than Stanley. Thanks to his bestselling books and colorfully written newspaper dispatches, his robustness was legendary. British and US readers possessed an intimate knowledge of his plucky adventures and near superhuman ability to survive the attacks of fierce African tribes, the ravages of tropical disease, the jungle's searing heat, the terrifying dangers of the unknown. So robust was this manly man that Africans had dubbed him *Bula Matari*, the "breaker of rocks." Writers routinely praised his "perseverance," his "dauntless spirit of enterprise," his tenacity in fulfilling "duties so manfully performed."[41] As a woman journalist put it, Stanley succeeded where others had failed, thanks to "his firmness and decision of character, [to] the exercise of these manly virtues."[42] A man of the pen, as of the sword, Stanley was no effete intellectual, no armchair geographer idly staring at his maps. For him, geography "was ever a military and manly science, dedicated to the subjugation of wild nature; its books and maps were weapons of conquest rather than objects of contemplation."[43] Such ideas fit perfectly with notions espoused in British public schools of the late century, namely that action, adventure, and the spirit of organized games vastly outweighed sedentary academic work.[44]

Despite this display of conquering manliness, which earned Stanley a great deal of support, he was not without his critics. According to his own newspaper dispatches and bestselling books, he had killed a large number of Africans as he traversed what he called the "Dark Continent."[45] Stanley's critics reacted not to his use of force, but to the apparent gratuitousness of the violence and the explorer's unrepentant celebration of what he had done.[46] Manly men needed to be tough and strong, but they also had to be just. In using muskets to attack Africans armed only with stones and arrows, Stanley had crossed an invisible moral line—not, it seems, for the majority of British men and women, but for those who believed manliness required a strong measure of self-control.

The mixed views of Stanley's achievements doubtless reduced, to some extent, his imperial prestige, though he remained an immensely popular figure. He won election to Parliament in 1895, earned huge sums on lectures tours in Britain and the United States, and was treated like royalty in his native Wales.[47] Overall, Stanley's immense fame and charismatic appeal allowed him to add luster and legitimacy to a British imperial project no longer lacking in public support.

Stanley's French rival, Pierre Savorgnan de Brazza, did much the same for France. In many ways, Brazza would outstrip Stanley as a colonial hero in part because he developed a reputation for peacefulness that sharply contrasted with Stanley's apparent record of violent excess, a record that, for some, called his manliness into doubt. After Stanley staked his claim to the Congo River in 1877, Brazza decided that he should represent France in challenging him and his British and Belgian backers for control of Central Africa. In 1880, Brazza and the main Congolese ruler signed a treaty the Frenchman interpreted as giving his country a huge swathe of territory on Africa's second longest river. Brazza won this agreement mainly through negotiation, though he nonetheless wielded the threat of force. French journalists ignored these threats, praising the explorer with near unanimity for winning France a huge colony "without spilling a drop of blood." Brazza had accomplished what writers labeled a *conquête pacifique*," a peaceful conquest now indelibly linked to the Frenchman's name. As a peaceful conqueror, he became the paragon of France's *mission civilisatrice*, the premise on which the Republic's imperial expansion could most successfully draw its public support.

Pro-colonial journalists understood Brazza's political importance, and writers for the popular press homed in on his near-mythological appeal. Reporters lingered over his exotic looks, the selfless sacrifice for France, personal bravery, and superhuman endurance in the wild tropical heat of Equatorial Africa. Without fail, accounts of his peaceful conquests emphasized the contrast between him and Stanley, between an Anglo-American villain portrayed as brutal and rapacious, and a French hero seen as pacific, moral, and good.

Under these circumstances, public adulation of the charismatic explorer was such that he could go nowhere without being saluted on the street. Brazza's long, taciturn face now stared down from shop windows everywhere, as cheap portraits of the explorer flooded Paris and the provinces. France's leading photographer, Nadar, captured Brazza's image as apostle of French civilization, and those images graced the covers of the country's illustrated press. Beyond the proliferation of images, merchants introduced an array of Brazza paraphernalia, creating a veritable *"mode Brazza"* in the 1880s.[48] People could buy Brazza

Illustration 1.3. Brazza, the "pacific conqueror." (*Source:* L'Illustration)

writing paper, pens, vases, commemorative medals, and books. Gentlemen du-
eled with swords made in honor of Brazza, and restaurants created menus celebrating the great man. Those who wanted to experience Brazza's presence more
directly could visit the Musée Grévin, France's answer to Madame Tussaud's,
where the explorer joined France's greatest celebrities in having his likeness im-
mortalized in wax.[49] We do not know exactly how many Brazza pens or vases
were sold, though it is clear that many tens of thousands of people gazed at his
waxed form in the Musée Grévin.[50] And there is good evidence that substantial
numbers of people from all walks of life identified with him, looked up to him,
and saw him as a hero to whom they could appeal.

Part of that appeal came from the kind of manliness Brazza seemed to
represent. As a manly but gentle explorer, a modest aristocrat who sacrificed
his fortune for France, Brazza projected an image of masculinity consonant
with the new Republic's egalitarian ideals. He fashioned himself as a military
man, but one with an uncommonly delicate touch. He was a conqueror who
seized territory without violence, a manly adventurer interested in the pursuit
of knowledge and the betterment of humankind. Brazza was, in short, a man's
man, but one with prominent "feminine" features as defined at the time: pa-
tience, tact, gentleness, subtlety, and charm.

This was precisely the kind of male embodiment the new Republic needed—
a manly man with the best qualities of women. Such a man could embody a nation determined to remain a world power and a Republic devoted to the rights
of man. The republican image of manliness differed from the dominant one
taking shape across the English Channel. There, the widely perceived threats
to empire and the growing fears of economic decline called for a tougher and
more martial response.

When Brazza announced he was looking for a small number of men to join
his third expedition in 1883, he found himself deluged with more than 1,500
applications.[51] One man wanted to join the expedition because "its goal was to
complete the pacific conquest that you have made for France."[52] His words suggest that the term *"conquête pacifique,"* so prominent in Brazza's speeches and
newspaper reports about him, had resonated with the public. Charles de Chavannes, who ultimately succeeded in joining the expedition as Brazza's private
secretary, wrote of having to wait for days to see the explorer, as he competed
with scores of others for the hero's attention.[53]

Brazza's mail was full of letters from people he did not know, letters calling
him a hero and exalting all he had done for France. A surprising number of
people sent him poems, some printed, some in script.[54] One correspondent
begged Brazza to save his ruined life. "Have pity on me," he wrote in verse,
"Alleviate my distress/ … / Be my protector,/ My support, my strength, and
my liberator."[55] If Brazza could help the poor savages of Africa, this secular
prayer seemed to say, he could surely do something for a countryman down

on his luck. Other writers became angry when Brazza appeared to ignore their appeals or if they were barred from seeing him when calling at his hotel. These followers of the charismatic Brazza felt an intimate connection with him, an "intimacy at a distance," that convinced them that he should notice them and respond to their needs.[56] The relationship was complex and ambiguous, since readers interacted with the newspaper but not with Brazza himself. This situation allowed individual readers to construct versions of the celebrity that suited their needs, images of the charismatic person uncontrolled by any direct intervention from him or her.

There is no need to cite more of these amateur poems; all suggest a popular endorsement of the Brazza image created by the explorer himself and by his friends and supporters in the press. Savorgnan de Brazza, the poems confirm, was a self-sacrificing charismatic hero, a great man around whom all French men and women could unite, a luminary whose contributions to civilization reflected the greatness of France and the liberty and progress of the Republic.

That Brazza's name and image became attached to everyday articles of consumption and the subjects of letters and poems both reflected and enhanced his stature as a national hero, a stature that conferred strength and legitimacy on the Republic itself. For this reason, France's political leaders had to take Brazza's image and popularity into account. During the Conference of Berlin (1884–1885), convened by Bismarck to resolve European conflicts over African territory, Jules Ferry, France's *president du conseil*, wrote his representative at the talks: "Even the most recalcitrant centers of opinion will approve of our arrangements at Berlin as long as we can ensure that those arrangements [do nothing to discredit] M. de Brazza. Brazza is popular; he has an enormous following, and he has come to represent the national honor. We need an arrangement that flatters the amour-propre of the French public."[57]

Brazza remained immensely popular throughout his life, serving as exemplar of empire and symbol of national unity for a French Republic in need of support. During his elaborate state funeral in 1905, thousands of ordinary Parisians poured out of their homes and businesses to pay the hero their last respects. "The entire nation is in mourning," declared *Le Journal*, "When a great man like M. de Brazza draws his final breath."[58]

Brazza's "*conquête pacifique*" resonated so widely that other French colonial figures inherited his legacy of public intimacy—with Hubert Lyautey foremost among his heirs. The French general and future minister of war fought in Indochina, Madagascar, and Algeria, before becoming proconsul of France's Morocco protectorate in 1912. He was one of France's most ardent colonialists, ruling Morocco almost single-handedly for thirteen years and ultimately presiding over the French Empire's premier commemorative event, the Colonial Exposition of 1931. Like Brazza, he became known for his peaceful conquests and for a manliness once virile and pacific, forceful and gentle, humane without being soft. In the colonies, Lyautey was said to wield an "iron fist in a velvet glove."[59] He excelled, wrote the *Petit parisien*, in "punishing brigands, restoring stolen goods, and bringing dissidents to order—and all this without firing any shots."[60]

Journalists and editors repeated comments such as these again and again between 1904 and 1912. Taken together, their articles reached tens of millions of French men and women, who learned not just about Lyautey's ideas and actions, but about his looks, dress, mannerisms, idiosyncrasies, and the like. Lyautey, wrote the editor of *Gil Blas*, "is tall and sharp, his svelte body proportioned harmoniously with his strong shoulders ... The silver-tinted hair [highlights] the glow of his thoughts."[61] In focusing so intently on Lyautey, as it had with Savorgnan de Brazza, the mass media of the era made possible an "intimacy at a distance," a familiarity gained without any direct interaction with the individual in question.[62]

Illustration 1.4. Portrait of General Hubert Lyautey. (*Source:* Author's collection)

The French archives contain vivid evidence of the role such "intimacy at a distance" played in making Lyautey a popular charismatic hero and celebrity and in attaching large numbers of French men and women to the colonial ideas and images he seemed to represent. One carton at the *Archives nationales* features about 500 letters to Lyautey congratulating him on his nomination as Resident General of Morocco in April 1912.[63] Most of the missives came from people who knew him only distantly or who had never encountered him at all. Among other things, the letters reveal the importance Lyautey had assumed in the mental worlds of a great many French women and men.

Several people wrote asking Lyautey to take them—or their sons—to Morocco with him, and others expressed their regret that they could not join his efforts. As one writer put it, "The task to accomplish is so elevated, so important to our country, that all those unable to accompany you must suffer a broken heart." In any event, "the hearts of all Frenchmen accompany you [to Morocco] and God is on your side." The writer, who had not seen Lyautey in many years, expressed the disappointments that can result from intimacy at a distance, "I would have been very happy to talk with you about this for a few minutes."[64]

Lyautey's appointment as proconsul of Morocco made him one of the most important people in France; many letter writers saw him as a celebrity and themselves as fans.[65] Several correspondents asked for his autograph, some enclosing a special card for that purpose. Others apologized for writing to him, insignificant citizens as they were. And dozens of writers revealed a deep emotional connection to the charismatic Lyautey and a personal, if vicarious, involvement in his deeds: "When this morning's newspapers brought me, deep in my provincial backwater, the news of your great [new] dignity ... I felt not just a joy but a profound sense of relief." For another correspondent, the emotional connection with Lyautey was such that "I will follow you, in my thoughts, along the path you have chosen. The path will be littered with obstacles, but it will take you into the realm of glory."[66]

For these writers, Lyautey was not just a celebrity, but a charismatic hero as well. Like the protagonists of ancient myth, he had undertaken a glorious quest, a quest revealing that he was the "indispensable man," the "necessary man," the "indispensable leader," the "man of all men of energy and courage."[67] As with other colonial figures anointed as heroes of the Belle Epoque, Lyautey seemed to offer guidance, protection, and inspiration in this prewar era of uncertainty and unease. For one writer, Lyautey was so heroic that "you exude for all of us the aura of Bonaparte on the eve of his conquest of Egypt."[68] "A great chapter in history is about to begin," said another, "and your name will be written on its biggest page."[69] "Without a doubt," wrote yet another, "the prestige of your name alone, a name that means loyalty, courage, protection for the humble ... will attract the [rebellious] natives to you and make them your servants."[70] They will, in other words, submit to Lyautey's *conquête pacifique*.

During a period of nationalist revival and looming fears of war, French men and women found themselves comforted by the "heroic" victories over Moroccan "rebels" and especially by the emergence of a potential savior in Lyautey.[71] Such feelings enabled him to embody in his person not just the French presence in Morocco, but the essential qualities of Frenchness itself. When Lyautey was elected to the *Académie Française* in October 1912, journalists framed this honor as evidence of his ability to incarnate the nation as a whole. "At pivotal moments," wrote the editors of *La Liberté*, "certain names appear before us. All at once everyone finds himself drawn to these names, and we all come together in a kind of national fervor. Today, that name is Lyautey."[72]

The letters to Lyautey and other similar documents demonstrate a broad, popular devotion to this colonial hero and suggest an attribution of charisma similar to what we have seen for Stanley and Brazza as well. If mass media made the dissemination and reception of charismatic figures possible, the medium was not, as Marshall McLuhan thought, the message.[73] Only certain kinds of people could evoke the emotional connections that enabled a great many of their countrymen and women to see them as embodying, as Edward Shils put it, "some *very central* feature of man's existence and the cosmos in which he lives."[74] This formulation might be made more historical by talking not of "existence "and "cosmos," but of the qualities most members of a given society at a particular moment in time consider fundamental to their sense of who they are and who they want to be. In the late nineteenth century, the best candidates for charisma were those who appeared to embody the essence of France or Britain, who extended their country's influence far and wide, and who could thus strengthen feelings of national belonging and pride. In attaching themselves to these figures, looking up to them, following them, and seeking the world through their eyes, a great many people attached themselves to their countries' empire as well.

CHAPTER 2

"So Writes the Hand that Swings the Sword"
Autograph Hunting and Royal Charisma in the German Empire, 1861–1888

EVA GILOI

In 1876, high school student Nicolaas von Cammenga approached Emperor Wilhelm I with a personal request:

> Most Serene, High and Mighty Emperor!
>
> May Your Majesty graciously allow me to direct these lines to Your Majesty, lines meant only to prove my deepest reverence and greatest veneration for Your Majesty. I have a request for Your Majesty, which, if Your Majesty graciously deigns to take notice of it, Your Majesty can easily fulfill. It consists, namely, in having Your Majesty send me a picture of Your Majesty, my dearly beloved Emperor and King. Until now, I have had a photograph of Your Majesty hanging in my room, but a [store-bought] picture—as Your Majesty no doubt knows—never has the same charm as one received from the hand of the person in question.[1]

Cammenga concluded his letter by assuring Wilhelm that it had always been his "dearest wish" to devote his life to Emperor and Fatherland. Unfortunately, the royal navy had rejected him because of his poor eyesight. He expected that, after finishing his schooling, he would "probably" join the army. Not a very forceful or vigorous young man—at the very least, he seemed tentative about his military commitments—Cammenga clearly hoped to connect himself to the charisma of monarchy by receiving a personal souvenir from the emperor.

Cammenga's letter fits squarely into the debate about whether hereditary monarchy was losing its charisma in the age of the "democratization of fame,"[2] or succeeded in retaining and reproducing it. The poles of this debate can be sketched out briefly. In his typology of charisma, Max Weber distinguishes between the charisma of the demagogue and that of traditional monarchy, which conferred upon each successive monarch a hereditary charisma (*Erbcharisma*) that superseded his personal qualities. Weber assumes that, in a modern world marked by routinized bureaucracy, on the one hand, and a demagogic politics of the street, on the other, royal authority based on the divine right of kings loses its persuasive power and becomes an anachronism.[3] In contrast, in his contribution to the *Invention of Tradition*, David Cannadine posits that European princes used their anachronistic status to effect a renewed mystification of monarchy. By the end of the nineteenth century, rulers succeeded in winning over their audiences by staging lavish, historicist spectacles.[4]

A similar ambiguity distinguishes the subfield of royal photography. Drawing implicitly on Walter Benjamin's concept of "aura"—in which reverence is based on the distance, inapproachability, and uniqueness of the object in question—historians often argue that the widespread distribution of royal photographs undermined the monarchy's aura by making the sovereign too visible and accessible.[5] Cammenga's case seems to support this view: the young man bought a portrait of the emperor and hung it on his wall, only to find that it lost its "charm." Nonetheless, this decline in aura—particularly at that moment, in 1876—is surprising. Only five years previously, Wilhelm I had performed the exceptional feat of winning the Franco-Prussian War and unifying Germany behind the Prussian throne. Against the backdrop of Wilhelm's popularity and heroic reputation after 1870–1871, the emperor's photograph could have acted as an icon—much like the images of saints—and retained a sacral aura. After all, the widespread distribution of religious images of saints (or Christ, for that matter) did not diminish their transcendent status.

What prevented the royal photograph from functioning like an icon was not the extent to which it was reproduced, but the social and ontological context in which it was experienced. Cammenga's photograph was devalued because of the way that it was distributed and consumed, rather than its reproducibility per se. The consumption of royal photography grew in tandem with the emergence of fan culture and memorabilia and became imbricated in their social practices. The carte-de-visite photograph, in particular as it developed after the 1850s, provides a prime example of how such photographic souvenirs determined the public's experience of royal charisma. From the perspective of the royal house, the carte-de-visite offered a means to encourage loyalty to the monarchy. Royal intentions notwithstanding, consumers appropriated the photographs and enveloped them in social practices that, while fundamentally pro-monarchic, personalized their experience of the monarchy in ways that undermined its regal aura.

Royal Memorabilia and Autograph Hunting: Breaking through the Social Barrier

By the later nineteenth century, an increasingly self-aware, self-assured audience of monarchy used memorabilia to satisfy expectations of access to the royal house. Monarchs had, of course, long felt the need to display their power before various audiences, and bolstered their legitimacy through spectacular means.[6] By the first half of the nineteenth century, however, Hohenzollern monarchs began to feel trapped into performing to a broader audience that insisted on being part of the royal display. Already in the year 1800, Queen Luise felt the effects of the Prussian public's sense of entitlement: despite complaining to all who would listen about the tedium of having to meet well-wishers on her tours, she felt that she had to press on because it was her "duty."[7] When her eldest son, Friedrich Wilhelm IV, embarked on his tours in the 1840s, his entourage commiserated with him for being a "martyr" enduring the "torment" of his subjects' attentions—for instance, the annoying, uninterrupted singing of the patriotic song, *Heil Dir im Siegerkranz*, to which the king had to listen for hours on end as he traveled from town to town. The king's entourage did not feel, however, that they—or he—could escape his subjects' attentions; they had to accept and acknowledge them.[8]

In the second half of the nineteenth century, the direction of movement reversed itself, as the public took the initiative to travel to see the emperor, Wilhelm I. Bad Ems and Bad Gastein, the two spas that Wilhelm visited annually, became a major draw for tourists, such that the path Wilhelm used for his daily stroll at Gastein was nicknamed *"der Kaiserjäger"*—a pun on the multiple meanings of *Jäger* as both fusilier and hunter—making *der Kaiserjäger* both the name of an Austrian infantry regiment and a reference to the crowds pursuing the emperor.[9] In Berlin as well, Wilhelm I was expected to show himself to the masses that assembled in front of his palace. He joked that *Baedeker's* travel guide had an entry on him as a tourist attraction, and that, even if he was conducting important state business, at a certain time of the day, he had to interrupt the meeting to go to the window and wave to the crowds.[10] Nor were such touristic expectations restricted to *Baedeker's*: by 1905, the guidebook *Berlin und die Berliner* featured ten full pages of tips on how best to conduct one's Kaiser-spotting.[11]

The escalating desire to see the monarch up close meant, however, that it became increasingly difficult actually to encounter him. As Berlin grew from a relatively small royal residence into a million-strong metropolis, and as ever more tourists were able to travel to the royal center, people had to jostle with one another to catch glimpses of the royal family. To bridge the widening gap between the desire for access and obstructed proximity, private entrepreneurs produced royal collectibles to satisfy the demand for contact, and thus capital-ized on their legal right to reproduce the emperor's portrait on consumer goods without prior royal permission.[12] In sum, while Berliners in the first half of the century most commonly experienced the monarchy through the objects they produced—as purveyors to the court, as artisans selling their wares to the royal house—in the second half of the century, the overwhelming majority experi-enced the dynasty as consumers.[13]

The boom in royal memorabilia developed not only against the backdrop of a general, intensified consumer culture,[14] but also the professionalization of the collectibles market from the 1860s onward, which had two primary effects on the perception of the monarchy. First, the new, impersonal mechanisms of sale—dealers, auction houses, official price lists, collectors' journals—that traded in royal relics and manuscripts deprived the royals of their unique status as they were commodified.[15] By putting predictable prices on the monarchy's relics and publicizing them openly, the collectibles market made the dynasty tangible, rather than numinous, and institutionalized, even routinized, the monarchy's mundanity. Second, on the collectibles market, royal memorabilia was traded side-by-side with souvenirs of other celebrities, encouraging con-sumers to make equivalences between what had formerly been separate catego-ries of fame. When letters by Wolfgang Amadeus Mozart or Johann Wolfgang von Goethe were sold at auction alongside those by Wilhelm I, the emperor was subtly compared to the two artists and often given a lesser value: royal documents consistently commanded lower prices than those of great musi-cians such as Ludwig van Beethoven and Richard Wagner.[16] When it came to photographs as memorabilia, the emperor resided in even more questionable company. Not only did the shop windows of Berlin display Wilhelm I's image alongside musical celebrities such as Franz Liszt and Niccolò Paganini, but also theater stars, circus performers, and women of the demi-monde.[17] Such juxtapositions drew the monarchy away from the unattainable distinction of 'royalty' and into the general cauldron of celebrity. The physical circumstances of the trade in royal memorabilia thus ensured that the student Nicolaas von Cammenga's store-bought photograph could not, by itself, act as a sacred icon exuding the unique, inalienable charisma of traditional monarchy.

Cammenga's case also seems to suggest, however, that royal photographs could be reinvested with charisma if they came directly from the monarch's hand. While royal letters and manuscripts sold at auction might no longer have carried a distinguishing, royal aura—and a store-bought photograph of the sovereign even less so—a photograph that the emperor personally signed, expressly for the recipient, carried a magical aura because of the conscious thought and effort that the monarch invested in the object. As such, the auto-graphed photograph gained a kind of 'kinetic' charisma, which lay not in the object per se, but in how it was handled. Through the deliberate act of signature, the autographed photograph was seemingly elevated above the status of a mere collector's item to being a carrier of the monarch's transcendent touch, much like a traditional relic.

This apparent equivalence between royal autograph and traditional relic lay only on the surface, however. In fact, in crucial ways, the autographed photograph was the opposite of a traditional relic because of how the autograph requestor treated the object. The act of asking for an autograph, in particular, was circumscribed by social practices that counteracted the kinetic charisma of the royal signature.

On the most fundamental level, autograph hunting required a conscious decision to break through the traditional social barrier between monarch and subject, a phenomenon that arose in Germany only from the 1870s onward. Of course, the desire for autographs of famous men had a much longer history, but one that largely excluded princes. In the sixteenth century, it became customary for students at German universities to keep a *Poesie-Album* (or *album amicorum*), in which to collect dedications from distinguished professors as souvenirs of their university days. Other members of the middle class gradually took up the custom, requesting dedications from prominent, emulation-worthy individuals; theologians, in particular, solicited inspirational verses from the great figures of the Reformation. By the eighteenth century, interest had shifted to cultural heroes—especially poets such as Goethe—seen not as men to be admired from afar (like the Reformers) but as kindred spirits in art. The designation *album amicorum* now took on an added significance, as famous authors and poets were regarded as peers within a network of Enlightenment men of letters. Album owners expected prominent cultural figures to write elaborate dedications in their albums to mark this belief in universal friendship, and then mixed these formal inscriptions in among those by personal friends and family.[18]

The emphasis on creative and emotional kinship placed eighteenth and nineteenth-century *Poesie-Alben* into the realm of intimate friendship, a realm not readily transferable to monarchy, at least not before the 1870s. Before then, few albums contained signatures of princes unless the album owner served the court in a direct, professional capacity—as courtier, tutor, or theologian to the court. Strangers may have besieged Goethe, Edgar Allan Poe, and even George Washington with requests for autographs, but not Friedrich Wilhelm III or Friedrich Wilhelm IV.[19] To assume this degree of candor in approaching the monarch was still unthinkable. Instead, the only real means of securing a signature from the king before the 1870s was to send him a gift in the hope that he would respond with a signed letter of acknowledgement. Such letters were difficult to obtain, as the monarchy had a longstanding policy of accepting gifts only from individuals personally known to the king, a policy that, although not always strictly enforced, conveyed a clear message of social distance.[20] Even if an individual managed to have an unsolicited gift accepted by the king, his act could elicit reproach from his contemporaries, such as when, in 1836, a *Landwehr* cavalryman sent Friedrich Wilhelm III a poem of his own composition. While the king appreciated the gift, the army's commanders censured the soldier's entire battalion for allowing him to dare to address the sovereign directly.[21]

The public's newfound willingness, from the 1870s onward, to request royal signatures in the name of intimacy and friendship, but without proffering gifts to the monarch first, thus represented a striking breach of social taboos. So novel was this development that state officials continued to feel uncomfortable with the idea of autograph hunting and regarded autograph requestors as "overly confident" and "brash" in posing their requests.[22] Officials also suspected autograph seekers of wanting to sell their prizes on the autograph market, although, ironically, they need not have worried: "mere signatures" commanded very little money, as serious collectors considered them beneath their dignity.[23] To have significant monetary value, even royal signatures had to be attached to letters of historical import.[24] Of course, material value aside, the monarch's signature could bestow social capital, as it did for a wealthy landlord who received a letter from Wilhelm I commending his charitable donations. Hanging the letter in his study, he forced his tenants to admire the object as they paid him their rent on the first of every month.[25]

In contrast to official anxieties, members of the public increasingly set aside lingering reservations about asking for royal autographs.[26] Like Cammenga, many people wrote to the emperor directly, asking him to send them an autographed photograph. Others took the initiative of providing Wilhelm with a photograph of himself, in the hope that he would sign it and return it to them. When he failed to do so, they descended on the royal offices to demand the pictures back.[27] They also began to engineer 'accidental' meetings with Wilhelm to create occasions at which to ask for an autograph.[28] This was one of the reasons why tourists ambushed Wilhelm in Bad Ems and Bad Gastein—to manufacture such 'chance' encounters, designed to break through the traditional social barrier between monarch and subject. The key to this newfound ability to regard the monarch through the lens of friendship, or what John B. Thompson terms "non-reciprocal intimacy at a distance," lay in the object onto which people wanted the royal signature to be placed: the carte-de-visite photograph.[29] As a physical, collectible object, the carte-de-visite was inscribed within social practices that undermined the traditional aura of monarchy.

Carte-de-visite Photographs and the Personalization of the Monarchy

Invented in the mid 1850s, by the time Wilhelm I ascended the throne in 1861, the carte-de-visite had become a Europeanwide sensation, especially for celebrity portraits.[30] Unlike the daguerreotype, the earliest form of photography, the carte-de-visite was the first photographic technique reproducible in mass numbers through a process that combined glass plate negatives with contact paper prints. It was therefore inexpensive, at least by middle class standards, and was small enough to carry around easily, both in its original 2.5 inch x 4 inch "carte" format and in the slightly larger 4.5 inch x 6.5 inch "cabinet" format. (Both formats will hereafter be subsumed under the term 'carte-de-visite'). Both size images were pasted onto a hard cardboard backing, making them durable and ideal as collectible items. Their stiffness meant that they could be handled, circulated, and traded without damage, and readily slipped in and out of the windows of photograph albums, now also produced in great numbers to house the pictures.[31]

As posed photographs, cartes-de-visite gave sitters the ability to determine their self-presentation through the images' backdrops and surrounding props, and allowed Wilhelm I, for instance, to draw upon the inherited iconography of painted royal portraiture.[32] The emperor could not, however, control how people used the cartes-de-visite they purchased. Instead, consumers introduced their own subjectivity into the act of circulating the objects, deciding how to handle them and where to situate them, symbolically and physically, in their daily lives. By personalizing the collector's experience of the monarchy, the carte-de-visite album placed the consumer at the forefront of his or her mediated interaction with the monarch.

Above all, collecting and positioning the royal carte-de-visite in a photograph album was a highly idiosyncratic act. As contemporaries noted, albums were often put together haphazardly as a result of the collector's day-to-day activities. A portrait of Wilhelm I might find its way into a family's album as an impulse purchase, based on what the consumer happened to see in a shop window while moving through the city, so that his or her daily business occasioned the acquisition. It could also come as a Christmas or birthday gift, its inclusion representing the bond between gift giver and receiver as much as the recipient's political beliefs.[33] Once acquired, the monarch's portrait could be placed at the front of an album to signal the family's political loyalties or to act as a model for emulation.[34] More often, it was located at different points within the album—middle, end, or anywhere in between—next to portraits of actors and actresses, travel souvenirs, or other collectible photographs, thus becoming part of the album owner's leisure activities, rather than an expression of outright political affirmation.[35] Through these idiosyncratic collecting habits, consumers communicated not only a self-conscious stance toward the monarchy, but also their very localized, personal life-circumstances.

Within the middle-class home, the photograph album was usually set out on a table in the parlor, where it fulfilled the same function as the room's other bric-a-brac: to prompt conversation with guests. Collectors thus used the monarch's image in the photograph album to facilitate sociability and build personal relationships, drawing it into the orbit of casual amusement and small talk, rather than setting it aside as an object of veneration.[36] Moreover, as a fixed image, the carte-de-visite allowed its owner to take it out and examine it at will, and to return the photograph to its album sleeve at any time. By its very nature, the object freed the possessor from the reciprocal obligations, or even sense of reality, that comes with face-to-face interaction, allowing instead for an "uncontrolled, shameless observation."[37] As John B. Thompson notes, collectors had "a great deal of scope in defining the terms of engagement" in this quasi-relationship. Their ability to slot the celebrities depicted in the photographs, including the emperor, "into the time-space niches of [their lives] more or less at will" lent the experience an intimate, if entirely one-sided, quality.[38]

Finally, the technological parameters of the carte-de-visite contributed to the public's willingness to cross the social barrier to ask the monarch for an autograph. Although royal portraits had been mass-produced as lithographs since the 1830s, people did not ask the king to sign his lithograph (as they asked other celebrities to do); royal autograph hunting arose only with the invention of the carte-de-visite. Although lithography and other graphic techniques did not disappear with the emergence of photography—in newspapers, photography did not displace lithography until the end of the century—the flood of cartes-de-visite after 1860 encouraged new expectations of the monarchy, expectations that the lithograph did not support. Specifically, what most distinguished the carte-de-visite from the lithograph was that, as a posed photograph, it narrowed the ways in which a celebrity could be depicted. The carte-de-visite thus represented a reduction in iconographic possibility that sharpened the focus on the portrayed person's "true self."

Since the publication of Johann Kaspar Lavater's *Physiognomische Fragmente* (1775–1778), portraits of cultural heroes—engravings, woodcuts, lithographs—had been studied to gain insight into the celebrities' innermost being. Such graphic techniques also offered the possibility of depicting the great man in action, or in the process of the creative act. As such, lithographic portraiture was used not only to reflect the actual countenance of the cultural genius, but also the emotions and artistic principles that his work represented. In the 1820s, for instance, the music critic Ludwig Rellstab noted that Beethoven's lithographic portrait showed him as having a "brusqueness, [a] tempestuous, unshackled quality" that Beethoven did not possess in real life, but which the portrait featured to bring it "into conformity with [Beethoven's] works."[39] In a nutshell: lithographs made Beethoven look like his music. This was a common expectation of lithographic portraiture, that it express the emotional tenor of a great man's work, and portray the artist's genius as much as the man himself.

The carte-de-visite continued the tradition of physiognomic realism, but not of depicting the creative act. Contemporaries felt that the photograph's unchanging, representative image encouraged a "quiet, close, inductive physiognomic study" of the individual in question, which in turn allowed the viewer to put himself "into the mind" of the celebrity, to "get to know him 'personally.'"[40] But the carte-de-visite's ten-second exposure time, based on the lighting conditions necessary to produce a good portrait,[41] meant that the sitter had to hold still with an inflexible facial expression: composed, inactive, and looking at a fixed point so as not to blur the image.[42] Only through external means, such as the props surrounding the sitter, could the carte-de-visite imply active emotion or the act of creation.[43] As an exception to this rule, actors could simulate movement by donning costumes and characteristic poses from their theater roles, re-enacting, in the photographer's studio, stage scenes halted *in medias res*. To contemporary viewers, such images were reminiscent of *tableaux vivantes*, the popular parlor game in which participants arranged themselves into scenes from famous paintings or operas. This was not, however, a pictorial technique open to a monarch as self-consciously sober as Wilhelm I, who would have considered any comparison to actors or parlor games as humiliating, and avoided such play-acting in his photographic portraits.[44]

The still, composed facial expression required by the carte-de-visite further lent the emperor's photographs a striking consistency, making his portraits look alike. This impression was heightened by the common use of photomontage, through which a given photograph of Wilhelm's face was pasted onto various different costumes—uniforms, hunting clothes, imperial robes—to make further elaborations of his image. Much like a paper doll, the emperor's clothing and accoutrements changed, but his facial expression remained ever the same. Due to this iconographic repetition, the emperor's face engraved itself onto people's consciousness as a standardized image, reflected in textual descriptions of Wilhelm's countenance, which became remarkably similar and almost clichéd.[45] Captured as he was in the carte-de-visite, Wilhelm's steady, unchanging portrait gave the illusion of a "true" self that could be fixed and fully, conclusively known.

Although aesthetic circles criticized the carte-de-visite's fixity as lifeless and dull, consumers often experienced the royal image as vibrantly alive.[46] When A. Braun and Co. produced a portrait of Wilhelm I in 1877, the *Neue Preussische Zeitung (Kreuzzeitung)* praised the photograph for being so realistic that it seemed as though the emperor were "about to step out of the picture and toward the viewer." In further describing the emperor's photographic face as filled with "a firm gravity, combined with gentleness, all the benevolence that characterizes each of the emperor's salutes, and a heart-warming friendliness," the newspaper emphasized that the image revealed Wilhelm's personal character traits, rather than his public actions as emperor.[47] In this way, royal photographs stood in striking contrast to lithographs of Wilhelm I published in the illustrated press, which depicted the emperor in action—on horseback reviewing his troops, for instance, as a metaphor for his military heroism. Because of its (com)posed nature, the carte-de-visite was not able to demonstrate such ideal attributes or regal aura through action, and instead focused attention on the emperor's personality.

The contrast between the carte-de-visite and the lithograph helps to explain the timing of royal autograph hunting as a social practice, and why people asked the monarch to sign the one and not the other. Lithographs that expressed the creative principles an individual represented also emphasized the king's regal aura and actions, keeping the barrier between monarch and subject intact. The carte-de-visite, on the other hand, enhanced the sense of "actual" being, of psychological lifelikeness, of a reality that could be grasped and touched. It encouraged the consumer to feel that he or she knew the emperor intimately, personally, and well enough to approach him directly.

Once they had broken through the social barrier, autograph hunters continued to personalize the act of autograph seeking. While there were some autograph seekers who styled their requests as acts of veneration—Nicolaas von Cammenga among them—more often, they asked for purely personal reasons. The Thuringian pastor Braunstein provides a typical example: against incredible odds, the two assassination attempts against Wilhelm I in 1878—on May 11 and June 2—coincided exactly with the minister and his wife's birthdays. In a letter to the emperor, Braunstein interpreted this coincidence as a personal "misfortune" for his family, because it became virtually impossible to celebrate the birthdays the following year—as though the emperor had somehow usurped the dates from the Braunsteins. The pastor requested an autograph from Wilhelm, with his signature and the two dates, as a way to reclaim the days of celebration. (Wilhelm granted the request).[48] Likewise, the South German pastor Karl Friedrich Gok solicited a signed photograph for the most intimate of reasons: he was born on the same day, almost the same hour, on which Wilhelm I's father had died. Gok requested the autograph because the coincidence of birth and death had been "so important to me all of my life." The autograph would confirm the significance of that coincidence for the pastor's entire family, as an "enduring memento for me and my descendants." Gok thus asked the emperor to validate his self-perceived connection to the royal family. (Although Wilhelm found the request "rather odd," he "could not bring himself" to reject it).[49]

Despite the overt language of reverence that often accompanied the requests, royal autograph hunting thus marked a deep shift in attitudes toward the monarchy. At first glance, the autographed photograph seemed to function like a traditional relic. Touched by the hand of the monarch, the autograph appeared to reinvest the photograph with the charisma it had lost in the process of commodification. However, unlike the traditional relic, the charisma of the autographed photograph was fundamentally relational: it was determined as much by the actions of the fan/collector as the status of the celebrity/emperor. The social practices surrounding the autographed photograph—the tendency to personalize the interaction, the illusion of "knowing" the monarch, the urge to break through the traditional social barrier—foregrounded the requestor at the expense of the monarch. The royal autograph became a means for the collector to validate his or her own person, to express his or her self-perceived connection to the social center. In the process, the monarch served as a *conduit* of charisma for the requestor, not as the proper subject of veneration or unique status. The manufactured intimacy of celebrity culture and its memorabilia undermined the charisma of traditional monarchy, no matter how grandiosely historicist its public spectacles became.

CHAPTER 3

The Workings of Royal Celebrity
Wilhelm II as Media Emperor

MARTIN KOHLRAUSCH

Only rarely has Wilhelm II, the last Prussian King and German Emperor, been portrayed as a charismatic ruler.[1] This may not be surprising, as nineteenth-century monarchs are usually regarded, according to Max Weber's ideal-types, as examples of traditional authority. Nevertheless, the reluctance to think about charisma and the Kaiser is regrettable, not least because Weber developed his concepts of authority against the backdrop of Wilhelm II's rule.[2]

At the time Weber pondered his ideas on charismatic rule, a dramatic transformation of the monarchy was underway, owing to the emergence of mass media in Germany. In what Walther Rathenau aptly branded "electro-journalistic Caesaropapism," Wilhelm II came to blend mass media and politics into a particular, charismatic form of government.[3] Within that system of rule, the monarch became, by his very nature, a special kind of celebrity. On the one hand, his extraordinary visibility made him a natural beneficiary of the new media society. But on the other, that new society subjected him to unprecedented constraints. Thanks to intense scrutiny from the press, any deviation from the requirements of his royal office, the demands of royal protocol, and heightened public expectations could have severe repercussions. The extraordinary political significance ascribed to the emperor in Germany thus cannot be understood without taking into consideration the media revolution. Such was especially the case because several of the projects linked so successfully to the Kaiser, at least in their initial phases, involved highly mediated topics.[4] Imperialism and construction of the naval fleet ranked high among the projects in question.

The dialectic between media and politics was particularly strong in the German case. Monarchies all across Europe exploited the opportunities offered by the rise of mass media at the end of the nineteenth century, but few enjoyed the

extensive royal prerogatives that the German Empire's unique political structure gave the Kaiser. Thus, Wilhelm II differed from both Queen Victoria,
whose global visibility dwarfed her meager political power,[5] and the Russian
Tsar, whose prerogatives exceeded even those of his German cousin, but who
played a comparatively restricted role in the media.[6] Wilhelm II combined political power, at least on paper and in the imagination of his followers, and mediated power, in the form of public presence, in a way that made the German
monarchy's resonance particularly intense.

Wilhelm II—a Charismatic Ruler?

Although most contemporary analysts left Wilhelm's charisma unexamined,
certain nineteenth-century scholars of constitutional law provide a telling exception to the rule. These scholars tried valiantly to fit the emperor into the
constitutional system, but without success. Their failure moved them to define
Wilhelm II as a 'Caesar': a Prussian hereditary monarch—and thus legitimized
traditionally—who also strove for additional legitimacy as a 'people's Emperor'
(*Volkskaiser*) through public speeches and direct contact with the public.[7] The
legal fiction of 'Caesar' allowed them to imagine the emperor as reconciling a
static constitution with a dynamic society: the democratic element in the constitution would reside in the monarch as *Volkskaiser*.[8] Moreover, these writers
believed that only an 'Integrator', a political force ideally identical to the monarch and ruling through plebiscitary means, could realize the social integration
of an increasingly fragmented German society. Georg Jellinek, one of the most
prominent law professors and a member of the circle around Weber, approv-
ingly described such a system as a "dictatorship of trust" (*Vertrauensdiktatur*), a
system in which the executive earned legitimation in a plebiscitary-charismatic
way and thus bypassed parliament.[9]

Such extreme expectations regarding the integrating role of the monarch
arose immediately upon Wilhelm II's accession to the throne in 1888. With
the monarchy redefined as a programmatic institution, the emperor was expected to take an active role in politics: reforming the school system, establishing a "welfare monarchy," and implementing the construction of an ocean-going
fleet, to name just a few examples. These projects had a strong charismatic dimension not only because they reached far into the future, but also because the
Kaiser was meant to implement them from outside the established administra-
tive institutions. One important implication of the Kaiser's new approach was
that support for him would be relative, tied as it was to the actual success of the
ventures entrusted to him.[10]

Friedrich Naumann, one of the empire's leading liberal politicians, highlighted precisely these features in his study, *Democracy and Imperial Monarchy*

(*Demokratie und Kaisertum*). For Naumann, the neo-absolutism epitomized by Wilhelm II was not an anachronism but rather the essence of modern power.[11] Naumann welcomed the direct engagement of the 'Caesar' as the "protest of the modern person of will (*Willensperson*) against constitutional theories." He regarded as historically necessary this new type of Imperial Monarchy (*Kaisertum*), since it alone would allow the Kaiser to create enthusiasm for new political goals that he, as the embodiment of the empire (*Reichsidee*) and its "future aspirations," was to introduce to the public on his travels and as "Grand Orator" (*Redner großen Stils*).[12]

These quotations suggest that Wilhelm II's style of rule—his speeches, his travels, and his symbolic emphasis on the divine right of kings—functioned as a practical measure meant to meet the demands placed upon him to act as 'Caesar' and 'Integrator.' Wilhelm's attempt to subordinate all aspects of politics and society to his influence (his 'personal regime'), to present himself as the focal point of the nation's life, and especially the eschatological rhetoric of the imperial speeches—the famous *herrliche Zeiten* (glorious times) the Kaiser promised to bring about—can all be seen as features of charismatic rule.[13] It would thus be misleading to see the charismatic monarchy of the legal scholars as merely an academic idea. Rather, as Naumann's interpretation shows, the legal fiction of 'Caesar' was predicated on an attempt to understand the monarchy's reinvigorated relevance and to interpret Wilhelm II's royal practices as an ideal form of modern power.

The recharismatization of the monarchy, and its basis in Wilhelm II's royal practices, grew out of changes in the media landscape of the late nineteenth century—although this media influence escaped the notice of most experts at the time. Few commentators joined the historian Theodor Oncken in recognizing the new reality brought about by the emergence of mass media and with them the groundbreaking structural developments that enabled the monarchy to attain new meaning and relevance. With these media in mind, Oncken described the Kaiser as the "leader of the nation" standing "in the centre of the garish light of day … visible every moment and sought out, observed and criticized, loved and rebuked."[14] From the moment of his birth, the future king and emperor was an object of constant newspaper coverage. Sentimental and sympathetic images of the monarchy, ever an asset for royal public relations, were multiplied exponentially through mass media.[15] Thus, although Germany's political and constitutional structures differed significantly from those of the United States or Great Britain, with respect to the media, the German Kaiser faced the same challenges of heightened visibility and audience expectation as the US President or the British Queen, while also engaging the media as a modern, 'charismatizing' form of power.[16] As the future Chancellor Bernhard von Bülow noted in 1893, the most traditional of all political institutions could both profit and suffer from the new "age of boundless publicity."[17]

The Kaiser and Mass Media

The development of modern mass media in Germany is too complex for a detailed description here; a brief sketch must suffice.[18] After 1880, the number of German newspapers rose dramatically, with many published several times a day. Overall circulation grew apace, as mass papers appealed to a broad range of social groups. The rapidity of this growth made the so-called media revolution more dynamic in the Wilhelmine Empire than elsewhere: media expansion started later, but once underway, the growth rate in numbers and circulation of newspapers exceeded that of the rest of Europe.[19] As politically neutral mass papers and tabloids entered the market, commercial concerns took precedence over issue-oriented reporting or partisan politics. This development in turn moved editors to dramatize topics for a broad audience and to echo the sensationalistic headlines of other newspapers.[20] As a result, newspapers across the journalistic spectrum—and not only the tabloid and popular press—tended to report in a more emotional, personalized, and sensational manner. This new journalistic form guaranteed that the Kaiser would have the spotlight focused on him.

This spotlight also took the form of visual media—photographs, film, and postcards—that demonstrated the extent to which mass media had transformed the presentation and perception of the monarchy. In 1913, a photographer's shop in Berlin advertised "267 heroic poses of the Emperor, all different." No fewer than twenty photographers received the right to serve as court photographers in order to meet the ever-rising demand for royal images.[21] In the new age of trademarks, the Kaiser became a particularly successful label; advertising pioneer Ludwig Roselius called him an impressive example of brand development.[22]

As a brand in his own right, the Kaiser found himself well situated to serve the needs of the early film industry. If professional movie actors generally remained unknown until the star system emerged around 1910, representatives of state—and the colorful German Kaiser in particular—were far more familiar. For this reason, Wilhelm II became the first German movie star, a *vedette avant-la-lettre*. When he appeared at the opening of the Kiel Canal in 1895, he may well have been the world's first politician to be captured on film.[23] By 1900, he had become the most filmed person in the world, and twelve years later, several leading international film companies celebrated Wilhelm as "Filmhelm," as "the most interesting personality ever caught by the lens of the cinematograph."[24]

To some extent, the technical parameters of early cinema facilitated Wilhelm's success as a "film star." The singular appearance of his uniforms and helmets distinguished him from other celebrities, confined to more ordinary garb, and made him more easily recognizable, even when a film's quality was poor.

Moreover, the highly regulated, choreographed character of royal ceremonies, the principal occasions on which the emperor was filmed, allowed cameramen to predict the Kaiser's movements beforehand, and thus to set up their equipment in locations ideally suited to capture him in action.

Beyond such technical considerations, the emperor owed his general success as a media star, in the press as well as in film and photography, to three further aspects of his public persona.

(1) *Peculiarity and distinctiveness.* No other actor on the German political stage was as visible as Wilhelm II. The emperor could build on the traditional reputation of the monarchy, on his political prerogatives and significance, but also on his singular, uniquely styled appearance, which stressed tradition and power as features exclusive to himself as monarch. Commanding a base for public visibility with which no other political contenders could compete, the Kaiser exhibited an odd mixture of glamour and the stiff dignity of Prussia's monarchical past.[25] By thus vulgarizing and romanticizing a whole body of royal heritage and invented traditions, the monarchy could deliver colorful and grandiose images, which parliaments or even presidents lacked. Such qualities further positioned Wilhelm as both a political figure and an object of entertainment.

Of course, mixing traditional and modern features indiscriminately was itself a significantly modern approach,[26] and, in Wilhelm II's case, the mixture was evident in the Kaiser's self-styled uniforms and often-ridiculed eagle helmet.[27] Indeed, it is a self-consciously dressed-up monarch who confronts us in countless postcards and collectible photographs. This imagery became so well known that it sufficed to draw the Kaiser's characteristic helmet to evoke the picture of the monarch and all the connotations attached to him.[28] Such visual shorthand was no doubt invaluable in an era of shrinking attention spans and rapid changes in the focus of media interest. Aggregating complex political problems in his person, Wilhelm II became a "concrete abstraction," fitting perfectly the reductive mechanisms of mass media.[29]

(2) *A new mode of political communication.* The monarch's media-affinity went beyond his celebrity status. Wilhelm II was the first German monarch to use speeches, which Weber regarded as a decisive feature of charismatic rule, to promote his political agenda.[30] These *Kaiserreden*, as they were dubbed, served both the media and the emperor, as they entered into a much closer and more intense exchange than ever before.[31] The monarch's rhetorical impulses led him to present his ideas in abbreviated form and through strong catchphrases. The Kaiser's talent—or fatal habit—of coming up with easily digestible 'sound bites'

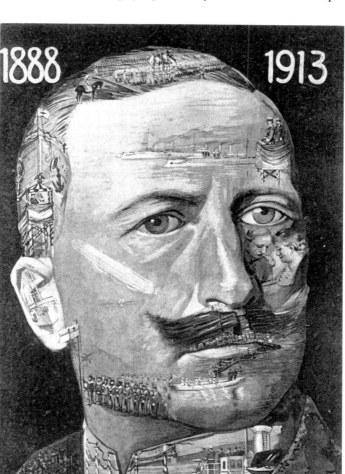

Illustration 3.1. The Kaiser's Portrait as Mirror Image of the Nation. (Postcard of Wilhelm II, 1913)

Under the left eye: 2. June 1880; Betrothal to the princess August Victoria
Under the right eye: Air-ship Zeppelin
Chin and Moustache: 10. August 1890; The taking possession of Heligoland by the Kaiser
Right cheek: 1. Jan. 1891, The hoisting of the German war flag on the East African Coast
Collar: 21. June 1895, opening of the North-east Sea Canal
Right temple: 2. June 1899, Christening of the Ironclad "Emperor William the Great"
Forehead: 2. July 1900, Despatching of an ironclad-Division to East-Asia. Farewell of the Kaiser to the soldiers
Upper part of forehead: Kaiser parade
Ear: Yacht-Hohenzollern
[English phrasing and spelling as on postcard. Source: postcard private collection M.K.]

suited the needs of the new mass media, already swayed by the great political influence the Kaiser commanded. The speeches filled a vacuum in the notoriously deadlocked parliamentary system of the Wilhelmine Empire.[32] His interventions also represented the opinions of a figure, the monarch, who provided an across-the-board point of reference better suited (at least in contemporary theory) to bridge the wide social differences among readers of the mass circulation newspapers than did the representatives of the various political parties.

The Kaiser's speeches thus regularly set the parameters of national debates, as the monarch gained a decisive role in shaping political consensus in an increasingly complex society. That the Kaiser's speeches were excessively criticized does not diminish their significance, but rather underlines the importance that contemporaries attributed to them. Even critical remarks regularly referred to an idealized communications model, in which the monarch presented a political topic to be approved, rejected, or modified by public opinion as expressed through the media. In sum, it was a system predicated both on Wilhelm's political status as head-of-state and his intense media visibility and celebrity. When peace activist Hermann Fried tried to win Wilhelm II over to his cause, he did so because he regarded him as "the most famous individual on Earth."[33] Fried based this assessment on the judgment that, as the literary critic Alfred Kerr noted in 1899, "in the past ten years no-one in Europe has been discussed as much as he."[34]

This media-based political model, which could be called 'direct monarchy' because of the way it circumvented parliamentary forms, proved immensely attractive. To many observers, the direct exchange between monarch and public, as facilitated by the media, seemed the fastest, most efficient, and thus most genuinely modern form of political communication, much more so than the seemingly complicated and indirect system of parliamentary debate, denounced in any case as "English" rather than German.[35] Moreover, since modern mass media permeated all strata of society, the concept of a 'direct monarchy' promised more widespread public participation than traditional political systems relying on indirect representation by political notables. Given the central role the media played in this new form of political communication, it is unsurprising that journalists of all political stripes eagerly endorsed the model of a direct exchange between monarch and his people.

(3) *Personalization and the human factor.* As a corollary to the emergence of the media monarch, a political public of millions of Kaiser-experts, all claiming an intimate knowledge of Wilhelm's character, came into being. The new public bridged party differences and brought about a widespread perception among Germans of a unified public sphere *vis-*

à-vis the monarch. It is telling that sensitive contemporary observers, such as authors Thomas Mann, Otto Julius Bierbaum, and Rudolf Borchardt, replaced the word "people" with "audience" when talking about the public's perception of Wilhelm II.[36] The audience knew what to expect of the monarch on stage, and consequently the Kaiser was increasingly described as an individual rather than as an abstract entity. The attribution of individual character traits was certainly not unique to monarchs of the late nineteenth century. Already in *ancien régime* France, commentators tended to 'humanize' the king by depicting him as a neighbor and family father, just as British observers attempted to integrate the king or queen into civil society.[37] In the case of Wilhelm II, however, this phenomenon developed a new quality. The personalization of politics fostered by the mass media was evident not only in the emphasis placed on the person of the Kaiser as a political actor, but also in the tremendous interest in Wilhelm's character and in what can be called the "construction of a royal individual," a process critical to understanding Wilhelm II's status as royal celebrity.

The Construction of the Royal Individual

There was a strong sense among contemporary German intellectuals that the *fin de siècle* was particularly individualistic, that this era placed great weight on subjective experience, and that a modern monarchy also had to possess an individualistic character. Wilhelm seemed to fit this characterization perfectly, as his unconventional views and impulsive nature gave him a highly idiosyncratic personality.[38] Wilhelm's distinctiveness was also closely related to the cult of the young emperor—Wilhelm II was only twenty-nine years old when he succeeded his father—fostered by a small brochure published by his tutor, Georg Hinzpeter, in time for Wilhelm's ascension to the throne.[39] In *Kaiser Wilhelm II: Eine Skizze nach der Natur gezeichnet (A Sketch from Nature)*, Hinzpeter promised to reveal the emperor's true character, addressing, with astonishing openness, the problems he had encountered in educating the heir to the throne with his "peculiarly strongly marked individuality."[40] In highlighting the emperor's individuality, commentators such as Hinzpeter meant that he was everything but a conventional person, and that he possessed a distinctiveness they contrasted positively to the horrifying sameness of mass society. In doing so, they broke with the tradition of using stock phrases to describe the monarch as "wise," "benevolent," etc., and instead stressed Wilhelm's very specific—i.e., individual—character traits.

What is crucial here is not whether Wilhelm II actually had a distinctive character, but rather the extent to which commentators sought to reconcile the figure of the monarch with the public's longing for a visible personality. When the *Hannoversche Courier* praised Wilhelm II for not being one of the many monarchs who cut off access to his "ego,"[41] it entered into a media discourse reflecting a deep shift in the public perception of the monarch. As one press commentator noted in 1894, it was difficult for people to imagine a king "who is a human being of flesh and blood like ourselves, with the same feelings." Commentators such as Alfred Kerr remarked upon the "strong sense of individuality" present in the Kaiser's speeches, while Bernhard von Bülow could note, with satisfaction, "an unimaginative conformist he is not." For his contemporaries, Wilhelm II was a man with every opportunity for self-realization, and who, as the poet and writer Rudolf Borchardt expressed it, "put something of the egocentric excess of his epoch into his concern for himself, into his self-scrutiny and self-penetration."[42]

These observations demonstrate a newfound obsession with the character and personality of Wilhelm II. Their prevalence further shows that the remarkable curiosity regarding the person of the monarch was no random development. It was necessarily linked with the emergence of a media-conscious public and the prominent brand-name product that was Wilhelm II. The mass media were much more interested in a personalized coverage of the monarch, which appealed to large audiences, than in the sober discussion of constitutional problems that interested relatively few. Treating the monarch as a person "subject to the vagaries of emotional life as any other man"[43] thus transcended an earlier hagiography that rarely referred to the ruler's actual personality. Wilhelm II appeared *vis à vis* the public as an object of almost psychological scrutiny.

The tendency to stress the "human nature"—that he was like "any other man"—did not contradict the equally prevalent image of his special, idiosyncratic personality. Both belonged to the process of adjusting the monarchy to the needs of mass media by overcoming the ruler's traditional aloofness. There was, however, also a strong temporal dimension to this process. The eccentric, neo-baroque image of Wilhelm II, presented early in his reign, worked well in establishing the brand of German Kaiser, but it aroused little sympathy. Gradually—though not systematically—this image was replaced by a more accessible 'humanized' image.

Only after twenty years on the throne did Wilhelm II enjoy his best moments in the public eye. These moments came when he presented himself as an 'ordinary man' with emotions and weaknesses. In November 1906, during the severe political crisis that preceded the notorious Eulenburg scandal—a grave affair within the inner circle around the Kaiser—Wilhelm II had a conversation with writer Ludwig Ganghofer reminiscent of today's at-home interviews with celebrities. Wilhelm II used the opportunity to explain "how his daily duties, which pressed down on him, tied him heavily" and to present sentimental details from his family life. Public response was extremely positive, as it was for a speech the Kaiser gave in August 1907 in Munster. Wallowing in self-pity, Wilhelm II declared: "During my long reign—it is now the twentieth year since I assumed office—I have dealt with many people and have had to put up with a good deal from them, [since] often unconsciously and, alas, also consciously, they have wounded me bitterly."[44] It remains surprising how positive the journalistic reaction was to this emphasis on monarchical subjectivity, even taking into account the hagiography inherent in publications about the monarchy.[45] Commentators believed that they had witnessed a deep transformation in the emperor's character: "Never before has he spoken to his people in this manner," as one newspaper noted.[46]

In the process, Wilhelm II became part of a strikingly modern culture of confession, which presented its own, new pressures requiring novel kinds of escape mechanisms. When, in August 1908, newspapers reported favorably on a poem titled "Resignation," written by the late Austrian Empress Elisabeth (also known as Sissi), they broached the broader problems encountered by royal stars in coming to terms with their exposed position.[47] During her lifetime (1837–1898), the unusually attractive Empress had captured the public imagination with her elaborate cult of beauty, which included special diets and a complicated hair-styling procedure, as well as her month-long absences from the royal court. Only seventeen at the time of her wedding, she had been in constant conflict with her mother-in-law, conflict that led to a deterioration in her marriage to the Austrian Emperor and years of wandering from one remote palace to another. In the process, she came to symbolize, in public consciousness, the suppression of the free individual through antiquated court ceremonial.[48] Her desire for freedom from the court, popularly interpreted both as a heightened sense of individuality and an odd reclusiveness, drew intense press coverage until her sudden death by assassination in 1898.

When Wilhelm discovered the Empress's poem ten years later, he carefully preserved it, and later donated it to the Empress Elisabeth Museum. German newspapers widely covered the event and paid particular attention to the place in which he had found the poem—Sissi's Achilleion palace on Corfu, which the Kaiser had recently purchased.[49] In these newspaper reports, Wilhelm's admiration for the poem linked him to Sissi in their common resignation to their fate as public figures, while the Achilleion became an emblem of royal fame and reclusiveness. For both the Austrian Empress and the German Emperor, the secluded, romantic locale served as a hideaway to escape the ever more pressing demands of the mediated world around them. Indeed, the fact that Wilhelm II erected a memorial to 'Sissi' in the palace park suggests that he deliberately tried to connect himself to the myth of one of the *fin de siècle's* most extravagant and celebrated royal stars.

A similar dialectic between privacy and publicity is evident in the royal travels in which Wilhelm II famously and excessively indulged. When embarking on his annual *Nordlandreisen* to the remoter parts of the Norwegian coastline, the Kaiser entered into a paradoxical game of hiding from the media, while at the same time allowing a number of professional photographers to make exclusive short films and snapshots for public consumption, bringing the Kaiser right back into the homes of his subjects. The Kaiser and the court thus increasingly stressed the private side of power through intimate pictures from the *Nordlandreisen*, while also appearing to show that he needed relaxation and an escape, only more so than everyone else.[50]

At the same time, the emperor's more traditional royal entries into places big and small connected him to the masses.[51] By routinely assembling enormous crowds, these well-staged events functioned like a self-fulfilling prophecy to confirm the Kaiser's celebrity status. Even beyond German borders, and particularly in Britain, Wilhelm II was able to attract mass audiences that, according to newspaper accounts, evinced "an absorbing interest in his doings."[52] Still, the huge audiences that greeted the Kaiser as he traveled across the German Empire also included those who normally opposed the monarchy,[53] so that his staged entries exaggerated his 'real' popularity. Individuals held various motives for attending these spectacular events, from the desire to demonstrate allegiance or opposition to the monarchy, to mere curiosity to see a famous individual and so to be entertained. The entries also provided ample opportunity for the media to multiply the events in pictures, postcards, and films, thus helping the court occupy a prominent space in illustrated magazines and early cinema. The emperor's public appearances as covered by the press—"world history unwinding from the print roll," as Rathenau described them—turned personality-based entertainment into a political act.[54]

Whether or not Wilhelm II pursued an explicitly elaborated media strategy—it is unlikely, in fact, that he consciously understood the mechanisms of mass media—the end result was the same. By presenting himself in a human way, the emperor lent himself to the personalization of politics in which the mass media's "society of self-disclosure" turned on the illusion of intimacy and the effort to present even kings as, at once, human beings and official persons. Such politicians-cum-private-individuals laid open their personalities in a "conversational mode," as Wilhelm II did in his talk with the writer Ganghofer, or in a "confessional mode," as in the Kaiser's speech in Munster.[55]

Within this mediated context, the emperor had to present himself as "one of us," as well as to live up to expectations of authenticity, a structural precondition of modern communication. If the monarch managed to present himself in an unpretentious and authentic way, he could be sure to meet the emotional demands of the new mass readership, as mediated, and cultivated, by the press. Of course, this accommodation to modern times took place selectively and worked against the background of Wilhelm II's marked personality—the Kaiser as a brand-name product. This development also implied, however, that the

Kaiser was increasingly judged as much on his personal qualities as on his genuine political actions. While it became ever more common during the course of the nineteenth century to judge monarchs on their achievements, in Wilhelm II's case, personal character also came into play. This is most explicit in the great scandals involving the monarchy, just at the moment when the Ganghofer conversation and the Munster speech sparked extensive discussions about the royal individual and his character.

The Scandalous Monarch

The so-called Eulenburg affair, the most significant political scandal of the Wilhelmine era, provides a good illustration of the new importance of the monarch's character, as well as the link between publicity and intimate knowledge about the monarch. In 1906, the immensely influential political journalist Maximilian Harden penned a series of articles accusing illustrious members of the imperial entourage, including Prince Philipp Eulenburg and General Count Kuno Moltke, of forming a camarilla around the monarch, characterized by homosexual inclinations and an "effeminate" foreign policy. Hoping to clear their names through juridical action, Moltke and Eulenburg became embroiled in a series of lawsuits that extended over a two-year period. Harden's highly public attacks cast the Kaiser's friends in a very negative light, and Eulenburg, one of the Kaiser's closest confidantes and most prominent figures of the Reich, found himself completely discredited.[56]

The lawsuits triggered a media interest unheard of until then. As the prestigious *Vossische Zeitung* picturesquely commented: "Lawsuit Moltke-Harden in the morning, Caruso in the evening. And everybody expects a feast. The demand for tickets for the drama in Moabit [the location of the court-room], of which one could not tell whether it would become a tragedy or comedy, is no less than for the first appearance of the king of tenors in the Berlin operahouse."[57] Surprisingly, press interest remained high throughout the entire two-year proceedings. And when the cases were reopened in April 1909, they returned immediately to the front pages.[58] The *Berliner Tageblatt*, hardly a vulgar, Grub-Street paper, alone published at least 150 articles dealing exclusively with the lawsuits and their political implications.

What can be observed here is a reciprocal dynamic between politics and sensationalist media. Without the connection to Wilhelm II, the Eulenburg case would never have received such broad interest, nor would the quality newspapers have reported it.[59] And without the sensationalistic aspect of homosexuality and the press interest it caused, the ensuing radical and open criticism of Wilhelm II would not have been possible. But the extremely explicit revelations made in the course of the trial, revelations about the homosexual practices of the men closest to him and their terms of endearment ("Darling") for him, proved disastrous for the Kaiser. Commentators concluded that Wilhelm II had either tolerated the special composition of his entourage or failed to recognize the problem. The first conclusion raised moral concerns, and the second questioned his ability to discern human nature. Both touched the core of the personal, and thus also the political, integrity of the monarch.

As the direct attacks on the Kaiser's entourage left him unshielded from an increasingly antagonistic mass press, the emperor found himself vulnerable to three kinds of critique—all linked to the emergence of a public, mediated monarchy described above. First, the scandal prompted a critique of Wilhelm II's performance, in which commentators depicted him as a political leader who failed to achieve the goals he had set for himself, and who, after twenty years in office (in 1908), lacked excuses for this failure. Tellingly, however, and this is the second point, the critique did not so much focus on concrete political blunders as on character traits, on problems that ranged from a lack of independence and discernment, to a naivety about human nature, to outright insensitivity. The Eulenburg scandal thus cast the monarch as an individual lacking the qualities necessary to rule. One could even say that the personalization of the monarchy, from which Wilhelm II, for a time, had profited immensely, boomeranged against him and created the decisive preconditions for the destruction of royal aura in the course of the scandal. Wilhelm found his standing undermined by the very mediatization from which he had earlier benefited so handsomely.

The third major line of critique turned on the Kaiser's failure as a communicator. It was no coincidence that an alleged camarilla around the Kaiser stood at the center of Harden's reproaches. The camarilla was criticized not so much as a source of faulty political decisions, but as an anachronistic obstacle to direct and transparent communication between public and monarchy. The problem, that is, was not the monarch's inability to realize specific political goals; judgments on this count varied along ideological lines. What opened him to widespread criticism was the far more damaging accusation that he had shirked his duty to engage in direct communication with the public.

Ultimately—and paradoxically—the third critique buttressed the idealized model of direct communication between monarchy and public through the aegis of the media. While the scandal provided a way to deal with frustrated expectations, it was simultaneously a conciliatory event ostensibly proving that "direct monarchy" worked. On the one hand, the scandal allowed for extreme criticism, as the *lèse-majesté* law lost its relevance in the course of the Eulenburg affair. On the other, the scandal, in the end, produced practical, relevant changes. Specifically, Eulenburg's removal from court, as a result of having been discredited, was interpreted as a reestablishment of direct communication with the monarch.

A similar mechanism can be observed in the so-called *Daily Telegraph* affair of November 1908, which was closely connected to the Eulenburg scandal. In a conversation with an English officer, Wilhelm II described the English as "mad mad mad as March hares" because they were so suspicious of him, and declared himself one of England's few friends in Germany. The conversation appeared as an interview in the *Daily Telegraph*, supplemented with revelations that the Kaiser had advised Queen Victoria in the Boer War, thus allegedly favoring England's interests over Germany's. The article caused a media storm in Germany, where editorialists received it with shock and profound irritation. The media outrage caused by the bizarre interview forced the Kaiser to announce a "declaration of subjugation," in which he promised henceforth not to deviate from German public opinion.[60]

The final balance sheet of the scandals reveals mixed results. While the institution of monarchy survived them with little harm, Wilhelm II's own, public reputation was badly tarnished. Not only was his personal character heavily questioned, but existing taboos inhibiting discussion of the emperor's conduct and inner circle disappeared. In that sense, scandal was the price that Wilhelm II had to pay for what initially had been his successful liaison with mass media. The more that politics became part of a dynamic business of entertainment, the more politicians, including the Kaiser, were judged as much by their character traits as by their achievements.

Conclusion: Royalty and Charisma

Despite the charismatic potential of the 'direct monarchy' model, Wilhelm II was unable to meet the hypertrophic expectations of a media society, or to function as the all-convincing agenda-setter for whom commentators had so greatly longed. At the same time, the appealing concept (from a contemporary perspective) of integrating the fragmented empire through an individual had clearly failed. What remained, and in heightened form thanks to the Eulenburg scandal, was a personalization of politics as fostered by mass media. This development led to a greater emphasis on charismatic forms of political leadership, largely imagined as a direct leader-to-people relationship facilitated by the media and applied even to traditional forms of political power. This form of 'relational charisma' differed significantly from the legitimate, traditional authority still dominant a generation earlier. Traditional royal attributes such as aloofness lost their significance in the new media-monarchy personified by Wilhelm II. The monarch became—at least in theory –a prime mover, an active player who operated outside of formal political structures to realize projects of direct personal interest to him. He did so by using the channels of mass media.

Ultimately, the demand for a charismatic monarchy helped bring Wilhelm II down. Even before Germany's defeat in 1918, numerous voices demanded a new ruler capable, first and foremost, of ensuring better communication between the media and the political center. Any monarch who wished to retain his legitimacy thus had to cultivate an image as the people's emperor and great communicator, as an individual with the qualities of character and personality that qualified him to rule. Only if we understand Wilhelm II as attempting to fulfill the demand for charismatic, media-based leadership, at the expense of the purely hereditary claims to legitimacy of traditional monarchy, can we explain the sharp decline in public support for his reign before, and especially during, the war. Wilhelm II's flight to the Netherlands in 1918 seemed to confirm a now-widespread view that he possessed too weak a character to rule effectively. While most postwar commentators deemed the aura of the institution and the inherited charisma of the monarchy of marginal importance, Wilhelm II's insufficient personal charisma proved decisive. This is why his flight could have such an overwhelming impact as the ultimate evidence of the monarch's fatal weakness. For us, it serves as a final proof of the personalization of the institution.

In this chapter, I have attempted to locate two seminal developments deriving from the emergence of mass media: the personalization and public promotion of the monarchy, which can be subsumed under the heading "celebrity," and the more political (in a stricter sense of the word) participatory demands, which can be subsumed under the heading "charismatic monarchy." Both lines were strongly intertwined and interdependent. The new mass media granted the emperor pervasive visibility, making him central to media culture and setting the basis for the monarch as 'great communicator' and the political expectations this concept awakened. The ever-rising tide of participatory demands was largely channeled into the new media monarchy with its mercurial exponent. Not only did this process reshape the monarchy itself, but it also enabled that traditional institution to influence the way that "participation through media" was integrated into the German political system. In this sense, writer Ludwig Thoma's democratic question of 1907—in reference to the Eulenburg scandal—seems strangely old-fashioned but also farsighted: "Why do we concern ourselves with His Majesty the Emperor's intimate acquaintances? ... The more we make the ruler's private life a public matter, a matter of the people, the more we distance ourselves from freedom."[61]

PART II

Celebrity as Performance

CHAPTER 4

From the Top
Liszt's Aristocratic Airs

DANA GOOLEY

"L'état, c'est moi"—Louis XIV

"Le concert, c'est moi"—Franz Liszt[1]

When Franz Liszt died in 1886, he was so famous that Eduard Hanslick, an influential Viennese music critic, claimed there was "no better known face in Europe."[2] Hanslick was a master of the double-edged compliment, and he chose his words carefully. He did not say that Liszt was the best-known *composer* or even the best-known *pianist*—these, in Hanslick's view, had already faded from public memory. It was literally the *face*, reproduced ad infinitum in journals, lithograph portraits, and other ephemera, that had created and sustained Liszt's pan-European celebrity. Hanslick's comment voices a suspicion that has dogged celebrated public figures since the early nineteenth century: that celebrity might attest to the image-making power of the media as opposed to the presence of authentic "inner" talent. Since their emergence in the early nineteenth century, the print and visual media have produced a nagging anxiety that charisma might be an illusion called into play by mechanized habits of spectatorship and material consumption, rather than an essence that pours forth from a talented individual and finds due recognition by discerning audiences.

Because Liszt is one of the first performers around whom this crisis of authenticity revolved, and because his career peaked along with the first media explosion, he is often seen as the nineteenth-century prototype of modern celebrity. His compelling visual iconography, at once wild, arrogant, self-fashioned, and exalted, gave rise to outlandish behavior on the part of his audiences as well as large profits at the box office. This circulation of Dionysian performance with desire and capital makes him appear as the first rock icon, an image that has been difficult to shake off, especially since Ken Russell's 1975 camp flick *Lisztomania*, in which the Hungarian virtuoso is played by The Who's Roger Daltrey. Cultural historians too have tended to see Liszt as a figure around whom pop stardom and mass culture originated. In a pioneering study of heavy metal, Robert Walser puts Liszt at the beginning of the line of *noir* virtuoso instrumentalists culminating in guitar heroes such as Randy Rhoads and Eddie van Halen.[3] Richard Leppert reads the romantic virtuoso as "an aesthetic analog to economic, political, technological and cultural modernity," whose performances fully engage the audience with industrial technology and the contradictions of bourgeois subjectivity.[4] And Lawrence Kramer argues that in Liszt's cultural context, "virtuosity helped form a series of epoch-making connections between mass entertainment, the construction of subjectivity, and the birth of stardom."[5] This emphasis on Liszt as a forward-looking figure might be seen as a postmodern rearticulation of the idea, propagated zealously by his acolytes in the 1850s, that Liszt was a prophet of the musical future.

Other recent interpretations revise this picture by presenting Liszt as a figure of historical transition with considerable debts to the musical past. Kenneth Hamilton complicates Liszt's reputation as "inventor of the solo recital" by showing that his incarnation of the concert drew on the older tradition of the miscellaneous program, mixing piano solos with vocal numbers and serious music with popular repertory.[6] Leon Botstein argues that Liszt's advocacy of symphonic music based on literary or philosophical programs was in part an attempt to restore, within the conditions of modern musical life, a facility of communication between composer and public that he had come to idealize from his education in Vienna as a young man.[7] In addition, Detlef Altenburg has demonstrated the depth of Liszt's commitment to reviving and renewing the "classical" legacy of Johann Wolfgang von Goethe and Friedrich Schiller when he took up his *Kapellmeister* position at the Weimar court in 1848.[8]

Here, I will similarly emphasize Liszt as a transitional figure by focusing on a dimension of his charisma that points historically backward: his aura of aristocratic grace and superiority. Liszt was fully modern in his use of print media to facilitate a sense of familiarity and emotional identification on the part of the audience, yet the drawing power of his aristocratic airs derived from premodern modalities of charisma that preceded the European media explosion and in significant ways survived it. In contrast to the tendencies of modern media, this aristocratic appeal is predicated upon the spectator's dis-identification with the performer: the spectator is impressed by and drawn toward the performer's appearance of innate elevation or otherworldly grace. Liszt's aristocratic aura had little to do with the sound of the music he played. If anything, his volatile, contrast-driven concert pieces worked against it. The sheer force of his virtuosity, so far ahead of that of his contemporaries, played a much greater part in elevating him beyond the normal. Yet as the case of Niccolò Paganini proved, extraordinary instrumental command was not quite enough to convince people that a performer was fully possessed of some deeper inner *virtù*. Liszt managed to build an impression of aristocratic elevation into his multifaceted persona principally by keeping his social networks extremely high and by staging his concerts in special ways.[9] By focusing on self-representative matters such as these, we might nuance our sense of what constituted "desire" in Liszt's audiences, which has too often been reduced to its evident erotic charge. In Max Weber's meditations on charisma, there is something intensely pure, inaccessible, or irretrievably "other" about the charismatic figure, and it is this dimension that an emphatically "modern" interpretation of Liszt may risk overlooking.

Two Publicities

Liszt's aristocratic aura was not just the product of personal appropriation or self-fashioning. It was in part the legacy of eighteenth-century musical culture, where courtly patronage was a major source of income and required that musicians emulate gentlemanly manners and graces. In the early nineteenth century, freelance career paths gradually freed musicians from the necessity of aping the nobility. But complete independence from elite patronage was rare for Liszt's generation, and the old habits died hard.[10] Two of Liszt's most distinguished contemporary pianists, Frédéric Chopin and Sigismond Thalberg, operated predominantly within networks of noble patronage, and both adopted markedly "noble" personal images. Well into the nineteenth century, kings and queens publicly rewarded virtuoso performers with gifts such as watches or tobacco boxes, in exceptional cases even awarding them with royal distinctions or medals.[11] This practice hearkens back to old, gift-based social customs that were evidently out of character with the modern, free market framework of public concerts. Rather than suppress such gifts in favor of a "modern" image of the concert, Liszt played them up, wearing his numerous medals and royal orders at public appearances. He gained considerable notoriety by wearing at a concert an honorary saber he had been granted by the Hungarian nobility in Pest, with matching national costume. Though proud of his talent and his social and financial independence, Liszt was receptive to the special status that could be conferred from persons of higher social status and wore its trappings onstage. Some have even argued that Liszt was plagued by feelings of insecurity about his unremarkable birth and incomplete education, prompting him to display his honors and titles in compensation.

Even as urban public spaces acquired the characteristics of industrial modernity, certain patrician markings remained. Liszt capitalized on those remains to arouse the enthusiasm of his audiences. An initial step in historicizing Liszt's popularity, then, is to extend the concept of "publicity" beyond its most common use today as a synonym for advertising. Jürgen Habermas's distinction between "representative publicity" (*repräsentative Öffentlichkeit*) and "civil publicity" (*bürgerliche Öffentlichkeit*) can help do this, not least because these categories are historically constituted.[12] Habermas's representative publicity is a quality of elevation or grace that a person of authority carries with him or her as a kind of innate "aura." It took the purest form in the feudal lord of the Middle Ages, whose subjects acknowledged his authority as a permanent, non-negotiable consequence of his inborn endowments. This static, auratic aspect of representative publicity had nevertheless to be produced and sustained from somewhere in the social domain. It could not exist without rituals of publicity, ranging from small details of physical behavior to major processional pageantry. As Habermas explains, the feudal lord "displayed himself, presented himself as an embodiment of some sort of 'higher power,'" even if this higher power in principle exceeded its realizations in performance.[13]

These rituals of representative publicity did not disappear with the decline of the Middle Ages, but "remained very much in force up to the beginning of the nineteenth century."[14] In the course of the eighteenth century, however, they were gradually divorced from their direct political functions. They were sublimated into a set of social codes—etiquette—showing "grace" and "superiority," but performed more and more in private spaces, behind closed doors, with less attention to an audience of spectators. The eighteenth-century salon was in this sense a descendant of the feudal lord's pageantry: it marked a physical space of endowed superiority, and placed the general public outside of that space—a social mapping, as we shall see, that was not lost on Liszt. The critical link between Liszt's talent and the aristocracy's habits of representative publicity is their shared emphasis on *performance*—social status produced and sustained in the medium of behavior and display.

The first performing musicians to incarnate celebrity of a kind comparable to that of Liszt were the *castrati* of the eighteenth century, who operated in one of the central institutions of representative publicity, the royal opera house. It appears that the *castrati* attracted the attention of all classes of the population, but symbolically and socially they belonged exclusively to the wealthy nobility and royalty, functioning as instruments in the display of elite power before audiences. Onstage, they played heroic and historical characters of sublime military and ethical virtue, delivered in the medium of extraordinary virtuosity that pushed coloratura figuration and vocal sustain to new limits. Their aura of awesome authority was reinforced by their historical association with the Roman church and by their exclusive traffic in high social circles. To the lower classes sitting in the parterre, the *castrati* offered little in the way of identification, but plenty in the way of admiration and awe. Similar to the religious *virtuosi* of the Middle Ages, they fascinated people through several orders of otherness, which were strongly reinforced by anatomical weirdness. Yet their high-class patrons took measures to ensure that this apparitional power would be framed as an extension of their social and political domination. The *castrati* were public without being an expression of a general will or taste, public by virtue of the nobility's control over public space and theatrical representations.[15]

In contrast, Habermas's civil publicity emerged gradually over the course of the eighteenth and nineteenth centuries and in many ways diverges from the "top down," performative characteristics of representative publicity. It is an inclusive sphere characterized above all by rational debate, discussion, and information concerning any events of "public interest" in the familiar sense of "general interest." Its representative and dominant institution is the press, which putatively carries the opinions and thoughts of the educated public working in collective agency, rather than imposing knowledge by decree from above. The differences between civil publicity and representative publicity can be illustrated with a brief look at the history of publicity posters for concerts. When public concerts started piling upon one another in London in the 1780s, and word of mouth or social networking no longer sufficed to guarantee a good audience, concert-givers began creating posters with an explicitly social form of address: "The gentry and nobility are invited to..."[16] Posters of this kind still obeyed the logic of representative publicity in that they presumed a social hierarchy and a nominally personalized mode of address (an invitation from X to Y). By contrast, posters advertising the concerts of Liszt and his contemporaries in the 1830s tended to isolate the event from specific social classes and exchange, with formulations such as "Mr. Liszt will give a concert this Saturday evening at the Grosser Redoutensaal," or simply "Concert de M. Liszt" together with a list of the pieces to be played. Posters of this kind frame the concert as a matter of "general public interest" that all viewers may choose to pay attention to or ignore—this nonexclusiveness or nonselectivity being the key to its "civil" character.

Musical performers wanting to give concerts for their own profit in the 1820s needed more than ever to use publicity posters and other print media, and thus found themselves immersed in the sphere of civil publicity. In many urban capitals, an open "concert marketplace" emerged that gradually established musical institutions outside the orbits of traditional patronage and of the relatively exclusive subscription-concert system. Tickets to musical events were available to the general public in a novel way, and concert artists depended on drawing them in. Paganini, Liszt, and other virtuosos did not have patrons financially backing them. Yet generally speaking, such performers could not and did not rely on civil publicity alone. Audiences still seemed to expect that the performer should represent some form of "higher power" through a reputation carefully built in elite salons, if not directly in the royal household. A virtuoso prepared his or her public appearances not through the media alone, but through a blend of media and private salon exposure, where oral publicity generated a core public for the concert. At his successful debut in Vienna, the young Chopin was congratulated onstage by a leading patron in the city's musical circles, Count Dietrichstein, giving the aspiring virtuoso from Warsaw a sort of social benediction long before the press could do the same.[17] A similar pattern of aristocratic approval preceding a public appearance can be found with Clara Wieck, Felix Mendelssohn, and even the notoriously asocial Paganini.

Representative publicity, then, remained a force in early nineteenth-century concert culture, even as a new, more commercial logic was taking over. It was still possible in Liszt's time, for example, to build a public performing career *primarily* through high-placed connections. An example is Lola Montez, the "Spanish" dancer who operated in precisely the same milieu as Liszt (and apparently had a fling with him in 1844). Montez was something of a latter-day courtesan, combining dance performances with erotic courtship in a manner reminiscent of the ballet dancers at the Paris Opéra. Unlike most other courtesans, she claimed (falsely) to be of noble origin and made the rounds of upper-crust salons, where her eccentric and powerful intelligence impressed many, while her assertive, frank breaches of decorum scandalized others. Montez's dance performances in London, Dresden, Berlin, and Paris were always prepared by immersion in the salons of the highest society, where she typically found a male patron or a series of vying protectors. When she made public appearances, it was principally these male admirers who led the applause and kept the flowers raining down upon the stage. But she had also prepared her appearances in the media with a fanciful biography identifying her as the exiled widow of a Spanish aristocrat who had become a political martyr. This combination of civil and representative publicity had an impact: in nearly every locale, audiences were initially carried away by her performances. But just as consistently, critiques would soon appear in the newspapers faulting her dances as sub-professional, and her public draw would diminish to the point where she could not offer many more performances. Here the domain of civil publicity, with its invitation to critical evaluation, revealed its increasing power relative to representative publicity. It did not help Montez's aristocratic aura that her Spanish dances (the nervous "spider" dance, for example) employed a choreographic vocabulary that drastically downplayed traditional ballet movements, accenting instead passionate, exotic, and sometimes bizarre movements that reminded audience members of popular dance hall entertainment.

Only in the United States, with its aversion to the trappings of European elitism, did something resembling "pure" civil publicity come into being in the early nineteenth century. The new power of media was demonstrated forcefully when P.T. Barnum began promoting Swedish opera soprano Jenny Lind for her 1850 American tour. Barnum had imported European virtuosos to the US for transcoastal concert tours already in the 1840s, but when it came to preparing Lind's tour, he outstripped even himself. According to rival impresario Max

Maratzek, who witnessed the whole thing, "a reputation was manufactured for her, by wholesale. It was not merely made by the inch, but was prepared by the cart-load."[18] Barnum's basic strategy strikes us today as unremarkable, but it was novel at the time: "He flooded the newspapers with portraits, sketches, letters, stories, many fictitious," and during the tour he added to these publicity genres a powerful innovation, the celebrity interview.[19] Lind's US reception was phenomenal right from her arrival at the New York harbor, which was meticulously stage-managed by Barnum, and the public's enthusiasm surged through the first months of her lengthy tour. Barnum's strategy of media saturation has a distinctly modern feel, and Joseph Horowitz sees it as the origin of a US model of publicity that he calls the "ballyhoo tradition."

Barnum's strategy in promoting Lind shows just how indispensable aristocratic aura was in the European context. In Europe, Lind's career as an opera singer put her in high social circles. But the US disapproval of inherited privilege meant that Barnum was forced into an extreme use of civil publicity to reconstruct and refocus Lind's character. The image Barnum created for Lind was a peculiar brew of genteel European exoticism and a Protestant American ethics of purity and sincerity. He trumpeted her charity and feminine virtue and shaped her concert programs to de-emphasize opera arias, highlighting instead unpretentious folk songs, self-accompanied on the guitar. In building up Lind as a figure for audience identification, Barnum deliberately downplayed her high-class aura: "When mobs of New York 'fashionable' congregated outside the hotel of the recently arrived Jenny Lind, he [Barnum] worried that so much *beau monde* attention would ruin his prospects."[20] The contrary holds for Liszt: his affiliations with the *beau monde*, together with his physiognomy and aspects of his concert style, were integral to his charismatic projection. In the examples that follow, I will focus on three moments in his career—his early concerts in Paris, his breakthrough concerts in Vienna in 1838, and finally his 1840 visit to London—to highlight the role his noble connections and social aura played in developing his onstage appeal, and to trace the independent functioning of civil and representative modes of publicity.

Liszt and the Resources of Publicity

Liszt's earliest public appearances in Paris as a twelve-year-old child prodigy took place in 1823 and 1824. They were arranged entirely by his father Adam Liszt, who was responsible for renting the hall, purchasing the candles, and having the posters printed. Although they were free enterprise events, Adam Liszt made little use of the press to advertise them. The task of rounding up a public, in Restoration Paris, meant going straight to royal circles, gathering prestige there, and letting it trickle down by word of mouth. One account from this early period reports, "after having played to the greatest acclaim before the Duke of Orleans, the present King of France, he [Liszt] became everyone's object of admiration, and the highest social circles fought for the privilege of paying homage to the astonishing child."[21] Another early biography announces, "An entire year went by, during which the young Liszt was like a doll for all ladies in Paris. He was in demand everywhere, flattered, caressed, spoiled, each of his droll or impertinent remarks … were found adorable … One evening at the Théâtre-Italien … every box vied for his company."[22] In such accounts, the desire to meet and hear Liszt radiates at least in part from its link to royal power, the Duke of Orleans, or the reflection of that power in the nobility's boxes at the Théâtre-Italien. The brief reviews we possess of these early concerts, furthermore, consistently draw attention to the fact that Liszt had been taken into the protection of the Duchesse de Berry, who had one of the most prestigious salons in Restoration Paris.[23] As a boy, Liszt's charisma was configured not around an individualized personality, but around the "borrowed" glamour of royal protection.

In the early 1830s Liszt developed the idiosyncratic personality for which he is best known today: he immersed himself in Romantic literature and philosophy, honed his compositional voice, and forged a highly original persona and stage presence that attracted both fascination and mockery. This romantic persona is often celebrated as a revolutionary break from the more traditional gentlemanly image that virtuosos such as Henri Herz and Johann Nepomuk Hummel projected. But this presumes a basic incompatibility between romantic and high-toned models of artistic identity. It would be overstating the case to claim that they have no symbolic or stylistic tensions between them—Liszt's hair was definitely "romantic" and not "gentlemanly"—but neither are they mutually exclusive. Chopin's music and persona, for example, accommodated appropriations by Romantics such as Eugène Delacroix, George Sand, Robert Schumann, and Liszt while at the same time endearing him to the conservative nobility in Paris. Romanticism's most stunning personality and Liszt's avowed model, Byron, was, of course, a lord himself. In addition, the boundaries between patrician and artistic models of superiority or innate grace blurred after the revolution of 1830. The revolution, together with the momentum of the Romantic Movement in the 1820s, catalyzed a redistribution of power in the Parisian *beau monde* at the expense of the traditional "aristocracy of birth." The term "aristocracy" broadened to embrace the ascendant power of financial and artistic elites, who were now being dubbed the "aristocracy of wealth" and the "aristocracy of talent."[24] Artists of modern sensibility who theatricalized their independence from old-fashioned patronage and emphasized the individuality of their gifts did not thereby align themselves with a bourgeois order. Honoré de Balzac, for instance, made his money from serial fiction, but he wanted to appear in Parisian society as a dandy and bankrupted himself in doing so.

Like many of his peers, he claimed "promotion" into the sphere of the social elites, preserving the notion of natural elevation above the popular, mediocre, or bourgeois.[25]

It might even be argued that Liszt was in the vanguard of this expansion of "aristocracy." The romantic cult of genius had already attributed innate superiority to the figure of the poet, but the worship of genius nevertheless emphasized the poet's solitude and had an anti-performative ethos.[26] Liszt differed from most literary Romantics in that, as a public performer, he could introduce into his art the codes of behavior that marked social superiority. In 1835, swimming in the philosophy of the Saint-Simonians, he published an essay entitled *On the Situation of Artists and their Condition in Society*. It offered a utopian vision of a reborn society in which artists had the role of priests, drawing society forward with inspiring images of the ideal, and thus liberating themselves from their historically subaltern social status (*subalternité*).[27] In the course of the essay, Liszt made it plain that the historical subjugation of artists to aristocrats needed to end, not by dissolving the nobility, but by raising the artist's status to a comparably elite level (the priest metaphor signifying status as well as visionary wisdom). Liszt's essay described an artist born with the "natural" gift of artistic inspiration and vision, not someone with whom the modern bourgeois spectator can establish identification. Thus, while the essay pleaded for the artist's upward mobility, it was not equivalent to the upward strivings of the bourgeoisie because it retained a firm distinction between "natural" and "acquired" superiority. The link Liszt tried to make between noble and romantic social stances is nowhere better captured than in his famous paraphrase of *"noblesse oblige"* as *"génie oblige."*

Aristocracy cannot be broadened without diluting itself, however. The moment a "peasant" genius such as Liszt or a "bourgeois" genius such as Balzac can appropriate "nobility" to his public advantage, the whole edifice of "natural" superiority stands at risk of collapse. The burgeoning media culture of the 1820s and 1830s loosened the bond between codes of conduct and situations of social performance by replicating these codes ad infinitum. The media converted such codes into free-floating signifiers, making them available for philosophical commentary (as with Honoré Daumier and Balzac) or experiments in identity formation (Liszt). In this discourse-ridden public sphere, charisma manifested itself less as an innate "aura" than as a self-fashioned identity—a "personality"—that appropriates public signifiers and masters them by folding them back "inward." The public sphere, then, has the potential to deconstruct representative publicity by annihilating the "natural." But by virtue of its poker-faced impersonality, the public sphere stimulates a reappearance of the numinous or auratic in the form of a publicly displayed personality.

In his unsurpassed analysis of charisma and social power, Max Weber made a point that helps explain the relationship between the modern form of charisma—organized around notions of personality and genius, and mediated in the public sphere—and the older logic of representative publicity. Weber opposed the "charismatic" form of authority to both the "patriarchal" and "bureaucratic" forms. Whereas patriarchal and bureaucratic authority are embodied in a group of people (e.g., the nobility or a parliament) whose practices have developed into an acknowledged status quo, charismatic authority comes from an individual person with a unique inner "mission" and appears indifferent to external influence. In its disregard for the established and the settled, for convention and tradition, charismatic authority is "revolutionary"; its bearer is paranormal and its appeal irrational.[28] Weber nevertheless identified a significant area of overlap between charismatic and patriarchal power: "both charismatic and patriarchal power rest on personal devotion to, and personal authority of, 'natural' leaders, in contrast to the appointed leaders of the bureaucratic order."[29] In other words, the masses—Weber's term for the largest social unit—behave toward both patriarchal and charismatic leaders with an attitude of deference to "natural" superiors, which is absent from the bureaucratic order, where authority is transparently and artificially invested by the populace. This illuminates the social psychology that enabled audiences of the early nineteenth century to see an equivalence between charismatic artists such as Liszt and traditional aristocrats (the patriarchal order), in spite of the radical or revolutionary aura that these Romantics sometimes carried with them. The prophetic powers of the romantic artist may threaten traditional social legitimacy, but they also position the artist unquestionably outside or above the secular bourgeois domain. Thus, as Lawrence Kramer notes, Liszt's sublime moments were commonly described using images of royal glory, and even the famous detritus collected by his obsessive fans, apparently dragging him down into the material realm, had a numinous undercurrent: "their connection with that body invests them with a fragment of its charisma on the model of the king's touch."[30]

By the later 1830s, as his concert tours got under way, Liszt began using media resources in a manner that anticipated P.T. Barnum's strategy for publicizing Lind. With an apparent lack of calculating purpose, he used the press to infuse his concert appearances with a sense of personal and biographical depth. He personally initiated the production of short, pamphlet-length biographies to be distributed in advance at the locales where he intended to play. These biographies, appearing in French and German, had a popular, slightly sentimental, and often lightly heroic tone.[31] Their aim was to initiate public discussion and produce an advance sense of intimate familiarity that his fleeting appearances could themselves never guarantee. Liszt was also among the first musicians (preceded only by Paganini) to employ an agent to handle press and organizational issues. The agent, Gaetano Belloni, coordinated the publication of Liszt's compositions with his public appearances, to help sustain

Liszt's public presence in commodified form.[32] Belloni also took care of distributing lithograph portraits, preparing posters, and making key press contacts for advertising. Additionally, Liszt kept his personality in the public eye by contributing to musical and aesthetic polemics in the press, thus publicizing his personal passions. With Liszt, the modern media became a phantasmic extension of the performer's presence, producing a desire for the concert in advance and producing memories of the concert in the aftermath, thus facilitating the spectator's capacity for identification and mitigating the ephemerality of the concert experience.

Practices such as these show Liszt as a celebrity of a recognizably modern kind. In contrast to Thalberg and Chopin, he was able to build mass audience enthusiasm without relying on the traditional model of representative publicity. When he launched his touring concert career in Vienna in 1838, for instance, he did *not* cultivate an elite social network and wait for trickle-down interest among the public. Instead, he generated advance interest in the press: papers and journals informed the Viennese public that he was eager to play a concert, not for his own profit, but to alleviate the distress of his fellow Hungarians, who had just suffered devastating floods in Pest. Vienna's public was prepared to receive a generous and sympathetic artist, better prepared than even Liszt anticipated—he was simply dumbfounded by the public's visceral reaction.

The continuation of the Vienna episode, however, shows that Liszt may have felt strong inner resistances to being identified as an artist working in the uncharmed, bourgeois-identified free market.[33] After the first concert, he started visiting the court. To his disappointment, he did not find there the openness to the "aristocracy of talent" that characterized the more fluid social life of Paris. Behind the glorious scene of his Vienna triumphs, he had to struggle to win the favor of the court. The cabal organized against him stemmed from his rivalry with Thalberg, the official court pianist, who had challenged Liszt's reputation in Paris two years earlier. Thalberg was of half-noble birth and had highly polished manners that attracted him to the traditional nobility in Vienna and Paris alike. His performance style brought this polish onstage: his head and body remained relatively still, though visibly inspired, while his fingers worked wonders on the keyboard. Liszt found this style irritatingly cold, far too gentlemanly, and hardly worthy of the great public attention Thalberg was getting. When Liszt found himself in the Viennese court, he could not help but feel out of place. On one occasion, his discomfort got the better of him: when Princess Metternich asked whether he had "made good business" at his recent Italian concerts, he replied, "I make music, Madame, not business."[34] This caustic comment soon made the rounds of the Viennese court aristocracy and turned them against Liszt. The court had once granted Paganini an honorary award, and had recently done the same for young Clara Wieck, but they would not award it to the troublesome Liszt. With time and cumulative effort, however,

Liszt eventually won over the court, enabling him to announce to his mistress Marie d'Agoult, "the Ostrogoth [Thalberg] has been quite relegated to second rank."[35]

Once in good favor with Viennese court circles, he literally started putting them onstage. Uncomfortable with the cavernous size of the *Grosser Redouten-saal*, one of the few available concert venues, he decided to reconfigure it as a pseudo-salon. He created a line of seats onstage around the piano, the so-called *cercle de distinction*, and filled the chairs with the leading ladies of Vienna's high society. This practice, which Liszt repeated on other occasions, has a strong whiff of representative publicity, of "displaying himself as an embodiment of 'higher power'" before an audience, and there is no evidence that anyone in the general public was repelled by it. By the end of his series of Vienna concerts, Liszt had become so closely associated with the high aristocracy that the popular journal *Der Humorist* waged a campaign to claim him "back" for the general audience. While other journals highlighted the pianist's Parisian wit and flair in the salons, the *Humorist* offered a counter-image of Liszt as a man of the Austrian people: "Even though the rush to his brilliant concerts here is comparable to other places, in terms of artistic recognition there has never been such an important, true and unfeigned understanding and respect for the genius as here: for here one does not go to concerts out of *bon ton* or fashion, which is for the most part what happens in London and Paris, but because one has a true feeling for the beautiful."[36] By privileging true inner appreciation above external glamour, these words model a "soul-to-soul" performer-audience bond that bypasses visual and social mediation, and thereby the entire order of representative publicity. While the passage seems to pit all of Vienna against the big cosmopolitan centers, the indirect target here is the cosmopolitan aristocracy *within* Vienna, with whom Liszt had aligned himself.

Liszt's visit to London in 1840 represents a similar oscillation in publicity strategies. As in Vienna, he gave his first concert with little preparation in the *beau monde*, something no other virtuoso could get away with or would dare try. The previous two years of steady concertizing, constantly reported in the press, had prepared the way for his phenomenal London success, without particular need to make a stir in the salons. And by this point he had accumulated the medals that testified to his superior status onstage. In a letter to Marie d'Agoult, he expressed pride in his independence from the *beau monde*: "I have refused to present myself at Lady Blessington's—I have absolutely no need of such people. My success here is unheard of."[37] Two days later he is even more proud to announce, "d'Orsay has come *to see me* and to invite me to go *to them*." Liszt had effectively reversed the older pattern in which interest in the *beau monde* trickles down to interest from the general public. No wonder he wrote to Marie half astonished: "Orsay's visit struck me as a unique thing [*une singularité*]."[38]

But this is only one side of the London episode. Soon, Liszt *did* join the brilliant society of Lady Blessington and Count d'Orsay, throwing himself into their uniquely dandyish and fashion-conscious world. In an intriguing letter to Marie, he requested that she send "the Hungarian ¾ coat with fur (please oversee the wrapping of this coat yourself)" and "a sort of bluish Turkish pant plus another morning pant of the same kind in white," plus "my Bovy medallion" and "my gray overcoat."[39] The pride Liszt placed in his independence from the legitimate aristocracy blended with a deep-seated admiration for that class's elevation and aura of superior grace. He did not need representative publicity, but he chose it anyway and used it to elevate himself beyond the prosaic domain of concerts for profit.

Blessington and d'Orsay, though legitimate aristocrats of blood, evidently subscribed to the expanded notion of aristocracy that included artists, men of

Illustration 4.1.
Lithograph by Josef Kriehuber, produced in connection with Liszt's Vienna concerts of 1840. The elegant costume is representative of Liszt's high-fashion dress of this period.

letters, and other people of talent. Liszt was amused to report to Marie: "Lady Blessington asserts that I resemble both Bonaparte and Lord Byron!!!"[40] Behind Blessington's close analysis of Liszt's looks lay Johann Kaspar Lavater's science of physiognomy, which read character and morality into facial and cranial features. She marked Liszt as a modern hero by comparing him to Byron and Napoleon, heroes of individuality and will rather than of magnanimity and military prowess. On the other hand, the "science" of physiognomy, while seeming to expand aristocracy beyond birth or blood, still defined superiority as innate, and not acquired or alterable. Because Liszt's performances were so visually focused, his physique fed into perceptions of his elite status. His long, slender hands were a marker of aristocratic grace, and they served as a privileged site of the spectator's focus.[41] In his more dandyish moments, he came onstage with kid gloves, gradually unveiled the hands, and "with a certain vehemence" threw them down before the piano in mimicry of ancient chivalric codes.

Illustration 4.2. Portrait by Ary Scheffer, 1835–1836, reproduced with permission of the Conservatory of Geneva. Elongated fingers give an "aristocratic" tinge to this typically romantic portrait.

Liszt's social gravitation toward highly placed people extended far beyond the Vienna and London episodes. Both of his long-term romantic partners, Countess Marie d'Agoult and Princess Carolyne von Sayn-Wittgenstein, had married into powerful noble families. Beyond his inner circle of musicians such as Hector Berlioz, Richard Wagner, and Hans von Bülow, a conspicuous number of his most intimate friends belonged to the highest social ranks: Olga von Meyerdorff, Princess Cristina Belgiojoso, Prince Felix Lichnowsky, Cardinal Gustav Hohenlohe, and Weimar's Grand Duke Carl Alexander. His friendships with journalists, poets, dramatists, philosophers, professors, and bankers—the more typical company of musicians in the nineteenth century (with the exception of opera singers)—were numerous but comparatively looser than with these highly placed people. No musician of the nineteenth century, in fact, felt so at ease in the company of the nobility and royalty. Mendelssohn, for instance, expressed a humble sense of privilege when he met the sovereigns of England and Saxony, and wrote excitedly about the occasions in his letters.[42] For Liszt, such encounters had already become routine in his virtuoso years.

Virtuosity and Social Crisis?

Although Liszt operated within the bourgeois public sphere and mobilized its media resources in forward-looking ways, his charismatic image also fed upon practices of performed social superiority inherited from the eighteenth century and still operative in the early nineteenth. The prevailing tendency to interpret Liszt as a projection of bourgeois desire brackets off aspects of his symbolic performative vocabulary that I have focused upon: dandyism, upscale hobnobbing, chivalric gestures, royal insignia, and physiognomic distinction. Even as widely publicized anecdotes about his life promoted among his spectators a sense of "intimacy at a distance," Liszt reached audiences by projecting an irresistible impression of blessed superiority that made him remote and untouchable. His romantic persona might best be viewed as an alternate aristocracy, branching out laterally from the traditional nobility and making comparable claims to natural leadership, rather than an oppositional identity resisting "from below" and calling the entire system of social hierarchy into question. British rockers of the late 1960s appropriated historical aristocratic costumes in order to subvert them, whereas Liszt appropriated them in an affirmation and recoding of their symbolic projection of elite distinction. Liszt made significant steps toward the system of modern, mass media-based stardom, but he was nevertheless a historically transitional figure, using representative and civil forms of publicity side by side. Only in the second half of the nineteenth century did his distinctive persona coalesce as a model of "artistic" superiority that erased or sublimated aristocratic resonances. Throngs of pianists came to

Weimar to study with him, imitate his mannerisms, and carry on his "message," thereby contributing to the routinization of his charisma.[43]

Liszt's aristocratic aura would have done him no good if there had not been some disposition on the part of his public to react favorably to it. It can be difficult to reconstruct audience attitudes with certainty, but it is clear that we cannot understand the appeal of Liszt's high-toned airs if we accept the traditional image of the nineteenth-century bourgeoisie as a smug and self-satisfied class. Peter Gay's massive study, *The Bourgeois Experience*, does much to challenge this received wisdom, showing that the Victorian middle classes were anything but certain, settled, or unconflicted.[44] They forged models of subjectivity and value that were contradictory and impossible to achieve in reality, positioning their experiences at a crossroads between behavior and intention. We might speculate that their enthusiasm for Liszt (not to mention Herz and Thalberg) stemmed from a well-concealed craving for the ease and security of elite social status that does not have to be acquired through education, discipline, and respectability. The literary critic Len Platt goes so far as to argue that the shadow presence of aristocracy was so strong as to be "Europe's 19th century other."[45]

Max Weber was disinclined to such psychological interpretation. His best-known thesis concerning charismatic figures is that they emerge at moments of social crisis, when the very basis of social and political authority is under threat. In some ways, Liszt combined the two principal forms of charismatic identity that Weber described: the heroic (embodied in the warrior) and the prophetic (the magician). Journalists and artists often described his virtuoso performances with images of military valor, leading to extensive comparisons with Napoleon and ancient emperors.[46] The same visual cues gave rise to portrayals of Liszt as a magician conjuring phantoms from the piano. Just as Byron brought his ideal visions to a kind of apotheosis by dying on the Greek battlefield, so did Liszt's intertwined identities as poetic visionary and valorous performer drastically magnify his appeal. Yet a performer like Liszt, no matter how popular, does not wield the kind of authority Max Weber described—his or her sphere of influence is simply too narrow. Even if we grant Liszt a generous measure of historical agency, his success is difficult to correlate with a major disruption of political and social authority. When such a crisis did come, in 1848, Liszt had already retired from the concert stage, and he kept quiet on the revolutionary cause.

The sociologist Richard Sennett, however, has argued that the early nineteenth-century cult of the virtuoso was indeed the response to a crisis—one of personality rather than of authority. The bourgeoisie, Sennett argues, constructed a model of personality with reference to interiority, feeling, and intimate relations, and found it impossible to reconcile this self with the conditions of modern urban public life, where anonymity, role-playing, external appearances, and aggressive competition ruled. The virtuoso's apparent capacity to "feel" authentically in public thus appeared to be a superhuman feat, and by applauding Liszt enthusiastically, audiences could themselves express strong feelings in public, if only temporarily.[47] Sennett's interpretation connects Liszt's charisma integrally with the logic of modernity and of bourgeois psychological flight. In retrospect, Sennett seems to have viewed the early nineteenth century in light of the crisis of public life and participation that marked the early 1970s, which led him to underplay the extent to which Liszt was resisted in his own time. Liszt was constantly being accused of arrogance, excess, histrionics, and triviality, suggesting that he was less a reflection of his time than a sort of critique of its limits. His virtuosity articulated a link between public performance and superior social status, which the bourgeoisie was in many respects trying to break down with its ethics of interior virtue and cultivation. His aristocratic airs, and the strategies of representative publicity from which they derived, expressed his resistance to the leveling inertia of modern media and secular enterprise, yet his enormous successes reveal just how compatible auratic authority and modern entertainment would turn out to be.

CHAPTER 5

Celebrity Gifting
Mallarmé and the Poetics of Fame

EMILY APTER

There are myriad approaches to investigating how celebrity is constituted and conferred. The symbolist writer Stéphane Mallarmé (1842–1898) offers a good case for testing approaches to the historiography of fame in nine-teenth-century France. Mallarmé can be seen as the prototype of a contempo-rary "I am not there" model of celebrity. A nobody in full view (photographed by Nadar, the subject of portraiture by Edouard Manet, Edvard Munch, and Paul Gauguin), he demonstrated an idiosyncratic form of media savvy that involves making a name for oneself through self-annexation to an international cast of creative, talented, beautiful people—writers, thinkers, artists, mistresses, pa-trons, family, and friends. The twentieth and twenty-first century notion of "celebrity gifting" (with gifting used as an active verb), though highly anachro-nistic in its historical ascription, arguably captures Mallarmé's very particular definition of the poetics of fame. It would seem that he turned the tradition of homage into a name-branding opportunity. Mallarmé entered tribute texts into an economy that assigned aesthetic value to proper names, which compounded the name recognition of "gifted" artists (Edgar Allan Poe, Charles Baudelaire, Paul Verlaine, Richard Wagner, Edouard Manet, and James Abbott McNeill Whistler, among countless others). As Mary Ann Caws notes with respect to Whistler (whose lecture, "Ten O'clock," Mallarmé translated into French):

> Mallarmé liked to have his name linked with Whistler's…. He wrote elsewhere to Whistler how happy he was to have a chance to put *"mon nom au-dessous du vôtre"* (my name beneath yours), and subsequently, on May 23, he insisted to the printer that when his name appeared on a poster advertising the translation, "let it be in very small type, so that I not seem to be profiting from the exhibition for my own good … All attention should be drawn to Whistler's name" (*Correspon-dence* 6). Repeatedly, they are both delighted to have their names *figure* in each

other's texts: Whistler in Mallarmé's *Médaillon* or portrait of him; Mallarmé in Whistler's margins, underneath his translations, or on his poster in small type.[1]

The rich relay between Mallarmé and Whistler (built up through acts of reciprocal translation that "sealed their friendship, like drinking from the same gourd") was seated in a larger network of names.[2] In a short piece on Poe, for example, Mallarmé uses Whistler and Villiers de l'Isle-Adam to position himself in relation to Poe.[3] And because Baudelaire and Mallarmé were both famed translators of Poe, Baudelaire and Whistler join the nexus of "stellar" names, despite the fact that at no point do they directly touch each other. Naming, *qua* medium of spiritual and creative blood transfusion, consolidates a celebrity confraternity. The poetics of names operates as a currency of transference, enabling embodied self-properties to travel from one gifted subject to another. Notwithstanding his reputation as a figure renowned for shunning the limelight, a figure whose very name was treated as shorthand for undemocratic social scenes and art at the farthest remove from populist engagement, Mallarmé, I will argue here, was "the first modern" of anti-market self-marketing. His biography, his work, and its reception together provide an exemplary framework for thinking methodologically about how to write the history of celebrity as a distinct form of modernity.

The historiography of reputation offers a starting point for such a history. Especially significant in the social history of art (as exemplified by T.J. Clark's study of Courbet), it has been a constant supplement to the archival reconstruction of exemplary lives in the biographical genre.[4] Jean-Claude Bonnet analyzed the phenomenon of "pantheonization" and the "great man" cult as crucial to consolidating national, post-revolutionary culture in France.[5] Building on a post-1968 current of historical research dedicated to restituting lost archives or effaced subjects of history (Michel Foucault on Pierre Rivière and Herculine Barbin, Jacques Rancière on the writings of workers, Michelle Perrot on the narratives of working-class women), Alain Corbin undertook in *Le Monde retrouvé de Louis-François Pinagot* the experiment of constructing the life of a wholly "fame-less" individual: a nineteenth-century shoemaker from Normandy whose legal tracks in civic life amounted to the bare minimum. Leo Braudy's *The Frenzy of Renown: Fame and its History* (1986), an elaboration of ideas seeded in his earlier book *The World in a Frame: What We See in Films* (1976), and Richard Dyer's *Stars* (1979) and *Heavenly Bodies: Film Stars and Society* (1986), examined fame through character construction, the psychology of role-playing, and the sociology of urban types.[6] Braudy and Dyer both subscribed to the central tenet that the theater of characterology formed the crucible of the star system. And it is undoubtedly to Braudy that we owe a historical field that might be called "Fame-graphy," based on his premise that famous people "are vehicles of cultural memory and cohesion.... By preserving their names, we create a self-conscious grammar of feeling and action that allows us to connect where we have been as a society and where we are going."[7]

In *Continental Drift: From National Characters to Virtual Subjects*, I argued that this grammar was crucial to surveying the *fin-de-siècle* proliferation of historically invested, exotically inflated character types, particularly the parade of larger-than-life female stereotypes consolidated during the Belle Epoque: the Courtesan, the New Woman, the Amazon, the Demimondaine, the Orientalist, the Socialite, the Streetwalker, the Suffragette, the Religious Enthusiast, the Femme Fatale, the Actress, the Cyclist, the Bourgeoise, the Colonial Civil Servant's Wife, the Coquette, the Fashion Plate, and the Adulteress.[8] Literature and history, I argued, formed a referential loop fusing historical female legends with the biographical properties of theatrical personae. Cleopatra-Sarah Bernhardt, Salome-Ida Rubenstein, Salammbo-Rose Caron, Sémiramis-Mme Segond-Weber, Sappho-Emma Calvé, Thaïs-Mary Garden—these portmanteau identities, often with a feminist-Orientalist or lesbian-Orientalist profile, became the predicates of modern celebrity. The naming function was always paramount: Émile Zola's "Nana," for example, names a generic prostitute, but the novel so particularized the historical type that the character became a "real" celebrity, giving rise to a new generic type—"*une nana*." The proper name of a literary character enters history via language, circulating in perpetuity as a common term of French vernacular.

Nana was a low-rent actor, and this detail is consequential. While there had always been press attention accorded social and political elites and avatars of the stage or society, the turn-of-the-century witnessed enhanced media interventions in the production of personae, and transformed bit players into egeria. Supplementing the mass diffusion of literary memoirs, courtesan autobiographies, and theatrical reviews in women's magazines, a nascent entertainment industry began to capitalize, internationalize, and technologize the marketing and management of national stars. Proust's Marcel registered the impact of this publicity machine's star production on the budding fan:

> But if the thought of actors preoccupied me so, if the sight of Maubant coming out of the Théâtre-Français one afternoon plunged me into the throes and sufferings of love, how much more did the name of a "star" blazing outside the doors of a theater, how much more, seen through the window of a brougham passing by in the street, its horses' headbands decked with roses, did the face of a woman whom I took to be an actress, leave me in a state of troubled excitement, impotently and painfully trying to form a picture of her private life.
>
> I classified the most distinguished in order of talent: Sarah Bernhardt, Berma, Bartet, Madeleine Brohan, Jeanne Samary; but I was interested in them all.[9]

While there has been considerable work on the psychoanalytic process of identification (emphasizing the star as focal point of affect, a template for subjective agency, a link to a larger community of fandom), less attention has been devoted to the study of celebrities as markers of historicity and cultural memory. Stars condense and personify temporal moments, as Andy Warhol knew well when he boxed up and dated treasure-troves of actuality—movie star pictures, foodstuffs, unpaid bills, unanswered letters, toothpaste containers, magazine ads—and labeled them as time capsules. Fame, like fashion, is thus revealed as a temporal by-product: it freezes ritual dailiness, small evental occurrences, and the intervallic spaces of sociability. In this sense, fame tempers the radicality of the "now," forcing temporality into the historicizing frames that Walter Benjamin associated with *Gedächtnis:* souvenir and calendar-time, Hallmark greeting cards that mark holidays and birthdays. On another level, though, fame implies timelessness or the untiming of historical measure and periodization. The capacity of a character to outlive the allotted duration of a programmed lifespan puts fame on a defiant course with respect to history. The star, even if he or she enjoys only fifteen minutes of fame, resists history's natural consignment of the individual to obscurity. The making of a name becomes a kind of historical blowback, a resistant spot of time.

I have already alluded briefly and in a more historical vein to how, in turn-of-the-century France, the phenomenon of "becoming a name" came about by hitching the legendary monikers of historical or allegorical characters to the sobriquets of the performers who played their parts. But this value of name is even more complicated in the case of a writer such as Mallarmé, who countered the publicity effect by encrypting his name. He embedded its sound values in a favored poetic lexicon that included words like "*âme,*" "*aile,*" "*plume,*" and "*stèle.*" He reveled in his own name, placing it under the allegorical legend of melancholia as a coded etymology for the one who cries painful tears ("*mal*" "*larmé*"), and he debased his name by using it as currency in poetic trifles and dedications: "*Quelqu'un par vous charmé/Stéphane Mallarmé*" (Charmed by you he may/be is Stéphane Mallarmé).[10] He also fetishized the names of other poets as a way of marking the importance of *the Poet.* As Roger Pearson notes: "Onomastic play is a major feature of the 'Tombeaux.' In 'Le Tombeau d'Edgar Poe,' the very title presents a quasi-hemistich of six syllables with an internal rhyme on 'beau' and Poe.'... while the name itself echoes through the poem in 'Poète and Poe' and through the repetition of its phonetic elements /p/ and /o/."[11]

The temptation here is to cast the cryptomanic Mallarmé as an agent of negative celebrity: he named, but often in such a covert fashion that he undermined the celebrity machine of name-production. To read Mallarmé symptomatically in this way is to cast him as an avatar of counter-fame, drawing on his conventional portrait as a figure of social withdrawal and impersonality. Certainly if we compare Mallarmé to Zola—the "universal" writer of the Republic of Letters and voice of French conscience during the Dreyfus affair—

Mallarmé's celebrity seems slight. Mallarmé's life, marked by failure and depression, was shaped by his career as a provincial *petit maître*. He was, after all, a teacher marooned in the Ardèche, the scion of a long line of functionaries, few of whom, as he complained to Verlaine, wielded "a pen for purposes other than to authorize a deed."[12] From early on, Mallarmé exhibited signs of the *arriviste*, claiming a more distinguished ancestral pedigree than he actually had, exhuming the names of minor poets in his family genealogy, especially on his mother's side.[13]

Mallarmé's father, Numa Florent Joseph Mallarmé, was a *sous-chef* in the administration of the Land Registry, who had worked his way up from posts in Mâcon, Baugy, and Amiens. By 1840, he had managed to secure the job of auditor of estates in Chartres. Like a type stamped out from Honoré de Balzac's *Physiologie de l'employé*, Mallarmé's father was a successful bureaucrat, bequeathing to his son an obsession with literary testaments, the power of numbers, and a desire to micromanage the real estate of his salon via a set of posthumous stage directions. These were communicated in cipher in the poet's never-published masterwork *Le Livre*, which instructed guests on where to sit and how many francs they should pay to channel Mallarmé's presence in a spiritual séance.[14]

Quietly provincial as it was, Mallarmé's biography contains no famous political stand. In *Faits Divers* (1893) and *Or* (1893, 1897) he tepidly criticized the bribery of politicians and newspapers by the Panama Company, which had successfully lobbied the Chamber of Deputies for a lottery loan. When the loan went bust, self-serving politicians pinned the blame on the engineer Ferdinand de Lesseps and did their best to deflect national ire onto the Dreyfus affair. A muted critic, as Barbara Johnson notes in her essay "Erasing Panama: Mallarmé and the Text of History," Mallarmé remained throughout this era of scandals "a mild-mannered reporter sending us delayed dispatches from nineteenth-century Paris."[15] For Fredric Jameson, this "reporting" was precisely what yielded a "materialist" Mallarmé, a "post-contemporary reinvention" of Mallarmé that takes full measure of his "seasonal" prose.[16] Jameson refers, on the one hand, to the way Mallarmé marked the *rentrée* with notations of fall happenings and concerts, plays and fashion, and on the other, to his recognition in "Crisis of Verse" that ordinary discourse had infiltrated the codes of literariness, creating a common language of universal *reporting*. Jameson renders Mallarmé's "universel *reportage*" as "universal journalism," placing emphasis on the influence of newspapers on Mallarmé's poetic language.[17] In this ascription, Mallarméan historicity jettisons politics in favor of ephemeral experience and the larger project of a new kind of "Book of the World" modeled after the Wagnerian *Gesamtkunstwerk*.

Zola's celebrity, by contrast, was soldered to the historical event. When, in 1892, he published *La Débâcle*, his novel about the Franco-Prussian War, Zola mobilized nationalists, monarchists, Catholics, and the military against him. At first the complaints were restricted to minor points of historical accuracy, such as whether or not the emperor actually wore face make-up on the front lines to disguise a glabrous complexion brought on by bouts of hemorrhoids and dysentery. Subsequently, though, reception of *La Débâcle* resembled a dress rehearsal for what Zola would face six years later in the aftermath of *J'Accuse*, as "patriots" unleashed vitriolic attacks on his ideological motives, excoriating him for sullying the reputation of the army and France as a whole. Zola countered with a long article in *Le Figaro*, refusing to withdraw his equation of defeat with misguided militarism. Zola's reputation as political enemy of the French state found its negative complement in his public image as a fame-chaser. Caricatures by Nadar and André Gill emphasize Zola as a literary "wannabe," worshipping at the foot of Victor Hugo, grooming himself for pantheonization. Nadar's lithographic *Panthéon* has been compared to Andy Warhol's celebrity silkscreens of Marilyn Monroe, Jackie Kennedy, Truman Capote, Troy Duster, Elizabeth Taylor, in turn considered the prototype for FACEBOOK.

No comparable output of caricature was devoted to Mallarmé. A review of journals of the period—*Le Journal, Ruy Blas, Le Figaro, L'illustration*—reveals scant material of a satirical nature directed his way, with the exception of a drawing depicting the poet as "the faun" applying himself to the Pan pipes. Where Zola was famous for being famous, or for wanting to garner fame in literary history, Mallarmé was famous for his obscurity, almost as if he were self-consciously playing the part of a secret in Georg Simmel's sense—the secret as most precious and thereby the most desired and jealously safeguarded asset.[18] As E.S. Burt reminds us: "he looked forward to a work structured around the 'Secret that each man has in himself,' to be offered to the 'reading of friends,' in both senses of the genitive."[19]

Unlike his predecessors, such as Alexandre Dumas, Balzac, or George Sand, Mallarmé's literary reputation was not based on mass appeal, large sales figures, a larger-than-life physique, a charismatic personality, colorful love affairs, or an exceptional life story. Though he inherited the crown of "prince of poets" from Baudelaire and Verlaine, he could never rival Hugo, who inspired a cult of Hugoliana of unimaginable proportions, comprised of countless commemorative artifacts and endless poetic imitations. Mallarmé's sociability in his lifetime was dominated by "the happy few" who attended his *mardis* at the apartment on the rue de Rome. And yet, this picture of limited influence must be revised when one recalls who was included in that "happy few": nineteenth-century artists such as Debussy, Rodin, Whistler, Renoir, Manet, Monet, Pissarro, Gauguin, Vuillard, and Morisot, as well as those who would set the aesthetic agenda for the new century—Proust, Claudel, Valéry, Gide. Any theory of fame must take full measure of the "who's who" in the "happy few." This entourage factor, crucial to the formation of aura around "stars" (no matter how reclusive), played no small role in securing his important place in literary history.

Equally important to the unique status of Mallarméan fame—and its peculiar longevity—was his historically crucial effort to cross avant-garde intermediality (journalism, photography, music, fashion, gameboards, avant-garde typography, etc.) with "the media" as understood in the contemporary sense of the celebrity machine. This marriage of aesthetics and publicity bears some affinity to the marriage between philosophy and television in the 1960's. As Tamara Chaplin has demonstrated, Jean-Paul Sartre, Raymond Aron, Jean Hyppolite, Alain Badiou, Georges Canguilhem, Paul Ricoeur, Jacques Lacan, Michel Foucault, and Gaston Bachelard were among the pioneer talking heads who seized on the televisual format as a timely medium for doing philosophy differently and for attempting emancipatory pedagogy. Foucault, on television, Chaplin writes, projected a "feral" quality, his body language vividly seconding the excited eddies of cognition. "There is no doubt that the man who once claimed that 'one writes so as not to have face' was blessed with an unusually photogenic talent for transmitting his ideas via the small screen."[20] Similarly with Badiou, the corporealization of thought proved to be thrillingly excessive, even posing technical challenges for the producers of early segments of "*L'Enseignement de la philosophie*" (Teaching Philosophy) in the mid 1960s. The medium had to catch up, so to speak, with the theatricality of the speakers, and until producers learned how to free up the camera, Badiou was constrained to the frame like a puppet through the attachment of a string to his foot.[21] Later, when the fixed camera was no longer a problem, television could track philosophers in the mobile environments of their daily routines. The small screen allowed a mass audience to glimpse the vivacity of philosophy as a worldly pursuit. If Mallarmé had mediatized poetics, the 1960s' philosophers televised thought. This transformative relation to new media, I would surmise, is part of what made Mallarmé so congenial to twentieth-century French philosophers, garnering him another radius of celebrity.

Such, in any case, was Marshall McLuhan's view. In his essay "Joyce, Mallarmé, and the Press," McLuhan credited the poet with having "formulated the lessons of the press as a guide for the new impersonal poetry of suggestion and implication. He saw that the scale of modern reportage and of the mechanized multiplication of messages made personal rhetoric impossible."[22] McLuhan traced the "newspaperwise" settings of *Ulysses*, the telescoping of space and time, the break-up of linear narrative, and the use of verbal montage in *Ulysses* and *Finnegans Wake* to Mallarmé's canny explorations of the newspaper format.[23] Mallarmé, filtered through McLuhan, becomes the premier forerunner of digital gamespace and telesthetic representation, themselves definable, according to the contemporary media theorist McKenzie Wark, as perception at a distance, the compaction of space and time, topography as topology. In this ascription of topology, vast territories are coordinated within the bounds of the line, whereby open frontier is enclosed in a field of calculation.[24] Roger Ansell Pearson likens *Un Coup de dés* "to a computer monitor upon which the words, stricken by a 'virus,' tumble down the screen."[25]

Redefining poetics in this way, Mallarmé provided an alternative to the nationally sanctioned *alexandrin* that seemed to have died with Victor Hugo. In doing so, Mallarmé opened versification to *vers libre* and to the cultivation of a language that could be documentary, yet released from the restraints of mimetic representation."[26] His defamiliarization of syntax and grammaticality, along with the revolutionary format of *Un Coup de dés*, not only contributed to Mallarmé's renown; it also earned him special status in the history of new media.

These dramatic innovations made Mallarmé a protagonist of what Badiou calls the twentieth-century's "prologue," the period from 1890 to 1914 that also featured the intensely compressed "polymorphic creativity" of Einstein, Freud, Schoenberg, Lenin, Conrad, Henry James, Joyce, Proust, Frege, Husserl, Wittgenstein, Picasso, Braque, Poincaré, Cantor, Riemann, Hilbert, Pessoa, Méliès, Griffith, and Chaplin. In this context, Badiou hails Mallarmé's project of "the Book" as an evental site: not just a new Bible, but a new form, unending and futural, yet comprehensive; the literary equivalent of a genome project in which letters and numbers are convertible and commutative.[27]

Badiou's appreciation of the "evental" status of Mallarmé's *Livre* not only revisits the old question of how aesthetic and political revolution are reciprocally imbricated; it points to the performative potential of poetry *as* philosophy. In *Théorie du sujet* (1982), *Petit manuel d'inesthétique* (1998), and *Conditions* (1992), Badiou activates the subtractive voids, empty spaces, and unconventional metrics structuring Mallarméan poetics to forge a mathematical ontology. Badiou elsewhere accords Mallarmé a unique status as a nomadic subject, an egalitarian of mind and thought comparable to the pre-Islamic classical poet Labîd ben Rabia. Overall, Badiou corrects Mallarmé's placement in a de-historicized philosophical continuum by returning him to the century, not his own nineteenth century, but the twentieth century that his avant-garde aesthetic proleptically scripted.

In their anthology, *Literary Debate: Texts and Contexts*, Denis Hollier and Jeffrey Mehlman acknowledge his capital importance in the twentieth-century history of theory by devoting a section to "the central case of Mallarmé." Mehlman argues that Mallarmé's enduring place in critical debate is surprising: "it might have been thought that the future lay with the ultraromantic lineage of Rimbaud (and the Surrealists) far more than with the diminutive English teacher and self-styled martyr to poetry whose centenary France celebrated in 1998." For Mehlman, the explanation is various and complex, attributable to Mallarmé's pursuit of "his oeuvre within a space fully as kaleidoscopic as the 'savage thought' Claude Lévi-Strauss had begun to explore during the postwar years. Reference, however precise, was strictly contingent, subordinate to the arch syntax of a repetitive structure."[28] Jacques Rancière's Mallarmé, according to Mehlman, deserves fame as the herald of a new secularism. He "is emphatically and self-consciously post-Christian; but unlike Sartre's Mallarmé, Rancière's is not a victim of that circumstance. For his is the project of a new communitarian cult, poetry, characterized by its rejection of *every mode of incarnation*."[29]

In locating Mallarmé firmly in the twentieth century (or its prologue), Badiou and Mehlman dispense with the cliché that Mallarmé's art was out of time. Svetlana Boym falls somewhat prey to this shibboleth when she sets up Mallarmé as the "pioneer of the modern myth of the death of the author that is passionately elaborated in contemporary criticism.... He continuously stages the poet's death, reenacts depersonalization and disfiguration, and performs a ritual purification of his poems to eliminate the anecdotes related to personal biography or history."[30] Boym builds on Roland Barthes's designation of Mallarmé as *the* writer in whom the Author, as a historical institution, "died." In 1968, Barthes contended in his famous essay, "The Death of the Author," that "for Mallarmé, as for us, it is language which speaks, not the author; to write is to reach, through a preliminary impersonality ... that point where not 'I' but only language functions."[31] Mallarmé's authorial death gives birth to the modern Scriptor, whose purpose is to trace a field that has no origin other than language itself.[32] For Boym, Mallarmé's fame lies in his exemplification of the cultural myth of the modern poet purged of biographical trivia; a model of fame "degree zero"; out-of-body, fully textualized, wholly dematerialized. Such poststructural accounts of his legacy offer a way out of simplistic biographical paradigms that emphasize ontogenetic determinism, narrow strictures of intention, or figments of unitary consciousness. But they unduly downplay the extent to which Mallarmé's oeuvre was socially situated. I would argue, contra Boym, that by attending more closely to the social Mallarmé, we see how he bequeathed a modern definition of worldliness and celebrity in his poetics of the gift.

Let us recall how many of Mallarmé's most significant works involved homage to great artists (Wagner, Puvis de Chavannes, Whistler) and tributes to dead poets: "Toast funèbre" (to Gautier), "Le Tombeau d'Edgar Poe" (1876), "Le Tombeau de Charles Baudelaire" (1895), "Tombeau" (to Verlaine) (1896). To these we must add the heartrending, unpublished "Tombeau" for his dead son, Anatole. Taking in the full range of his tribute texts, not just those dedicated to famous poets, but also trifles such as "Dons de fruits glacés au nouvel an" (gift baskets to all of the nice ladies: Mesdames Dauphin, Madier de Montjau, Seignobos, Gina, Marie et Paule) or micro-sized signature-events such as Mallarmé's rhymed addresses ("Les Loisirs de la poste" and "Recréations postales"), one becomes aware of the extent to which the act of gifting shaped Mallarmé's entire corpus. For Richard Sieburth, these "miniature commemorations of occasion," these "dedicatory squibs written on albums, photographs, fans, Easter eggs, jugs of calvados or pebbles … represent Mallarmé at his most sociable and most puckishly anti-monumental."[33] A cursory sampling confirms this reading, the first a riff on the name of Edmond Deman, the Belgian editor who published Mallarmé's *Les Poèmes d'Edgar Poe* in 1888:

> Avec l'éditeur Deman
> On n'a pas d'emmerdement. (OC I, 327)
> (No unnecessary demands/With the editor Deman)

In other dedicatory verses, the fetish writer Poe is invoked, forging a link among literati:

> Aux encans où l'or aime braire,
> Le prodigue Darzens a beau
> S'exténuer comme un libraire
> Je lui signe, moi, ce *Corbeau* (OC I, 315)
> (At the auctions where gold loves to bray/The prodigious Darzens/In vain exhausts himself selling books/For him, I sign this *Raven*)
> Louÿs
> Ta main frappe au
> Sépulcre d'Edgar Poe. (OC I, 316)
> (Louÿs/your hand hits/Edgar Poe's tomb)

> Muse, qui le distinguas,
> Si tu savais calmer l'ire
> De mon confrère Degas (OC I, 316)
> Tends-lui ce discours à lire
> (Muse, who gives him distinction/If you know how to defuse/the rage of my comrade Degas/Give him this speech to peruse)

Evident here is how each text is constructed around a proper name, enabling Mallarmé to insert himself inside a social network of friendship and celebrity. There is something erotic about this act of circulating in and through others to reveal the void in the subject. As Wayne Koestenbaum, himself a premier theorist of celebrity, observed: "Mallarmé used poetics as a laboratory for new forms of interpersonality—call it social intercourse.… Mallarmé hotly pursued the No One, the evaporated catalyst of speech: Everything in his prose 'moves toward some supreme bolt of light'—some orgasm—'from which awakens the Figure that No One is.' What happens if you write a party and the No One you are shows up?"[34]

Leo Bersani's interpretation of Mallarmé's relationship to his literary network had similarly emphasized the paradox of a "signature" impersonal interpersonality:

> Neither hostility nor attachment is especially evident in Mallarmé's tributes to Gautier, Baudelaire and Verlaine; rather, the poetic *hommage* provides the occasion for an emotionally and intellectually neutral moving away from the poets being honored, a movement which is the consequence of nothing more than the decision to make of them the object of a poem. Just as the project of naming the world results in the activity of *misnaming*, so the tributes to other poets inevitably become missed tributes. The *Tombeaux* poems are, by virtue of the very project which inspires them, *hommages manqués*. For Mallarmé, poetry is the dispersal of subjects; and it is as if its practice were therefore incompatible with the explicit monumentalizing intention of the *Tombeaux* poems, and perhaps even with any serious claim to the authority of a personal signature. Mallarmé's own initiation into writing, as we have seen, moves him away from himself, even leads him to announce his own death. The posthumous tribute is, for this always respectable man of letters, a satisfyingly oblique way of generalizing his experience of writing as the loss of authorship." [35]

Bersani's recuperation of "affective impoverishment," non-familial relationality, and the tribute *manqué* as strategies for disabling the deferential posture of oedipal indebtedness is interesting not merely because it allows him to elect Mallarmé "first author" in the "death of the author" sequence, but also because it affords a fresh perspective on the aesthetics of immortality acquisition. Making a name for oneself, in a modernist, poststructuralist vein, herewith entails the addition of subtracted, neutralized proper names. The work's fame derives from de-famed artists' names, and comes at their expense.

Suggestive as Bersani is, a new current of research on the social Mallarmé encourages us to read the Mallarméan signature very differently, that is to say, as part of a publicity machine of a piece with the mass marketing of consumer objects, commercial culture, and fashion. [36] In this scheme, when Mallarmé signs himself "the Raven," he espouses the house brand of "Poe," much as he would the house of Worth in *La Dernière Mode* (his foray into popular journalism). One could also say that by appending the properties of other proper names to his own, Mallarmé was engaging in a practice that might now be identified as "celebrity gifting." [37]

When the word gift is used as a transitive verb, as in "to gift someone" or "to gift a charity," it usually refers to a marketing ploy. The name of a celebrity is donated to a gift to enhance its purchase. "Gifting," defined by this close fit between nominalism and superadded value, began to enter mainstream usage in the 1980s, when retailers recognized they could tap into the star power of Academy Award presenters, and use them as human advertisements to market products. Valuable swag bags were distributed at high-profile events. Jewels and gowns were common "gifted" items, but gradually the merchandise branched out into non-wearable offerings. One article about this practice noted that Gwyneth Paltrow "expressed surprise on the red carpet of the Golden Globes at having received a cruise to Antarctica and Tasmania in her gift basket. (Estimated value: $22,000)." Paltrow wanted to "re-assign" the cruise to a charity, but the question arose of its new worth. At what price could the cruise be valued now that it had been "Gwynethed?" The self-properties of "Gwyneth-ness" had been bestowed on the item, just like "Poe-ness" was added to Mallarmé's gift to Louÿs. In both cases, the process of gifting relies on the value of nominalist self-property, rendering transparent the investment potential of limited edition, celebrity proper names.

Damian Catani has stressed how the mimetic desire to acquire what famous people own puts fashionability and ownership into potent relation:

> Bourgeois snobbery dictates that greater value be attributed to those works owned by people of a high social rank than to those belonging to individuals of more modest means. Being more attentive to provenance and ownership than to inherent aesthetic value, the bourgeoisie narcissistically sees the work of art as a status-symbol rather than as an inherently worthy object of beauty ... in bourgeois society an artist's reputation is defined by the money-spinning potential, fashionability and social provenance of his or her work.[38]

In affixing his name to the names of other famous poets, Mallarmé entered into a competitive economy of name making and name ownership in which proper names—and *dons*—served as the Mallarméan currency of fame. Even his English phrasebook *Les Mots anglais*, with its preponderance of expressions focused around the psychic economy of gifts, attests to his attraction to the theme:

> A slight gift, *small thanks.* (OC II, 1221)
>
> One gift well given recovers many losses. (OC II, 1221)
>
> What is bought is *cheaper* than a gift. (OC II, 1226)
>
> What is *freer* than a gift? (OC II, 1226)

In gifting others, one might say, Mallarmé gifts himself to eternity. Gifting, it would thus follow, is relevant to the historiography of celebrity because it renders transparent the process by which names serve as predicates of psychic transference, conferring properties that are themselves vested particulates of fame.

The intuition that Mallarmé may have given us the prototype for celebrity gifting came to me at a New York Public Library exhibition on the "artist's book." Entering the gallery, I was confronted by a famous headshot of Mallarmé, photographed by Nadar. What riveted my attention was an extravagant cravat that made the poet look gift-wrapped. The *don du poète*, in this case, was not a tribute text, but rather the visual offering of himself dressed as a luxury package. The impression grew as I surveyed other portraits of the poet.

In another Nadar photograph taken sometime after 1889, the effect of exotic packaging was even more pronounced. The high, upstanding collar supporting the poet's head suggested a proud offering of genius. The cravat's knot, which resembled a perfect Christmas bow, was artfully tied so that the folds created mysterious craters and sculpted shadows, like origami art or a Lacanian knot diagramming psychic topology or a subjective Matheme. The tie also seemed animalistic, moving and shimmering with reptilian sheen and shape, with tie-ends that hung like tails.

In still another Nadar photograph, titled *Stéphane Mallarmé en châle* (142), the cravat resembled a velvet dragonfly that had flown to his chest and stuck there. The cravat forms a counterpoint to the checkered shawl, draped tent-like over Mallarmé's shoulders and arms, the fringe falling over the jacket like a waterfall. In this picture, there is a visual relay of cravat-shawl-plume as Mallarmé assumes a "writer's pose," his pen poised in one hand over the page, inviting the viewer to decipher the upside-down-words on the sheet.

In Edvard Munch's *Portrait de Stéphane Mallarmé* (1897), the poet's goatee is inserted into the V-shape of the bow, which itself inverts the swags of the drooping moustache. The overall effect is to meld the man and tie, as if the cravat were integral to the subject's very being.

These images of Mallarmé formed an interesting contrast to Manet's portraits of Poe (1860–1862). In these sketches, the wings point down, away from Poe's face, like a black bird in flight. The moustache and the cravat visually rhyme with each other. I began to detect a family resemblance between the raven gracing Manet's illustration of 1875 (the one used for a bookstore poster of Mallarmé's translation of "Le Corbeau") and the shape of Manet's drawing of Poe's cravat. In his *autographies*, Manet establishes a formal relationship among poet, raven, head of Pallas, and tomb. The raven appears to haunt the text, just as the English original of Poe's language doubly haunts the French translation, first in Baudelaire's voice, then in Mallarmé's. The latter made different versions of his translation of "The Raven," one emphasizing the frightening sight of the bird as "specter" sitting on the bust over the bedroom door:

> Car je suis forcé de convenir qu'aucun homme vivant
> De ceux qui vivent encore n'eût été riant de voir l'oiseau sur la porte de sa chambre,
> L'oiseau ou le spectre sur la statue sculptée sur la porte de sa chambre
> Avec un nom comme "Jamais plus!"
> (Forced am I to concede that no man alive/Among those still living would laugh at the sight of the bird above the bedroom door/The bird or specter on a sculpted statue atop the bedroom door/With a name like 'Nevermore!')

Illustration 5.1. Munch. Portrait of Mallarmé.

Another version, substantively different, diminishes the moment of fear and stresses the animality of the bird:

> Car je suis forcé de convenir qu'aucun homme vivant
>
> N'a jamais eu le bonheur de voir l'oiseau sur la porte de la chambre,
>
> Un oiseau ou un animal sur le buste sculpté sur la porte de sa chambre.
>
> (Forced am I to concede that no man alive/Ever had the pleasure of seeing the bird above the bedroom door/A bird or an animal atop the bedroom door.)

Putting the versions together, a clearer allegory of death emerges. Funereal sculpture, busts, tombstones, the finality of the word "Nevermore," these markers of death are taken into the body of Mallarmé's poetry and become part of his own bid for poetic immortality.

Ultimately, it proves impossible to reckon with Mallarmé's art of the gift without acknowledging his profound Poe complex, itself an almost plagiaristic appropriation of Baudelaire's Poe complex, satirized by one critic as "Poedelaire."[39] In a letter to Henri Cazalis, written at a moment of crisis early in his career (1864), Mallarmé announced: "Toutefois, plus j'irai, plus je serai fidèle à ces sévères idées que m'a léguées mon grand maître Edgar Poe." (From here on, the further I go, the more faithful I will be to those severe ideas legated to me by my grand master Edgar Poe) (OC I, 654). Mallarmé describes reading "The Raven" as an experience of absolute poetic ejaculation that triggers the sensation of deathly impotence. He implores "Matter" to deliver him from Impotence, hoping to transpose the severity of the sepulchral statuary into the idea of creative death (OC I, 655). Alluding to Poe's *Philosophy of Composition* (translated by Baudelaire as "Genèse d'un poème"), Mallarmé seeks to revive his extinguished creative spark by following Poe's procedures for obtaining poetic effect, but to no avail. A suicidal despair grips him, a despair commensurate with the goth power of Poe's raven to haunt him ("je sens mon tort et avoue que je suis hanté", emphasis in the original). (OC I, 655)

Gauguin's *Portrait de Mallarmé* of 1891 accesses the poet's lifelong, hallucinatory raven fantasia. Here, the raven is perched on Mallarmé's head, as if the raven-cravat had migrated, in the pictorial sequence I have sketched, from cravat to winged moustache, and from moustache to head. Thomas Hanson's essay on Mallarmé's hats lends credence to this (admittedly fanciful) focus on headgear and sartorial trimmings as the signage of celebrity gifting.

> The top hat is a concentrating container which gathers heads and thoughts.
>
> Mallarmé has and is [a hat]: he himself clearly thinks of the top hat, not simply as an object or instrument detachable from its wearer, but rather as an integral part of late nineteenth-century man…. The hat as 'lid' is reminiscent of the 'mowing down' effect which negates transcendent values (symbolized by diadem and plume) and thwarts man's aspirations toward the infinite above. The hat is both 'part' of us and a countervailing force dampening our impulses.[40]

Illustration 5.2. Gauguin. Portrait of Mallarmé.

Hanson draws a connection between the hat and Poe, reminding us of Mallarmé's description of Poe as he who "burst into gems of a crown."[41] In contrast to the hat, which connotes creative explosion, the cravat suggests a funeral garland forming a chain of election: Poe–Baudelaire–Mallarmé. Mallarmé's fascination with the deaths of other poets and the restaging of their negation is no longer conceived, then, as a Bloomian agon of symbolic father-killing, but rather as a ticket into the pantheon of poetic celebrity. The tribute is made in the fiduciary sense of that word, as a down payment for posterity or a mortgage on future illustriousness.

My intention has been to demonstrate the importance of "gifting" to the historiography of fame. Mallarmé transformed the conventional epitaphic genre into a model of modernist subjective signature that doubled as a strategy for bestowing himself on posterity. To make this argument is to suggest that "gifting" be placed within successive transformative stages in the history of fame, taking us from an Aristotelian construct of biographical exemplarity and afterlife (summed up in his famous words: "Considering human affairs, one must not … consider man as he is and not consider what is mortal in mortal things, but think about them [only] to the extent that they have the possibility of immortalizing") to a capitalized model of celebrity.[42] In this most recent model, fame warrants inclusion on the list of those commodities—sexuality, culture, history, heritage, nature as spectacle or rest cure, originality, and authenticity—that, according to David Harvey, entail "putting a price on things that were never actually produced as commodities.[43]

CHAPTER 6

Rethinking Female Celebrity
The Eccentric Star of Nineteenth-Century France

MARY LOUISE ROBERTS

Does female celebrity in the nineteenth century warrant our particular attention? Does it differ significantly from male celebrity or can it be deemed impervious to gender norms? In *The Frenzy of Renown*, Leo Braudy left such questions aside, focusing his history of fame mostly on men. Though he never denies that societies could celebrate women, he does not examine what happens when they do. It is this question that interests the historian Lenard Berlanstein, who argues that celebrated women, and actresses in particular, evoked more attention than did their male counterparts. Because celebrity in the nineteenth century was defined as the recognition of individual self-achievement, Berlanstein reasons, and because women's role at the time was to be barely seen, let alone heard, celebrity status was more problematic for women than for men. As a result, female celebrity was more provocative than male celebrity, moving critics and commentators to pay a great deal of attention to actresses, who were frequently condemned as a dissolute lot.[1]

Taking Berlanstein's argument as my starting point, I want to reexamine the prospects of a specifically female celebrity. What did it mean for a famous woman to draw attention to herself in a society that regarded femininity as a matter of self-restraint? How did female celebrities break with restrictions placed upon them as women? How did they live comfortably in the limelight; that is, how did they manage their celebrity? Using the examples of two spectacular women—Rosa Bonheur and Sarah Bernhardt—I will consider *eccentricity* as a strategy of female celebrity. I will argue that both of these women, one an artist and the other an actress, deployed eccentricity as a *posture of celebrity*, a posture that helped them manage their fame. Their embrace of eccentricity as a personal style represented some acknowledgement on their part, whether conscious or not, that they had become culturally unintelligible to their public, precisely because they were female celebrities. Their strategy, then, was to play with such unintelligibility and deliberately to become *strange* in an amusing way. In the process, they became comprehensible— and hence more acceptable—to their public.

I have chosen Bonheur and Bernhardt because they stood out as two of the most celebrated women in nineteenth-century French society. Bonheur was a renowned painter of animals, most famously "The Horse Fair" of 1853. Not only was she the most recognized woman painter of her day, becoming in 1865 the first French woman to receive the *Légion d'honneur*, but she also gained great commercial success.[2] Like Bonheur, Bernhardt was an international celebrity, at the peak of her fame arguably the most famous woman in the world. By the 1890s, Bernhardt had become far more than an actress: she was also "the Bernhardt," *la Divine*, the Eighth Wonder of the World. Besides bringing Paris

Illustration 6.1. Sarah Bernhardt.

to its feet in such plays as *Cleopatra* and *Hamlet*, the actress opened her own Parisian theater, where she acted and produced plays when she was not touring the world. Audiences in Odessa, St. Petersburg, Buenos Aires, San Francisco, Honolulu, Sydney, Grand Rapids, Antwerp, Budapest, and Cairo, to name only a few, flocked to see Bernhardt and acclaim her genius. And this when the actress never spoke anything but French on stage.[31]

It was no coincidence that both women established reputations for being eccentric. To do so, both built upon their professional status as artists and exploited the new media technology of their era. Bonheur attracted attention as an *excentrique* in the 1850s by jaunting about Paris astride a horse in trousers and a jacket. Men of position scheduled to rendezvous with her in the Bois de Boulogne took one look and galloped off in the opposite direction.[3] Bonheur also attracted gossip by keeping an entire menagerie of animals in her

Illustration 6.2. Rosa Bonheur with her lion, Fatma.

backyard, including lions, almost forty sheep, goats, horses, oxen, mules, and a wild boar. Similarly, a wide range of contemporaries saw Bernhardt "as always in love with eccentricity."[4] "Scour the annals of the theatrical arts," dared the drama critic Francisque Sarcey, "you will never again see as strange a spectacle as this turbulent, treacherous life."[5] Like Bonheur, Bernhardt lived with large beasts, such as pumas and alligators, and gave them the free run of her home on the Boulevard Péreire in Paris. The actress was also known to eschew a bed as her sleeping place in favor of a coffin.[6]

As eccentrics, Bonheur and Bernhardt lacked accountability for their actions, a fact that was key to the success of their image. Both women presented themselves as "victims" of the celebrity surrounding them. Bernhardt, in particular, made herself out to be the hapless prey of the reporter, whom she condemned as "a veritable dung-beetle."[7] "Since the very creation of reporters," she wrote with her usual flair for understatement, "there is no person on this earth who has suffered as much from them as I did on my first tour."[8] By portraying herself as a casualty of the press, Bernhardt disavowed authorship of her own eccentric image. Such a denial was crucial to the credibility of the eccentric *qua* eccentric, since the behavior was not supposed to be intentional. Bonheur and Bernhardt had to appear to do weird things out of a whim or instinct rather than conscious intent. In this way, they were not held accountable for their actions. As creative artists, both women sought lives that were inventive and unscripted. The particular brand of blamelessness they gained through their eccentric behavior made their lives more livable precisely in these terms.

Bernhardt led a scandalous life that hardly needs rehearsing here: she engaged in prostitution as a young child, bore an illegitimate son, had one brief, disastrous marriage, and counted lovers by the dozen. And yet, with the exception of her anti-Semitic enemies, she was prized by the vast majority of French people, who viewed her as maddeningly fickle, but ultimately adorable—an artist who led her life "up so high" that she could not be judged by normal standards. Bonheur enjoyed the same blamelessness of the eccentric. Like Bernhardt, she was hardly a model of the domestic feminine. Bonheur shunned marriage and lived openly with two women—the first, an inventor, and the second, a US woman from San Francisco who was half her age. In an era when no woman dared put a cigarette to her mouth, she was a chainsmoker. And yet Bonheur was "forgiven" because of her eccentricity. While some critics singled out Bonheur's so-called masculine face as a warning to women seeking an art career, there were many more who, as Tamar Garb has put it, "indulged her personal whims by dwelling on their eccentricity, their very oddness."[9] Again, tolerance sprang from the general view that an eccentric could not be blamed for her behavior, which was beyond individual intent or will.

By using the technologies of celebrity (newsprint, photography, magazine copy) to market themselves as eccentrics, these two women not only managed their fame, but also, notably, got away with mortal sins against true womanhood. How can we understand this immunity in a society notorious for its restrictions on female behavior? Because eccentric behavior was not taken seriously in the nineteenth century, historians have largely disregarded it as well.[10] My aim in this essay is to question the putative innocence of eccentricity. What were the politics of eccentricity? How did eccentricity figure in the efforts of women, such as Bonheur and Bernhardt, to sustain a creative and possibly critical relation to gender norms in the nineteenth century? How specifically did it help them to manage the problem of female celebrity? Historians have devoted enormous attention to nineteenth-century gender norms, regarding them as a contested but relatively stable set of ideals and practices controlling the terms "male" and "female" during this period. Such norms, historians have argued, were either enacted or rejected by women in their social behavior. The eccentricity of Bonheur and Bernhardt reveals the overly mechanistic way in which we have understood "resistance" to gender norms. Not only did individual women maintain infinitely variable relations to such norms, thus defying the notion of the "normal," but they also produced these norms even as they challenged them.[11] On one level, Bonheur and Bernhardt appear to have used their eccentricity to escape preexisting normative "rules." But such an argument overlooks the fact that eccentricity could not be understood without reference to convention. As such, eccentricity reinforced as well as challenged the stability of norms. The purpose of this chapter, then, is not only to examine how Bonheur and Bernhardt as "rebel" eccentrics managed their celebrity, but also to complicate our understanding of how individual women sustained a creative relation to gender norms.

In being dubbed eccentrics, Bonheur and Bernhardt represented a new breed. Although human beings have exhibited strange behavior since the beginning of time, the very notion of the eccentric individual did not exist before the modern era. Originally, "eccentric" was an astronomical term that referred to a planet whose axis was other than centrally placed. Planets in eccentric orbit felt the pull of gravity from other stars as well as the one they were orbiting. As a result, their paths diverged from a normal ellipse or circle; an eccentric orbit followed an arc that was remote from where it was supposed to be. "Deviation from a centre, in fact, is the very thing which constitutes eccentricity," wrote a British cleric in 1859.[12] Eccentricity was about location, measured precisely by its aberration from a normal orbit. It was produced by and served as an index of normality.

The term "eccentric" had no figurative meaning at all in England until 1685, when a poet, thinking to compare a human to a star, used the metaphor of "the brightest, yet the most excentrick Soul."[13] This figurative meaning as "odd and whimsical" gained strength in England during the eighteenth century, crossed the Channel to France in 1817, and from there traveled to Germany in the 1830s. Even then, one could still not be an *"excentrique"* as a type until the 1840s.[14] In the 1850s, however, the word became fabulously *chic*: French writers and poets flocked to variants of the word "excentrique."[15] For example, the French novelist George Sand, notorious for her cross-dressing and steamy love affairs, used it in record numbers in her 1855 autobiography, *Journal de ma vie*, to describe her penchant for "walking away from every convention in the world."[16]

Eccentricity as a mode of behavior was thus "invented" in the late eighteenth and early nineteenth centuries. It coincides, then, with the emergence of a bourgeois democratic state in France. This chronology makes sense if we consider that eccentricity is grounded in individualism—the central value of bourgeois liberal society—and can be defined as a kind of hyper-individualism. To use the astronomical idiom, an eccentric feels the gravitational pull of some inner, highly individualistic force moving her into another orbit. An eccentric person, like an eccentric orbit, was located somewhere other than where she was supposed to be, and thus indexed normative behavior. Clearly, then, eccentricity was a product of the normative society that distinguished modern bourgeois liberal culture. The very imposition of homogenous norms on human behavior created the possibility of differentiation at the level of the individual. The new emphasis on conventional behavior gave rise to the eccentric, who materialized

the limits of normative behavior, appearing to resist them but, in fact, reinforc-
ing them. Eccentrics such as Bonheur and Bernhardt engaged precisely these
tensions between the norm and the exception, between sameness and difference, which lay at the heart of nineteenth-century liberal society. They expertly
navigated the reverse gravitational forces of convention and individualism. As
artists, they inhabited socially marginal spaces where, according to Jerrold Seigel, they helped act out and resolve the contradictions of bourgeois society.[17]

As stars, they also steered their lives into eccentric orbits. Like eccentricity,
"stardom" was a recent import from the astronomical lexicon and also an invention of the nineteenth century. Again, England stood in the forefront, using the
word "star" in 1824 to describe an actress who, by name alone, could pack a
theater. Although the French noted this English usage as early as 1844, neither
"*star*" nor "*étoile*" entered the French vocabulary until the late 1870s, precisely
at the heyday of Bonheur and Bernhardt's careers. Neither word is included
in the *Littré* of 1875, but Émile Zola referred to "*La Blonde Géraldine, une
étoile d'opérettes*" in his 1880 novel *Nana*.[18] Although female stars were more
provocative than their male counterparts, they were also more popular. Both
controversial and exciting, they were condemned and loved in a way male celebrities were not. By 1902, *La Vie en rose* observed that it was now female *étoiles*,
not theatrical pieces, which determined the size of an audience, particularly
those "veritable suns, around which revolves all of Paris theater."[19]

Bernhardt was such a sun. When she married in 1882, her husband was
dubbed "a satellite of a star."[20] In the 1880s, when she left the state-sponsored
theater to begin her international tours, one journalist wanted to know "why
she left the Comédie-Française to become a wandering star?"[21] Another contemporary had her say, "I am the morning star; I am the evening star, I am the
star of the day, ... I am she who shines."[22] To say that Sarah Bernhardt also
knew how to craft a star image would be an understatement. As is well known,
the actress pioneered the marketing and publicity of the star system, becoming
notorious for her manipulation of the press and advertising industries. Quite
apart from her profession as an actress, Bernhardt staged a self that was all illusion and artifice, a surface play of images behind which the "real" Bernhardt
became impossible to locate. "A vagabond comet," as one admirer described her
in 1896, Bernhardt created and recreated herself according to her own whims
and those of her managers and publicists.[23] She became the model of subjectivity as pure performance, a star constantly in orbit.

And so it was with Rosa Bonheur. Although "stardom" was mostly confined
to the theatrical world, Bonheur nevertheless became, according to Daniele
Digne, "the artistic star" who "knew the tedium of the star system," indisposed
by fans who sought her autograph, her photograph, and even the locks of her
hair.[24] In an age when women artists were dismissed as "unnatural," besides
entirely lacking in talent, Bonheur became an international star artist, whose

work was commercially successful in the United States and England as well as France. As Gabriel Weisberg has observed, Bonheur "well understood that in order to market her paintings successfully, her dress, demeanor and public image—in addition to her paintings—were crucial to shaping perceptions of her accomplishments as an artist. Bonheur was one of the earliest painters to use modern methods of self-promotion to establish herself as an international personality."[25] Such methods included interviews and biographical portraits in the new mass press, replete with photographs of her "at home" in her studio at Fontainebleau. British and US magazines lavished attention on the artist's clothes, her animals, and her chateau. The press copy generated often exceeded the public's attention to her paintings but increased their value in the process. Bonheur also used other media stars to stage her celebrity. When the Wild West Show brought Buffalo Bill to Paris in conjunction with the Universal Exposition of 1889, Bonheur recognized a kindred spirit. She smothered the famous cowboy with attention, and famously painted his portrait.[26]

It became impossible to fathom the star power of either Bonheur or Bernhardt without reckoning with their bizarre habits. Building on already culturally embedded links between the artist and capricious behavior, both women flaunted their oddness. For much of her career, Bonheur played up her unconventional appearance and mannerisms in the media through press interviews and articles. As the critic Judith Grainger has put it, she "knew the advantage of public image and used her eccentricities to build a controversial and somewhat mysterious persona to enhance her reputation."[27]

Like Bonheur, Bernhardt considered herself first and foremost an artist; the fantastic whims of the artist were her only master.[28] Her fans ate it up. "In an era when the marvelous seems to have vanished from sight," wrote her contemporary Claude-Roger Marx, "she has also known to remain far-away, to preserve a mystery not exhausted by the years."[29] Marx evoked a common perception of Bernhardt as somehow outside of the normal order of things. As another critic put it, "Sarah's fantasy and her pride have carried her up so high that her life is no longer visible; nor can we communicate with her. Everything up there is superb but unreal, made only for the charm of the imagination."[30]

Adding to Bernhardt's eccentricity was her apparent ability to hover on the peripheries of society, pulled away from the center by the force of her own unpredictable desires. Indeed, another, older meaning of eccentric derived from the Greek "*ek*," meaning "out of," and "*kentron*," meaning circle; eccentrics lived outside of the circle and "out of the way." As artists, both Bonheur and Bernhardt were already identified with the social margins, a marginality Bonheur underlined by choosing to live on the periphery of Paris. Many of Bernhardt's closest friends had their roots in the theatrical and literary underworld of Parisian life, among them, Jean Lorrain, René Vivien, and Oscar Wilde.[31] In addition, some critics, especially anti-Semitic ones, claimed her half-Jewish origins "gave her face the troublesome grace of the bohemian or gypsy," and "link[ed] her to the Orient and to the primitive world."[32] Because of its geographical remoteness to Europe, the Orient itself was considered eccentric. As the figurative meaning of eccentricity took root, Europeans linked the eccentric, peripheral location of Northern Africa and the Middle East to its culture, which they deemed lacking in normative disciplining. As a result, the Orient became to them a "reservoir of infinite peculiarity," to use Edward Said's phrase.[33]

Through the new technologies of mass newsprint and photography taking shape in urban Europe, eccentrics also emerged in the late nineteenth century as a new modern "type" or social being. Europeans hardly had to wait until the *fin de siècle* to witness humans behaving outlandishly. Nevertheless, eccentricity was novel in two ways. First, it served a new purpose, which was to materialize the limits of normative behavior in a bourgeois liberal society marked by disciplining and regulatory controls. Second, eccentrics were now produced *as images* in a mass press particularly preoccupied with the curiosities of the everyday. As Vanessa Schwartz has shown, the daily newspaper, as well as serial novels and guidebooks, "incessantly conjured a never-ending festival of modern life."[34] This set of images produced a new social being—the eccentric—who came to symbolize not only modern "spectacle," but also the modern response to the legislation of identity.

Eccentricity can be defined as an inability to fit easily into any reproducible norm or by the unwillingness to be "regulated by ... central control."[35] If we take the contemporary example of superstar Michael Jackson, we note that Jackson's eccentricity derived from his visual failure to meet normative expectations of race and gender. Jackson's eccentricity originated precisely in the fluid visual space he occupied between black and white, male and female, human and animal. Both Bonheur and Bernhardt became unintelligible in this way, by failing to match normative expectations. They existed at the margins without going too far beyond them, just recognizable enough to be "odd" without being "normal." Eccentricity was largely generated through visuality. While we can easily envision an eccentric outfit, we have more difficulty conjuring up an eccentric novel, poem, or comment.[36] To be eccentric was to present a queer (in the sense of illegible) spectacle of oneself. More specifically, the illegibility of Bonheur and Bernhardt's images rested in their *androgynous* and *therianthropic* qualities, that is, their ability visually to merge male and female, and human and animal forms.[37]

Both Bonheur and Bernhardt donned men's clothes. Bonheur's famous excuse for her *travesti* was that she needed to dress like a man in order to visit the slaughterhouses to sketch animals without being harassed.[38] But Bonheur by no means limited her male costume to the slaughterhouse; she consistently wore a male style of dress at her chateau. Her friend Joseph Verdier recalled a female neighbor's chagrin when his fiancé took a stroll with the artist one day. She soon dropped by to scold Monsieur Verdier for letting his fiancé walk unchaperoned with a man, and a handsome one at that.[39] But to describe Bonheur's clothes as "male" or to say that she simply "cross-dressed" is not quite right, for her costume was neither really feminine nor masculine. In 1853, an observer described her dress as "a compromise between that of a woman and a man."[40] "Impossible to guess her sex," declared Eugène de Mirecourt in 1856.[41] For her part, Bonheur enjoyed her ability to keep everyone guessing. "They wonder to which sex I belong!" she once wrote gleefully to her sister.[42] The key, as Bonheur's companion Nathalie figured out, was to create a costume unique to the artist alone. She instructed Bonheur to wear something as "distinctively yours" as Napoleon's cap was to his image. In response, Bonheur created a uniform consisting of a Breton-style smock, a vest, simple pants, and a little cap. Contemporaries deemed it "queer" and "odd," but also amusing.[43] (See Figure 6.2.) Bonheur's costume became eccentric rather than scandalous because it was recognizable as hers alone, and thus inhabited a unique site on the peripheries of gender norms.

Bernhardt also trumped normative expectations concerning gender and dress. (See Figure 6.1.) Like Bonheur, Bernhardt claimed that her cross-dressing was a professional hazard—she found male roles to be richer and more complex than feminine ones.[44] Some of the most successful moments of Bernhardt's career took place in men's clothing.[45] At the peak of her career, she played Hamlet as well as the Duc de Reichstadt in Edmond Rostand's *L'Aiglon*, both to high, if not unanimous, acclaim.[46] While rehearsing for *L'Aiglon*, Bernhardt played with gender roles in her press appearances. For example, when someone asked her about her ability to rehearse until 3 or 4 A.M. as the Duc, she responded "Bah! Don't be surprised. Now that I've cut my hair short, I feel I have the strength of a man."[47] As the Duc, she drew this response from a reporter concerning her short hair and male costume: "She wears it with such ease that the 'real' men beside her have the air of being disguised."[48] The effect of Bernhardt's *travesti* was to render masculinity as queer as herself. This denaturalizing effect explains why Bernhardt was one of the most caricatured personalities of her day. As a mode of representation that admits to its own mimicry through parody, caricature perfectly captured Bernhardt's inclination for parody rather than to inhabit any normative identity. Her eccentricity signaled a tendency to *stage* the culturally inscribed limits of gender identity rather than "naturally" reproduce them.

Androgyny was an important signifier of eccentricity that firmly established both Bonheur and Bernhardt as strange in the public eye. But it was the two women's theriomorphism that marked them as truly, verifiably eccentric. While eccentricity was certainly not the sole province of females in the nineteenth century, there were arguably specific female traits of eccentricity. One of them was a peculiar relationship with animals, particularly cats. The association of women and cats dates back to medieval times, when black cats were burned as witches.[49] The witch, as the icon of the marginal woman in the early modern era, was probably the closest precursor we have to the female eccentric. Witches were believed not only to harbor cats in large numbers, but to transform themselves into cats, the better to cast spells on their victims. Lonely old women were said to keep cats, particularly black cats, as *familiars* given to them by Satan at the time of their initiation into witchcraft. Historians have noted how many of these prejudices survived into the nineteenth century.[50] Even in the twentieth century, according to a recent popular study on eccentrics, "the stereotype of the eccentric woman is an old lady in a big house with a hundred cats."[51]

Both Bonheur and Bernhardt loved animals. As noted above, Bonheur was known for keeping a menagerie of animals in her backyard and even in her own bedroom. An otter, brought back from the Pyrénées, would sometimes escape his tank and crawl between the bed sheets.[52] Over her lifetime, Bernhardt's menagerie of pets included, if we are to believe the reports: three domestic cats plus a tigress, lynx, wildcat, lion, cheetah; three greyhounds (two Russian, one Italian), plus four other dogs (bull mastiff, poodle, terrier, and wolfhound); two horses (Vermouth and Cassis); several birds, including a hawk; six chameleons, a parrot, a boa constrictor, and two pet alligators from Louisiana. Bernhardt killed one of the latter by feeding it too much champagne; the other she shot dead after it swallowed her beloved Manchester terrier. Bernhardt procured many of these animals while touring and getting them back to France was not easy. A London hotel initially refused to house a tigress due to the vicious rumor that she had eaten two waiters.[53] Even in Paris, Bernhardt's menagerie became a problem when she allowed the cats to walk freely about her house. Alexandre Dumas *fils* once lost his straw boater to a puma while waiting five minutes for Bernhardt in her studio. In 1894, one terrified reporter told the tale of finally gaining entry to the actress's house, only to be introduced to her two jaguars, Antony and Cleopatra.[54]

As these stories suggest, Bernhardt had a special place in her heart for cats. On a theatrical tour in London in 1879, she set off to Liverpool to acquire a lion. She returned instead with a cheetah. Much to everyone's chagrin, she let it loose in her backyard in Chester Square. Her biographer Cornelia Otis Skinner describes the response of her entourage of friends: "Madame Gué-rard screamed and crossed herself, the butler dropped a tea tray, de Nittis kept flailing the air with his cane, Doré walked with stately alacrity into the house and everyone else, including Sarah, burst into maniacal gales of laughter. Passers-by peered in amazement over the garden wall and scores of faces appeared at windows in the dignified houses surrounding Chester Square."[55] The next day, London papers summed up the scene as a "witches' Sabbath." Returning to France across the Channel posed a challenge, as the cheetah forced a near mutiny on the boat.[56]

While Rosa Bonheur did not live with countless cats, she favored extremely large ones, including several full-grown lions.[57] According to one art critic, Bonheur had an "obsessive interest in lions."[58] In 1873, the director of a small zoo near Melun invited Bonheur to make studies of a lioness in their possession. Bonheur sketched "Pierette" again and again, but because she tired of traveling to the zoo, she went on to "rent" a lion named Brutus, and then had two shipped up from Marseilles. She kept these for about two months, then donated them to the Paris zoo. In 1884, Bonheur again took in two lion cubs, one of which, Fatma, lived with her for three years.[59] She frequently gave them the run of the yard and of the house. Bonheur delighted in the trouble Fatma got into when she chose to wander around and make a shambles of her bedroom.

To keep big cats as pets was a performative gesture. When Bonheur and Bernhardt brought a large wild cat into a domesticated space, they expressed a desire not only to cause trouble, but also to attract attention. Keeping wild animals was dangerous as well as strange; it demonstrated the kind of death-defying behavior already associated with bohemian artists, with their abuse of drugs and alcohol.[60] In domesticating such animals, the two women also put on view a bravura akin to circus performers who conquer predators. The lion was known in the nineteenth century as he is today: "the terror of the forest" in La Fontaine's phrase, who could make animals tremble at his mere smell.[61] Bonheur bragged that, unlike many of her male visitors, she felt no fear whatsoever approaching a four-hundred-pound predator. In order to avoid fights with dogs and visitors, she once had a night cage built for one of her lions. "But," she qualified, "she was so tame that I let her put her paws around my neck, I took her head and embraced her. She was a model of obedience and docility." Fatma was similarly slavish. He followed her around "like a poodle," she once observed. When she and her companion Micas went to the train station to pick up the cubs from Marseilles, they did not tell the male train workers that they had been guarding the lions. This was because, explained Bonheur, "they would have died of fright retrospectively."[62] Bonheur's fondness for predators helped to stage her androgyny: she used them to launch herself in the public eye as manlier than men.

Besides being dangerous, wild animals were exuberant in famously unpredictable ways. They engaged in such "uncivilized" behaviors as chasing, attacking, biting, and relieving themselves indoors. Such behaviors were funny inasmuch as they disrupted the "normal" course of life—causing screams, grasps for high furniture, repellent smells, and agonizing embarrassment. In short, feline behavior launched an all-out assault on the orderly disposition of nineteenth-century bourgeois liberal society. At the same time, such animal behavior—like eccentricity itself—was blameless; one could not blame an animal for behaving like an animal. The Romantics believed that the animal escaped the pull of normative disciplining altogether: its center of gravity was located elsewhere—in instinct and survival. What was considered "undisciplined" be-havior among humans was "normal" or "natural" for animals. Animals, in other words, were born eccentrics.

Through their menageries, then, these women used animals not only to thumb their noses at bourgeois probity, but more fundamentally, to call into question the very logic of the cultural norm. What was normal and what was uncivilized? The two artists also turned upside down the nineteenth-century domestic imperative: that women maintain the home as a private oasis of com-fort and tranquility. Home could hardly serve as a haven in a heartless world if you had a dangerous predator stalking your living room. Bonheur and Bern-hardt's insistence on keeping undomesticated animals uncaged in their houses troubled their guests and neighbors, who were upset over the presence of lions that *should* have been restrained, yet *were not*.[63] Both women allowed normally confined creatures to do as they please, even at the risk of being dangerous. Could not the same be said for them? Out of orbit, out of cages—the two women's delight in large cats was nothing other than vicarious gender trouble once removed. In leaving wild animals only partially "domesticated," they cre-ated a living model of their own rebellious relationship to the French domestic ideal.

Living with wild animals, Bonheur and Bernhardt situated themselves on the peripheries between the animal and human worlds. Bernhardt's mansion in Paris was moreover decorated with animal furs from the far reaches of the globe. The gadfly Jean Lorrain recalled beaver from Brazil, buffalo from Can-ada, and bear from South America; he described Bernhardt's studio as "an ac-cumulation of hair in every shade and from every provenance."[64] According to Skinner, Bernhardt bought the lion while in London because "she was fed up with meeting so many people. She had always found animals more interesting." As Skinner wrote, Bernhardt "could handle a supposedly savage beast such as a lynx or a cheetah with fearless ease. Even reptiles held a fascination for her. When she played Cleopatra, she more than once insisted upon using a real snake for the final scene." Bernhardt once even schemed to graft a tiger tail onto her own spine. Hoping to lash it about when she was angry, she nevertheless allowed her friends to talk her out of it at the last minute.[65]

Similarly, Bonheur presented herself to the mass press as a romantic figure living amid her animals on the edge of the Fontainebleau forest (the periphery again). Her letters were full of animal similes in which she compared herself to a rat, a dog, a tortoise, a mule, a boar, and a bear.[66] Speaking of Bonheur's love of animals, Arsène Alexandre remarked: "The animal is an enigma; he offers the beauty of life in movement, of instinct unspoiled by what makes men so insufferable, that is, education."[67] As a hermit living on the edge of the forest, Bonheur relished her animals' lack of "education." "Since I've been in By, living constantly in the midst of my animals," she once told her companion Anna

Klumpke, "I scarcely have time to play the grand lady; so my visitors will have to take me as I am."[68] To live among her animals was the truth of her identity; to be *une grande dame* was to play an imposed role.[69] "I need the society of no one," she wrote in 1886, "What can the world do for me? A portrait painter has need of these things, but not I, who find all that is wanted in my dogs, my horses, my hinds, and my stags of the forest."[70] Through her choice of artistic subject, Bonheur also positioned herself on the social peripheries. Although painters of her era commonly portrayed domesticated pets or interactions between animals and humans as a way of mediating between the natural and the social, Bonheur's art focused almost completely on a natural world cut off from human society.[71] As John Ruskin famously noted, Bonheur focused almost exclusively on animals, and did not articulate human faces.[72]

In sum, both Bonheur and Bernhardt's eccentricity consisted in their failure (whether intentional or not) to fit easily into any reproducible norm, whether male or female, animal or human. A famous cartoon by André Gill represents Bernhardt precisely in this way—as an androgynous, theriomorphic fantasy creature, dressed in a man's suit, with the torso of a human and the legs of a mule. Bernhardt's much publicized habit of sleeping in a coffin, it could be argued, also located her on another and perhaps ultimate periphery, the periphery between life and death. These *miscellaneous* identities (in the sense of sundry, unclassifiable) allowed Bonheur and Bernhardt to remain just outside the gravitational force of normative cultural systems. Precisely as miscellaneous, recognizable but not categorizable, the two women eluded expectations that they would follow the usual female circuits of marriage

Illustration 6.3. Cartoon of Sarah Bernhardt by André Gille.

and motherhood. They were eccentric stars whose orbits were predictable only in their unpredictability. In this way, their provocative, unconventional celebrity images became intelligible *on their own terms*. Eccentric stardom enabled Bonheur and Bernhardt to pursue their own trajectories—to lead inventive, creative lives even in a universe where female movement was radically proscribed.

In astronomy, eccentric stars are doomed because their orbits ultimately end in collision and extinction. And so it was with female eccentricity as a style of celebrity: it burnt itself out by the beginning of the twentieth century. During this period, Berlanstein argues, the media focus on stars became even more obsessive, but at the same time, increasingly emphasized the *ordinariness* of actresses' lives. Journalists begin to domesticate actresses by sanitizing their lives and making them models of proper domesticity. Readers of such magazines as *Fémina* were treated to photos of pristine actresses in their immaculate bourgeois foyers, holding forth on their love for their children. Berlanstein considers this development a good thing, describing such images as "a liberating message." The domestication of actresses signaled "the acceptance of women in the public sphere," as the new woman entered higher education, took on respectable paid employment, and enjoyed independence.[73] But how can the transformation of the actress into a domestic mother signal the rise of the new woman? And how can becoming ordinary—subscribing to normative female behavior—become suddenly liberating, when it was the very uniqueness of stars that had, in the first place, freed them from the restrictions of womanhood? One wonders how these changes affected the actresses themselves now that they had to portray themselves in "ordinary" terms. Was it not more fun to be eccentric?

As we have seen, there was nothing innocent about eccentricity at all; its most clever disguise was its apparent unimportance. As a posture of celebrity, eccentricity helped both Bonheur and Bernhardt manage their fame as specifically *female* stars. At the same time, eccentricity had its limitations, for it relied on the capitalization of culture—the rise of sophisticated technologies of image production and promotion, and with it, an ever-quickening thirst for novelty and surprise. In this type of mass commodity culture, eccentric stars were doomed, their orbits destined for mimicry and ultimately a collapse into cliché. In addition, as a behavior, eccentricity was an incitement, but also itself a means of normalization. The mere classification of female eccentricity was a normalizing judgment of hyper-individualization: to say that such-and-such was an eccentric was also to reaffirm conventional behaviors. In this sense, eccentriciy was its own worst enemy.

PART III

The Politics
of Fame

CHAPTER 7

Byron, Death, and the Afterlife

STEPHEN MINTA

"*Quand on nous a annoncé la mort de Byron, il nous a semblé qu'on nous enlevait une part de notre avenir.*"[1] Victor Hugo's anguished response to the death of Byron was echoed across Europe. Jane Welsh, the future wife of Thomas Carlyle, wrote of her own reaction: "My God, if they had said that the sun or the moon had gone out of the heavens, it could not have struck me with the idea of a more awful and dreary blank in the creation than the words 'Byron is dead!'" While Carlyle himself felt "as if I had lost a Brother!"[2] The intensity can only strike us as remarkable, not wholly explicable—and certainly not explicable simply as an immediate response to Byron's death. For here, as one among a myriad of examples, is the French poet and statesman Lamartine, reflecting on Byron while he was still alive: he called him "Esprit mystérieux, mortel, ange, ou démon" (Mysterious spirit, mortal, angel, or devil), and conjured a fascinated image of Byron reigning with Satan in the infernal darkness.[3]

Terms such as *charisma* and *fame* may appear inadequate to account for these extraordinary impressions, produced across a vast audience of both men and women, of people of widely differing political persuasions, and from countries with very different traditions. In this essay, I want to compare reactions to Byron in England and in Greece, as a way of throwing light on the different ways in which his life and death could be read. In England, he early secured a contract with his readership that, in the eyes of many, he subsequently betrayed. England's relation to him was dark, fascinated, and unhappy. In Greece, on the other hand, there was no such contract, the relationship was much simpler, yet still intense and enduring. The comparison suggests ways of thinking about how fame and charisma are constructed, how they link, and how they differ.

Charisma and Fame

Charisma and fame: the two terms are so frequently allied in the modern world that it is easy to forget how recent is the semantic alliance. In origin, they relate to two very different areas of experience. It is, at first sight, tempting to define that difference as one between the religious (charisma) and the secular (fame), and to view their close proximity in the modern age as the result of the progressive secularization of the charismatic. But, though there is some truth in this, even the briefest history of the two words suggests tensions between them that are more complex and less monolithic.

Charisma and fame both derive from very ancient roots. The proper noun *ka-ri-si-jo* (Χαρίσιος), which appears on Linear B tablets at Mycenae and Knossos in the second millennium BCE, already contains the underlying sense of χάρις (*kharis*, 'grace', 'favor'), which is at the heart of charisma. As a name, Kharisios has an exact equivalent in the Latinate proper noun 'Grace'. *Kharis* in Homer is often a gift from the gods, characteristically a gift that makes the receiver more beautiful and seductive. Here, for example, is the goddess Athena at work, endowing Odysseus with her favor as he encounters the young virgin Nausicaa: "as when a man overlays silver with gold … and full of grace is the work he produces, even so the goddess shed grace upon his head and shoulders. Then he went apart and sat down on the shore of the sea, gleaming with beauty and grace; and the maiden marveled at him."[4]

The reiteration of 'grace' here foreshadows the future history of charisma in the modern age, as Odysseus receives that indefinable, inexplicable gift that renders him irresistible, both to Nausicaa and to the audience of the epic. The transformation in Odysseus as brought by *kharis* is something so powerful that it cannot be explained except through the intervention of the god. It is far more than any human being, even one as resourceful as Odysseus, could ever hope to achieve for himself. As a result, there is always something potentially unnerving or transgressive about the process, something that is profoundly against nature. Yet, at the same time, we vaguely sense that what the goddess has achieved here, through her gift of *kharis*, is an idealization of nature—nature transformed by divine intervention into its otherwise unattainable best.

The derived term χάρισμα (*kharisma*) enters relatively late the Greek language. As far as we can tell, its function is, from the beginning, entirely religious. The Apostle Paul sprinkles liberally the term across his epistle to the Romans and it is most famously embedded in the binaries of Romans 6.23: "For the wages of sin is death; but the gift (the χάρισμα) of God is eternal life." Charisma was always a term of high seriousness, the 'grace' or 'favor' of God, the divine gift that indicated the worthiness of the recipient and that manifested itself in powers of healing or of prophecy. The *Oxford English Dictionary's* (*OED*) first attestation in English of the word *charisma* dates from 1641 and it continues to retain a uniquely religious sense into the twentieth century.

If the essence of charisma is gift, fame is all about talk. The Indo-European root of Greek *pheme*, Latin *fama*, has the basic sense of 'to speak,' and it is preserved in such English words as 'blaspheme' and 'telephone.' The *OED* offers, as one of its definitions of 'fame': "[t]he condition of being much talked about," which retains the root meaning. *Fama*, in Latin, originally means both 'good fame' and 'bad fame,' since, quite logically, talk can go in either direction. Its shift toward the positive is a creation of the imperial age. Greek *pheme* also has a contested history. It can be divine, an "utterance prompted by the gods," "a voice from heaven," but in the following fascinating passage from Homer's contemporary Hesiod, the ambiguities surrounding the idea of talk are fully in play: "Avoid the wretched talk (*pheme*) of mortals. For talk is evil: it is light to raise up quite easily, but it is difficult to bear, and hard to put down. No talk is ever entirely gotten rid of, once many people talk it up: it too is some god."[5]

The paradox is wonderfully expressed. Talk may be light and trivial, but through that promiscuity of articulation at the heart of fame, through endless repetition and circulation, it acquires a power that is somehow god-like: the power and the price of fame.

The recent history of charisma is one of rapid assimilation to the secular. Already by 1920, it had passed from theology into sociology with Max Weber and, according to the *OED*, the first English secular reference dates from 1930.[6] By the 1950s, it had been adopted into the language of literary criticism: Lionel Trilling talks of charisma as "the charm of power" (1950); after which, it began a swift process of semantic extension, or, as some would say, dissolution. Applied frequently to John F. Kennedy, it became, in the 1960s, the term of choice in the mass media to denote the otherwise indefinable aura with which they graced certain public figures. Increasingly, it came to evoke the power of almost anything that hints at a miraculous gift by association. So we find, in 1967, an invitation to "the real charisma" of "classic tennis clothes."

In the twenty-first century, it is a word with a denuded, perhaps unglittering future. Joe Klein overhears someone saying, at a public meeting addressed by Barack Obama: "We know he's got the charisma. We want to know if he's got the brains." It might seem as if, by its endless extension, the term charisma is destined to lose its power to evoke the *mystery* of attraction. Christopher Caldwell's patrician regret at the semantic decline is, in this context, comprehensible. Writing recently in the *New York Times*, he says: "Once it is untethered from its roots in revelation, charisma can appear as mere celebrity."[7]

"Mere celebrity," however, begs all of the important questions. We know that nothing is stranger, or more problematic, than celebrity. As Roland Barthes reminds us, in the famous essay "Le Visage de Garbo," the "mere" face of Valentino was enough to drive spectators to suicide, torn by the paradox of the face's apparent accessibility and its simultaneous quality of being utterly beyond reach ("*où le visage constituait une sorte d'état absolu de la chair, que l'on ne pouvait ni atteindre ni abandonner*").[8] We can recall Lady Liddell's reported remark to her daughter, on seeing Byron on the roof of St Peter's in Rome: "Don't look at him, he is dangerous to look at."[9] Or one thinks of Prime Minister Tony Blair's shrewd encapsulation of the Valentino paradox, when he referred to Diana, Princess of Wales, as the "people's Princess," in the immediate aftermath of her death. This image suggested someone who could reach out to all, who belonged to all, yet who remained every inch the Princess she had become by her marriage, rich, unattainable, and living in a fairytale.

In truth, the supposed devaluation of the word *charisma* is less interesting than the fact of its extraordinary secular rise over so brief a period. It remains in our time one of the most slippery of terms, but clearly one whose need is widely felt. Charisma is always power, and so it is always potentially disturbing, not least because it is so difficult to rationalize. Sometimes it appears that it is the touch of a hand, the movement of an eyebrow, or the inflection of a voice that is the source of power, and that troubles the rational mind. Fame is often explicable, but it might be the case that true charisma never is, that it remains, in that sense, a gift from the gods.

Charisma is problematic in a secular age. Only in modern Greek has the word been assimilated to the manageable and the concrete. Contemporary Greek knows the secular usage now common in English (one may talk of a man with 'many χαρίσματα'); but a primary meaning is the simple, solid, and altogether uncontroversial one of 'gift': "this watch was a gift (χάρισμα) from my mother." Greek has effected in this way a kind of democratic revenge on the elitism of charisma, rejoining, if at a considerable remove, the reassuringly ubiquitous sense of charisma that we find in I Peter, 4.10: "As every man hath received the gift (χάρισμα), even so..."

The power of fame and the power of charisma are often intertwined and mutually supportive, but it is important to acknowledge how much they may differ in terms of the way we experience them and of our attitude toward them. People do not run the marathon today because it recalls a famous victory of the Athenians over the Persians in 490 BCE. The fascination of the marathon is tied to the almost certainly false account of a runner (often named as Pheidippides), who allegedly brought the news of the victory over the Persians to Athens, and who then died on arrival, with one of history's most famous sound bites on his lips: "Greetings, we win."

It is the supposed death of the runner, as he uttered his sound bite, that endows the event with something more than fame, that gives it a kind of superhuman, god-like quality. The historical Pheidippides appears to have done an epic run from Athens to Sparta, which is an infinitely greater feat than any supposed marathon. His achievement is now commemorated annually by the race known as the Spartathlon, but it is the marathon—which he did not run—that holds the imagination. Every runner in a marathon shares, not in the fame of a real Athenian victory, but in the agony and loneliness of a fictitious predecessor. The heroic impossibility of the task is confirmed by the death of that first protagonist, and the result is an identification far darker and more potent than would derive from any simple historical connection. Pheidippides is like the medieval martyr who exalts and terrifies by the example of a heroic sacrifice. This is the world of the charismatic.

Lord Byron

If there is, obviously, a certain anachronism in projecting a secular charisma back into earlier periods, the very slipperiness of the concept in our time allows us a measure of freedom. In any case, as I have suggested, it may be that true charisma is never wholly secular and never completely severed from its origins in the divine. But however we may seek to define our terms, there are few nineteenth-century figures who offer wider insights into the power of fame and charisma than Lord Byron. He became famous overnight at the age of twenty-four, as he himself recalled ("I awoke one morning and found myself famous"), and by the time of his death in 1824, he was one of the most talked about figures in Europe. He established an early contract with his readers and then tested it almost to destruction. He was self-consciously transgressive, and indulged in sodomy, incest, and the love of boys. Brought up in Scotland in no grand style, he unexpectedly became a great English lord and maintained an ambiguous relationship with England for all of his life. After scandal, humiliation, and the separation from his wife, he abandoned England forever after 1816. He died famously in a small town in Greece during the War of Greek Independence.

Presence, magnetism, Castiglione's *sprezzatura*, Elinor Glyn's 'it'—Byron had them all in great measure. Edward John Trelawny said of him: "he was rich as a gold mine, in every direction you bored into him you could extract wealth, and he was never exhausted."[10] Meanwhile, Mary Shelley confided in her diary her sense of helplessness, trapped between two of the most charismatic figures of the century: "I do not think that any person's voice has the same power of awakening melancholy in me as [Byron's] … when [Byron] speaks & Shelley does not answer, it is as thunder without rain, the form of the sun without heat or light … & I listen with an unspeakable melancholy—that yet is not all pain."[11]

That melancholy, of course, was the basis of Byron's initial contract with his readership, his form of "public intimacy." If he indeed awoke one morning to find himself famous, following the publication of the first two cantos of *Childe Harold's Pilgrimage* (*CHP*) in March 1812, it was a result that had been both carefully prepared and tantalizingly manipulated. "Fame is the thirst of youth," after all.[12] Byron's remark about his sudden fame suggests effortlessness, unselfconsciousness, and an aristocratic insouciance. It implies that the fate of something as fundamentally unserious as a literary work is entirely due to what is happening out there, rather than from within, due to the responsibility of those growing new middle classes with their appetite for long narrative poems and—at least so far as women were concerned—the leisure to read them.

But Byron also had a shrewd sense of his poem as, in our terms, a marketable commodity. The first edition sold out in three days and he made a fortune from the *Childe*. The work was new. Though owing something to the eighteenth-century topographical poem, it went far beyond. Walter Scott said it was "certainly the most original poem which we have had this many a day." It appeared to speak directly to its readers. Scott talks of "the novelty of an author speaking in his own person" (1818).[13] At once, the push-pull quality, which is one of the defining attributes of charisma, is established. The poet is both distant and intimate, withdrawn and exposed, casual and committed.

From the opening sentence of the preface, *Childe Harold* hints that everything we are going to hear about is real: "The following poem was written, for the most part, amidst the scenes which it attempts to describe. It was begun in Albania…" Even today, Albania is probably the least known country in Europe. Then it was still more a marker of the absolutely exotic. That Byron in fact spent no more than ten days in the country and went barely fifty miles beyond the frontier was of no consequence. He knew how to make the most of it. "Albania," he wrote to a former tutor, "I have seen more of than any Englishman" (apart from William Leake, he had the grace to add in parentheses), "for it is a country rarely visited from the savage character of the natives."[14] Albania was wild, remote, a place where transgression of various kinds was endemic; it was a "rugged nurse of savage men!"[15]

Byron visited the court of Ali Pasha in Tepelena. Ali, though nominally dependent on the Turkish Sultan, exercised, in practice, an almost unchallenged power over his subjects. It was the first time Byron had encountered a society in which sex with young boys was common and apparently removed from moral prejudice. He was obviously taken with the heady mix of power and what was, for him, transgressive sexual freedom. In England in his day, sodomy was still a capital offense. In the published version of *Childe Harold*, Byron manages discretion: the reader feels the excitement, and may well be tempted by the alliance of the erotic and the exotic, but is not forced to take a path that is unwelcome or unthinkable. The contract between writer and reader holds. What took place on the "soft voluptuous couches" of Ali Pasha's court is never made explicit.[16]

It is only in some cancelled lines that the truth of Byron's experience is now made inescapable for us:

For boyish minions of unhallowed love
The shameless torch of wild desire is lit,
Caressed, preferred even to woman's self above.[17]

These lines were replaced, for publication, by much more conventional thoughts about the position of women in Albanian society:

Here woman's voice is never heard: apart,
And scarce permitted, guarded, veil'd, to move,
She yields to one her person and her heart,
Tam'd to her cage, nor feels a wish to rove:
For, not unhappy in her master's love,
And joyful in a mother's gentlest cares,
Blest cares! All other feelings far above!
Herself more sweetly rears the babe she bears,
Who never quits the breast, no meaner passion shares.[18]

Contemporary readers of the *Childe* were spared confrontation with the truly transgressive nature of their adored author. He hinted at a crossing of borders, but his readers were not forced into the recognition of just how far Byron had gone. As every pop star or film star knows, there is always a limit, sometimes crossed by design and sometimes by inadvertence, beyond which the fan base rapidly begins to peel away. Byron, both in life and in art, was to test the boundary in radical ways and his publisher John Murray was fully alive to the marketing consequences.[19]

A generalized wildness, the hint of sexual transgression that is unspecified, an exotic location, and the gloomy, melancholy central figure—all invite a reader of the *Childe* to identify the "real scenes" of Albania with the character of Byron himself. But Byron teasingly refuses to allow that illusion of access. "It has been suggested to me by friends," he writes provocatively in the preface, "that in this fictitious character, 'Childe Harold,' I may incur the suspicion of having intended some real personage: this I beg leave, once for all, to disclaim—Harold is the child of imagination." Naturally, every reader wanted to believe, in reading the *Childe*, that genuine access to the poet was what they had had. The young man mysteriously unloved, who yet "gather'd revellers from far and near," who hated his native land, who, most importantly, had sinned, and who then "sick at heart" had resolved to "visit scorching climes beyond the sea."[20] Here is the outline of that autobiographical myth that so affected contemporary readers.[21] It was one that Byron was to develop in different directions, not least after the self-imposed exile of 1816, when, increasingly, he was to draw both on the example of Milton's Satan and on Milton's own personal and political history.[22]

In the immediate aftermath of the publication of *Childe Harold*, Byron became a star, with all the trappings we associate with it. The Duchess of Devonshire wrote to her son in Washington: "The subject of conversation, of curiosity, of enthusiasm almost, one might say, of the moment is not Spain or Portugal, Warriors or Patriots, but Lord Byron! ... [*Childe Harold*] is on every table, and himself courted, visited, flattered, and praised whenever he appears ... in short, he is really the only topic almost of conversation—the men jealous of him, the women of each other."[23] Women who read the *Childe* wanted to redeem Byron from his sins, from his unhappiness. To look into the depths of his heart and to save him from himself was a challenge that proved irresistible, not least to his future wife, Annabella Milbanke. The temptation was all the more pressing since Byron had apparently experienced things so terrible that they must never be unmasked:

> Through many a clime 'tis mine to go,
> With many a retrospection curst;
> And all my solace is to know,
> Whate'er betides, I've known the worst.

> What is that worst? Nay do not ask—
> In pity from the search forbear:
> Smile on—nor venture to unmask
> Man's heart, and view the Hell that's there.[24]

Such a reverse invitation has enormous power. Annabella, young and virginal, lacking experience, though gifted with a great intelligence, inevitably struggled to acknowledge that it was precisely the hint of darkness that made Byron so charismatic. She believed she was in the presence of a darkness that could be comprehended and so redeemed. The reality of sodomy, boys, and incest fell far outside her imagination, or her recognition of what might be possible in a man's life. So it did, presumably, for many or most of the contemporary readers of the *Childe*.

From all this it might seem as if Byron had calculated everything surrounding the publication of *Childe Harold* with one known end in view. But it is one of the strange features of charisma that it must never be felt as calculation, and, indeed, there is an apparent paradox in Byron's approach. Certainly, he appears supremely confident in his ability to draw in the reader through the persona of the Childe. Byron had wanted fame from very early days. But, as his biographer Leslie Marchand noted, it was as a political orator and statesman that he imagined he might one day be famous.[25] Until the time of publication, Byron remained apprehensive about the possible effect of the *Childe* on his political future and uneasy about how much of himself he had allowed to surface. To become famous as a poet was something he had never seriously considered, perhaps never allowed himself seriously to consider.[26]

Moreover, he was the Childe and he was not. His relationship with his hero was as complex as the relationship between any novelist and any persona. Here is Byron writing to Charles Dallas: "I by no means intend to identify myself with *Harold*, but to *deny* all connexion with him. If in parts I may be thought to have drawn from myself, believe me it is but in parts, and I shall not own even to that ... I would not be such a fellow as I have made my hero for the world."[27] What matters is that the public was seduced by the Byronic persona. They were drawn in by the darkness and then, just as surely, when the darkness appeared too terrible, many recoiled in outrage.

But my concern here is not to retrace the chronology of Byron's relationship with his reading public. I am interested in what happens at the point of Byron's death. With death a process of construction or reconstruction can begin in earnest. Death enables the survivors to focus, to make their choices from someone else's life—whether bizarre or logical, sympathetic or treacherous. Death allows for degrees of conscious and unconscious concealment, as we prioritize some aspects of a life and bury others. Above all, the drama of finality allows the dross, real life's essential cement, to float free, so that the supposed significance of a life can take the place of the messiness of reality. Byron's last surviving letter from Greece enquired after the state of his bank balance and complained that Lord Blessington had bought a boat from him and never paid. That could have been savored, after his death, as a defining moment—proof of Byron's dogged commitment to the cause of Greek Independence with all of its financial burdens—but it is never recalled. On the contrary, the story began to be written about almost immediately as one of tragedy and failure. Only in Greece, as we shall see, was the perspective radically different.

The process of redefinition after death can be extraordinarily swift. Lady Diana, Princess of Wales, died on a Saturday night in Paris. Her death led to what the BBC called "an outpouring of grief never before seen in the UK." An estimated 2.5 billion people watched the funeral in sixty countries and forty-four languages. More followed the funeral procession than had attended the celebrations in London to mark the end of World War II; and, there was widespread satisfaction that the Queen had felt obliged, for the first time in history, to lower the union jack on Buckingham Palace to half mast.

Yet all of this apparent consensus of grief was the creation of only a few hours. On the Sunday morning following the death of Diana, the London *Observer* found itself stranded by the sheer speed with which the emotional landscape had changed. On that morning, the newspaper published an article that had been written before the news of Diana's death reached London. The article concluded, in a way that was not uncommon in newspapers and magazines while she was alive: "if her [Diana's] IQ were five points lower [she] would have to be watered daily." While the *Sunday Mirror*, successfully joining in the overwhelming grief, forgot that a few weeks earlier it had described Diana as "trivial and brain-dead."

It is with this context in mind that I turn to the leader in the London *Times* for Saturday, 15 May 1824. It is a fascinating piece. Not because it is especially perceptive or productive of insights, but because it enables us to catch the moment of indecision before consensus has formed. A courier had reached London the previous day, bringing the news of Byron's death in Mesolongi. From the opening three words, it is clear that the leader writer is aware of how insecure Byron's position is: "With unfeigned regret we announce to our readers that Lord Byron is no more."

"Unfeigned." There is a world of defensiveness here. One would only write in this way if one suspected that the word "regret" alone might raise doubts or provoke some suspicion of insincerity. And those doubts are almost immediately acknowledged: "We know not how many of our countrymen may share the feelings with which this news has affected us. There were individuals more to be approved for moral qualities than Lord Byron—to be more safely followed, or more tenderly beloved."

The writer clearly knows what he feels: "there lives no man on earth whose sudden departure from it ... appears to us more calculated to impress the mind with profound and unmingled mourning." Byron was "[t]he most remarkable Englishman of his generation." And yet the writer thinks of the perhaps numerous readers who may not share his opinion and his grief, whose view of Byron as the devil incarnate may be unnuanced by time. Their potential rejection of the language of mourning must be accommodated: "Lord Byron was doomed to pay that price which Nature sometimes charges for stupendous intellect, in the gloom of his imagination, and the intractable energy of his passions. It was his proper nature to ascend: but on the summit of his elevation, his leading passion was to evince his superiority, by launching his melancholy scorn at mankind."

This anguished doubt as to which way England would turn now that Byron was dead is unsurprising. Byron had not been in England for eight years; he had made it clear what he thought of the country. In 1819, he had written to his publisher, John Murray: "I am sure my Bones would not rest in an English grave—or my Clay mix with the earth of that Country:—I believe the thought would drive me mad on my death-bed could I suppose that any of my friends would be base enough to convey my carcase back to your soil—I would not even feed your worms—if I could help it."[28]

Then there were all of the stories that had filtered back from Italy about Byron's sexual promiscuity, stories which appeared to confirm how right polite society in England had been to ostracize him. Shelley, wide-eyed, had reported that Byron was sleeping with "people his gondolieri pick up in the streets"; that he was associating with "wretches who … do not scruple to avow practices which are not only not named but I believe seldom even conceived in England."[29] As Marchand put it in his biography: "It was not what he had done but what he had frankly proclaimed to the world that made him in many eyes no longer an Englishman, or an English gentleman."[30] Moreover, the beautiful young man was no more. Visitors to Venice in 1818 were able to confirm "the multiplied anecdotes of Lord Byron's metamorphoses into a fat, fat-headed, middle-aged man, slovenly to the extreme, unkempt, with long, untied locks that hang down on his shoulders."[31]

All of this was an unprepossessing basis for constructing a heroic return. And, indeed, the English, unlike the Greeks, have never felt secure about Byron's status. The role that was quickly allotted him was that of the returning failure. This allowed for a wide spectrum of interpretation. At one end, he could be the flawed, sometimes even the tragic, hero, the one with so much promise who threw it all away in the end, but who remained a great man, at least in death. At the other end, there was failure, *tout court*. A number of those who had been close to him in Greece fostered the latter version: men like Julius Millingen (though his criticisms were tempered by some recognition of Byron's qualities), Trelawny (who was outrageous in his condemnation: "I wish he had lived a little longer," he wrote to Mary Shelley, "that he might have witnessed how … I would have triumphed over his mean spirit"), and Leicester Stanhope, who told John Cam Hobhouse that in Greece Byron "did little—but shoot pistols—& ride—and drink punch." Hobhouse himself, one of Byron's oldest friends, remarked that, had Byron lived, "I am not sure that he could not one day or the other have had cause to regret that he had not fallen by the fevers of Messolonghi."[32]

The great crowds who greeted Byron's funeral procession are largely mute for us, but doubtless many savored the romance of Byron's hostility toward the English establishment and identified with him against the society that refused to welcome him home. The denial of a burial in Westminster Abbey, the relative lack of "people of quality" along the course of the funeral cortege, these must have done something to increase a sense of commitment among those who were there. Byron's own sense, in March 1823, that he was "at this moment the most unpopular man in England," may or may not have been accurate at the time.[33] But the anonymous crowds who turned out for him were, by their very presence, a confirmation of how much he was, as the *Times* leader indicated, "the most remarkable Englishman of his generation." Each person who attended must, no doubt, have made his or her own complicitous pact with Byron's transgressions—to overlook or to deny. Or perhaps, now that Satan's child was dead and there could be no further sin, the transgressions were suddenly an intimate part of what brought them there.

So England remade Byron, placing him at myriad different points along the broad spectrum of failure. The situation has changed little today, though the emotions are, of course, less engaged than in 1824. A recent film about Byron ends with a series of darkened shots of what is supposed to be Mesolongi in the rain. Fletcher, Byron's servant, is heard to say, "Fucking Greece," as if that summed up all of the wrong choices, all of the futility of dying in a corner of an obscure foreign field. Or here is F. Rosen's imperious judgment: "Byron was vulnerable [in Mesolongi]: a poet, entirely out of his depth in military matters … He lacked ideological commitment in a setting that required it, if any progress (of whatever value) was to be made."[34]

Byron, it seems, always falls short for the English. He should have remained a poet; or he should somehow have acquired some military sophistication. Better still, he should have been a real hero and died fighting, as the *Times* leader lamented: "Had he but died in battle against slaves and infidels, for a Christian people struggling to be free, his own fame would have received its full consummation, and his wishes, as is well understood, their complete fulfilment." Byron himself, indeed, appeared to encourage such a view from beyond the grave. His poem, "On This Day I Complete My Thirty-Sixth Year," written in Mesolongi in January 1824, was widely reprinted in newspapers after his death:

> Seek out—less often sought than found—
> A soldier's grave, for thee the best…

The rest of the poem makes clear that this apparently heroic choice was the result of grief and frustration over an unrequited love affair—with the Greek boy Loukas Chalandritsanos. But, inevitably, this is not how it could ever have been read in England.

After the anguish, despair, and failure of the English Byron, the Greek construction is a stimulating contrast. In England, by a process of romantic denigration, Byron's death in Mesolongi appears as a futile, if entirely compelling, rain-drenched conclusion. The reputation of the poet wallows to no purpose in the mud of a small western Greek town. Through Greek eyes, though, Mesolongi is quite different. It is one of the holy towns of Greece. Its fame has been built partly around the legend of Byron's 'sacrifice,' but it is the actions of the people of Mesolongi themselves that have secured its enduring memory. Two years after Byron's death, on 10 April 1826, almost the entire population of the town took part in what is known in Greece simply as the 'exodos,' an attempt to break through the lines of besieging Turkish forces. In a war where unadulterated heroism was in short supply, the exodos gave Europe the image of a struggling people who were entirely worthy of their independence. Byron had made Mesolongi famous all over the world by dying there. When Mesolongi fell, in the course of the exodos, it only needed Eugène Delacroix's *La Grèce sur les ruines de Missolongi* (1826) to complete the cycle of its fame.

Through English eyes, again, the few months Byron spent in Mesolongi have little meaning, except as the prelude to the dramatic finality of his death. Greek archival material, which has long been available but scarcely ever examined in this context, enables one to think of Byron's role as part of an evolving process, one simply cut short by the pure *accident* of death. The political situation during the brief period of Byron's return to Greece in 1823–1824 is highly complex. It was in constant flux, as the country moved toward civil war in November 1823. Against such a background, it is easy to see why the story of Byron's last months is so often written as one of mere confusion and chaos.

What is clear from Greek archival material is that, while Mesolongi was in a disastrous state when Byron arrived, the prospects for the medium term were encouraging.[35] There is plenty of material on which to build a story of the pointless, the anarchic. The town was suffering from the effects of three years of Turkish depredation. It was full of fighting men, but they had no supplies, and there was a large contingent of Suliote warriors who had not been paid for nine months. Mavrokordatos, the Greek political leader who had been sent to Mesolongi, wrote to the legislative authorities just before Byron's arrival. He was at his wits end to know what to do and concluded: "All hope ... now rests with the Lord," by which he meant, of course, the Lord Byron.[36]

But though things were difficult, Mesolongi was not the obscure place that invariably, and necessarily, emerges from the English accounts. Even when Byron and Hobhouse had passed through in 1809, it had been quietly prosperous. The Independence War had transformed it into the most important town in Etolia and it would provide independent Greece with five Prime Ministers in the course of the nineteenth century. It is also clear that Mesolongi was never envisaged as a final destination, either by Byron or by Mavrokordatos. They were largely in agreement about what they wanted to do and where they believed the Greek Revolution should be going, and Mesolongi was simply a place where they happened to come together. Already in December 1823, Mavrokordatos supposed that Byron might come to Mesolongi and then go on to the seat of government in the Argolid[37]; this was still a possible outcome a few months later, as Pietro Gamba noted on 18 March 1824.[38]

The key to Byron's position in Greece, and the reason for the encouraging nature of the medium term prospects, is contained in a long letter from the Metropolitan Ignatios, then in exile in Pisa, to Mavrokordatos in Mesolongi. The letter is dated 16/28 February 1824.[39] Ignatios is clear about the dangers of the current situation. He speaks of those in Greece who failed to recognize that the future independence of the country depended, not on their capacity to win a final military victory, but on the international position of Greece. To win English support for Greek independence was now crucial, given that the political climate had dramatically altered with George Canning's appointment as foreign secretary in 1822. Under his predecessor, Lord Castlereagh, British foreign policy had been hostile to any form of insurrectional or revolutionary change. Now there was political space, if Greece could learn to use it intelligently.

The great fear in England, as Ignatios knew, was that Greek independence and a declining Turkey would give Russia a free hand in the east. Greece and Russia were traditional allies and many liberals in England saw current events in Greece as simply the proof of Russian territorial ambition. The topic was still being hotly debated in England a half century later. Ignatios argued that English fears could be turned to Greek advantage; that an independent Greece could be offered to Europe as a buffer against Russian expansionism. "This truth," he wrote, "England first and alone is capable of understanding." But a divided Greece, one headed toward civil war, would clearly fail to convince England of its reliability as a European ally.

Ignatios had recognized how valuable Byron might be in this context.[40] A visual and high-profile symbol of the importance of the English connection, he had money, and, if he were prepared to use his influence in favor of the Western Greeks, it would privilege their situation. This was all the more the case, since in February 1824, Greece was successfully raising a loan on the London market. Byron was to be one of the commissioners responsible for the distribution of the proceeds. His presence in Greece and commitment to the cause could only reassure investors; and the loan was Greece's best hope of securing unity, since it had been the financial weakness of the center that had allowed local elements to achieve disproportionate influence.

All of the evidence suggests that Byron was fully prepared to play a role both symbolic and practical in Greece's internal affairs. How close his thinking was to that of Ignatios is suggested by the remarks attributed to Byron by Gamba:

> I cannot ... calculate to what a height Greece may rise. Hitherto it has been a subject for the hymns and elegies of fanatics and enthusiasts; but now it will draw the attention of the politician ... The English government deceived itself at first in thinking it possible to maintain the Turkish empire in its integrity: but it cannot be done; that unwieldy mass is already putrefied, and must dissolve. If any thing like an equilibrium is to be upheld, Greece must be supported. Mr Canning, I think, understands this, and intends to behave towards Greece as he does with respect to the South American colonies. This is all that is wanted; for in that case Greece may look towards England with the confidence of friendship, especially as she now appears to be no longer infected with the mania of adding to her colonies, and sees that her true interests are inseparably connected with the independence of those nations, who have shown themselves worthy of emancipation, and such is the case with Greece.[41]

Byron mattered to the Western Greeks because he was famous, because he was English, and because he shared, in large part, their patrician view of the direction that the revolution in Greece should take. In death, Byron's fame in the Greek tradition is secure. On the south side of the Zappeion Gardens in Athens, at the intersection of two traffic-choked avenues, a nineteenth-century statue of Byron shows him gazing into the eyes of a personified Hellas. While in Mesolongi, in the Garden of the Heroes, Byron's statue has a central place, surrounded by the memorials to the Germans, Swedes, US Americans, Poles, French, Swiss, and other foreigners who gave their lives for Greece. A visit to Mesolongi for Greek school children remains a lesson in history, democracy, and good governance. In all of that, Byron had a role to play. In Greece, he was a famous man who came to lend a hand.

By contrast, in a deeply conservative England, Byron could only have been mad, bad, and dangerous. He sold himself to his reading public with *Childe Harold*, perhaps without fully realizing what he was doing. Thereafter, he had a contractual relationship with his middle-class audience, one that they demanded should be personal. And, as in all such relationships, the disappointment, when he let them down, was intense. In England, he remained charismatic in his failure. In the clearer light of Greece, his fame still flourishes under a sign of freedom.

CHAPTER 8

The Historical Actor

PETER FRITZSCHE

After the Battle of Waterloo on 18 June 1815, visitors from across Europe thronged to the field of battle outside the city of Brussels. In the very first weeks, the site was still littered with the debris of decamped soldiers and the remains of the dead. In *A Visit to Flanders in July 1815*, the Englishman James Simpson reported that all around him "lay the melancholy remains of the clothes, accoutrements, books, and letters of the dead." Indeed, written materials "were spread over the field like the rubbish of a stationer's shop." Charlotte Eaton was also struck by "the quantities of letters and of blank sheets of dirty writing paper" strewn about. They "were so great that they literally whitened the surface of the earth." In no time, she added, people living near Waterloo had made fortunes plundering the belongings of the dead, selling to visitors "the most moving French and English letters from the friends of the fallen."[1] These lost and retrieved letters are the remarkable evidence of how history had become a mass medium that authorized, made poignant, and gave value to ordinary testimony. History had become, literally and figuratively, a whitening or representation on the motley, dirty surface that stretched out across the fields at Waterloo and beyond.

The forth and back of letters to soldiers and friends, the traffic from corpses to plunderers and on to collectors, their citation in correspondence, memoirs, and history books—all of these phenomena indicated the extent to which Europeans shared a collective historical consciousness in which ordinary experience was "telling" or poignant, generating, in turn, "intimacy at a distance." It was the new figure of the historical actor who produced and consumed the testimony of letters. History had become much grander. This was so not only because the revolutionary and Napoleonic era affected so many more people, who as a result felt compelled to join up in the review of history in vital, democratizing gestures; history was grand also because it could not be comprehended from a single vantage point and required, for the sake of veracity, the testimony of innumerable witnesses. This kaleidoscopic perspective made history an ongoing, embracing conversation that only made sense with the continuous addition of vernacular renditions. The placement in history of ordinary witnesses turned them into minor celebrities, unauthoritative but poignant, "telling" representatives of the "spirit of the age." Precisely because the nature of the revolution was open to contest, it could not be understood without introducing a variety of contestants with subjective, one-sided positions. In an argumentative, democratic age, many more historical actors crowded the stage of history to expand the notion of celebrity. The era of the witness corresponded to the age of history; it was not the particular product of the Holocaust.[2]

There are three important historical productions that made the post-battle rubbish at Waterloo possible. First, the revolutionary and Napoleonic Wars were massive in scale and intensity. They mobilized hundreds of thousands of men who crossed the line from civilian to military life. These citizen-soldiers brought into army life new middle-class skills, such as the ability to read and write; in turn, they found in the armies to which they were called unexpected, extraordinary, and difficult experiences that they sought to set down to memory; and they also left behind families and friends whom they missed and with whom they wanted to communicate.[3] Second, the correspondence in this period indicated not just the displacement of war but also the desire to report on historical events, an understanding of which both writer and reader shared. Correspondents believed they were witnessing a common visible history that had become profoundly animate in this revolutionary period. In other words, letters relied on a mailing address, but also required a historical address. The movements of history are what contemporaries came to realize they shared, and, when contemplated over the years, these effects created distinct experiences of generation, class, and nation. And third, the commodification of ordinary testimony in the form of lost letters bought and sold or of old stories retailed again and again over the course of the nineteenth century registered a new, avid interest in the point of view of the individual witness. History was increasingly recognized as a comprehensive process that swept up writers and readers, yet it took the form of countless perspectives, each with a certain authority and none authoritative in the traditional sense. The whole business of revolutionary history was the struggle to figure out meaning in the course of fast-paced events, which revaluated precisely the variety of subjective perspectives. By destroying *authority*, the revolution *authorized* unending debate about the constitution of society, the viability of political forms, and the direction of history itself; hence all of the books, the blank sheets, and the letters among the dead on the field of battle in 1815. The revolutionary issue of representation was pertinent to texts as well as to parliaments and enabled the enfranchisement of often-incompatible perspectives and thus the accreditation of partial, incomplete histories without which the turbulence of the era could not be comprehended. In this "leveled, uncertain new world of the nineteenth century," the ordinary witness was the exemplary witness.[4]

Many of the English visitors to the battlefield at Waterloo had been to the continent before. From the start, the French Revolution was accompanied by a new visual regime in which spectators flocked to consume the extraordinary, monstrous, unnatural, sublime, and thus inherently dramatic events taking place in France. Numerous eyewitnesses, such as Helen Maria Williams, provided well-received letters from Paris beginning in 1789, and during the first real cessation in hostilities between France and Britain—the Peace of Amiens between autumn 1801 and spring 1803—thousands of English tourists descended onto Paris. An estimated 10,000 sightseers, including two-thirds of the members of the House of Lords, made the eight-to-ten hour journey across the Channel to Calais and continued on with an arduous fifty-four hour expedition overland by carriage to Paris. With the Louvre, the imperial court, and of course Napoleon, Paris was also newly outfitted with a touristic infrastructure of reliable hotels, restaurants, and guides. The first of its kind, a *Practical Guide During a Journey from London to Paris*, offering "maps and useful tables" for the entire journey and a "description of all the objects deserving of notice" in Paris itself, was published already in 1802.

In the main, these objects of notice were landmarks of the revolution and the consulate: new installations such as the Pantheon, the Champ de Mars, and the convent of Petits Augustins that now housed the monuments that had survived the vandalism of the republic; but also old terrain, the Place de la Revolution where public guillotining had taken place during the Terror. Inspecting "the very spot" on which the king and queen had been executed some ten years earlier, Sir Samuel Romilly noted that the places were still overwritten with "the words, UNITÉ, INDIVISIBILITÉ DE LA RÉPUBLIQUE, LIBERTÉ, EGALITÉ, FRATERNITÉ." "The words *'ou la mort'* followed in all these inscriptions, but are now effaced," he added. Effaced too from municipal monuments were inscriptions to "la Roi."[5] So popular was the destination of world revolution that Charles Lamb mocked the pretensions of his friend Thomas Manning who was in Paris in February 1802:

> You cannot conceive … the strange joy, which I felt at the Receipt of a Letter from Paris. It seemed to give me a learned importance, which placed me above all, who had not Parisian Correspondents … You cannot write things so trifling, let them only be about Paris, which I shall not treasure … Have you seen a man Guillotined yet?[6]

Napoleon's declaration of war in 1803 interrupted the touristic spectacle until it resumed after Waterloo. The ensuing decade marked a crucial shift from the Great Tour to modern mass tourism. Every year after 1815, thousands of tourists followed James Simpson and Charlotte Eaton as well as luminaries such as Walter Scott and Lord Byron. Waterloo, alongside the sights in Paris, became a standard stop on continental travel itineraries written up in John Murray's popular *Hand-Book for Travellers* or organized later in the century by Thomas Cook. Karl Baedeker, himself a veteran of the German armies who had fought against Napoleon, also cashed in on the growing interest in history-themed tourism with his line of guidebooks beginning in the late 1820s. The Napoleonic Wars prepared nineteenth-century tourism in crucial ways. (Similarly, after World War II, Arthur Frommer's travel guides catered to his fellow soldiers stationed in Europe, then to veterans returning to the continent, and eventually other tourists.)

Tourists desperately sought relics from the Battle of Waterloo, attracting the interest of relic merchants who set up shop on the site and eventually requiring advice on how to avoid pushy salesmen or fraudulent antiques. To accommodate the vast majority of curious spectators who could not afford a European trip, Madame Tussaud exhibited in London her collection of "full-length portrait models" in wax, which included guillotined heads, the bathtub murder scene of Marat, and the main political and military characters of the period as well as a full-sized, sharp-bladed guillotine. Her sons later expanded the collection to include Napoleonic memorabilia, which could also be seen in London's popular Waterloo and Napoleon museums in the years after 1815. On both sides of the Atlantic, the twenty-five years of the French Revolution remained the object of extraordinary interest, creating a new sense of historical drama in which children replayed the Battles of the Nations with smartly painted tin soldiers on apartment floors, and characters named Toussaint and Napoleon could step out of Émile Zola's 1885 novel *Germinal* and Heinrich Mann's 1918 novel *Man of Straw*.[7]

Some English observers—and present-day writers—understood Waterloo as the resolution of the revolutionary drama and the closure of the apocalyptic struggle to renew obligations to custom and country, and thereby offer a final, complete vindication of Edmund Burke. The literary critic Jerome Christensen even attributes "the end of history" and the long deferral of alternatives to the post-revolutionary restoration of British society after Waterloo.[8] But this argument for interpretive rigidity about the revolution and the political quietude that followed in its wake misses the perceived states of fluctuation that drew visitors to the battle site at Waterloo and that animated popular interest in contemporary history. First of all, it was Napoleon, the vanquished loser, and not Wellington, the triumphant winner, who attracted the lion's share of popular interest in the 1820s and 1830s. "Waterloo" entered popular vocabularies as a byword for rout, loss, and the unlucky gamble, not for victory and empire. The word testified to the consciousness of fragility in political design. Wellington himself admitted that the battle was very close and could have gone to Napoleon's advantage. What made the revolution so interesting was the evidence for calamity it provided: the destruction of the old order, the Reign of Terror, the unsupportability of republican rule, the lure of military dictatorship, the fall of kingdoms and empires on a continental scale, and the continual compounding of hope and disappointment in a twisted course that meandered through millions of households and that came to an end only with Waterloo. Madame Tussaud advertised her historical showcases with a reference to the ongoing "French Revolution, ever changing, ever new."[9]

With the focus on Napoleon, the emphasis was on a careening process described as "without measure, without proportion, without standard."[10] Contemporaries repeatedly insisted on the unprecedented, surprising nature of revolutionary events for which there were no adequate historical models. History was reprised primarily in the conditional tense in terms of what might have been, what could have happened, what was still possible. The tidiness of the "end of history" is completely out of place here. In this regard, Napoleon's astonishing "One Hundred Days" provided liner notes for the entire period. Even after Napoleon's death in 1821, the specter of the return of revolution haunted conservatives, who admitted not to the end of the French Revolution, but to its incorporation into "every monster; the revolutionary spirit has traveled around the world in a thousand forms."[11] "There will be no separate revolutions," wrote François-René de Chateaubriand in the last lines of his memoirs, only "the great revolution approaching its end."[12] What did Thomas Carlyle and Robert Southey talk about when they last met? More than a half-century after the storming of the Bastille, the topic was, Carlyle remembered, "the usual one," that is the "steady approach of democracy, with revolution (probably explosive) ... [the] steady decay of all morality, political, social, individual; this once noble England getting more and more ignoble and untrue," until it "would have to collapse in shapeless ruin, whether for ever or not none of us could know."[13]

This drastic description gave history sublime qualities that dramatized the contemporary condition. However energetic the attempt was to grasp hold of events by framing them inside historical continuities, such as the march of progress or the spread of enlightenment, or embedding them in a dehistoricized natural landscape of cycles, seasons, and stages, the fact of revolution, and the memory of the unpredictable event, continued to slip out. The revolution was not easily digestible; as Linda Orr points out, historians had enormous difficulty assimilating into "the logic of history the cup of blood, heads bobbing on pikes, and the slash of the guillotine."[14] This excess is what visitors went to see at Waterloo or Paris's Place de la Revolution or Madame Tussaud's on London's Baker Street.

The historical sublime was underwritten by the multitude of parts that ordinary people played in the French Revolution. The high drama was consistent with the massive mobilization of the revolutionary years in which hundreds of thousands of soldiers participated in battles of unprecedented size and in which tens of thousands of people, on the move as refugees, felt the marauding gestures of history and identified with both the soldier and the exile to make sense of their uprooted lives. Like Jane Austen, with her brothers in the British navy, and Dorothea Schlegel, with her son in the Prussian army, contemporaries looked upon soldiers as their own representatives and as contemporaries. In a remarkable letter, Schlegel described an encounter in August 1808 with soldiers on a market boat from Cologne to Koblenz. At first, she was disgusted and frightened, but Schlegel began to recognize the sons of fathers, the friends of neighbors. "You can imagine my feeling," she wrote, "when you let go of my hand yesterday, and I had to climb down into that hole, where I was greeted with the tobacco smoke from a half-dozen soldiers' pipes." For several hours, she sat quite still: "[I] pulled my hat deep over my face and pressed myself into the corner," and feeling sorry for herself, "everything that was dear to me and pained me rose up through my body in the boldest colors." Ashamed of her tears, however, she "pulled herself together," and looked around: "And there sat a whole bank of the most honest-looking, good-hearted faces in French uniform across from me and to my side. They were Germans from the Rhineland who had served in the previous war against Austria and Prussia, were slightly wounded, had taken their leave, and were now returning to their various homes." This was the first time she actually saw the soldiers or talked to them, and in her melancholy state, Schlegel recognized her own faraway home in theirs. "Lots of brave, nice people," she declared, "not at all so bad when you get to know them." Now it was not the smoke that bothered Schlegel, but the "soldiers' poetry" that attracted her: "very astonishing portrayal of the motives and characters of each and every hero."[15] Schlegel's hours under deck circumscribed a decade-long process around 1800: everyman had become a poignant representative.

Contemporaries also saw their losses reflected in the fate of the French émigrés. "In all the novels which deal with the French Revolution," observed Agnes von Gerlach from French-occupied Berlin, "it is always the case that unhappiness separates families and divides lovers, and now I find this to be the case." Indeed, after the fateful Battle of Jena in 1806, she had written: "My son is being held prisoner and he reappeared here the day before yesterday safe and sound ... Henri, the son of my brother, is also apparently prisoner. My brother Eugen was slightly wounded and returned to Brieg. My brother Henri has probably been taken prisoner, but we don't know for sure."[16] The particular misfortunes of the exiles resonated with a much wider range of readers for whom "hybrid chronicles that track[ed] the convergence of an individual destiny with national destiny" corresponded to a general sense of displacement in what was quickly short-handed as "the age of revolution."[17] The very comprehensiveness of the revolution and the wars privileged the point of view of soldiers and exiles.

What is more, the experience of the revolution was fundamentally oppositional. "Never before was the spirit of the times so subject to passions and preconceived ideas"; "everyone has his party," complained the editors of the *Politisches Journal*. In the somewhat stilted language of "*Partheylichkeit*" and "*Unpartheylichkeit*," they put their finger on a key aspect to the French Revolution, namely, its dramatization in ideological positions incorporating highly contested visions of the future. There was no such thing as a quiet point of objective perspective: "nonpartisanship itself appears partisan."[18] Contemporaries increasingly saw the historical process in terms of their opposition to others, their self as a claim on history. As they debated the merits of the revolution's aims, friends broke apart. "Knebel is raving mad," wrote Charlotte von Stein to her friend Charlotte Schiller: "we had such a falling out that he doesn't want to see me again." Even families divided into ideological camps: "I side w/ Father—against Mother + Ferdinand," and against the revolution, confessed Regina Beneke, a young woman in Hamburg, in 1794.[19] The arguments went on for twenty-five extraordinary years, right up to the eve of the invasion of Russia, when Count Pierre Bezukhov and the Vicomte de Montemorte disagreed about Napoleon at Anna Pavlovna's soiree in the opening pages of Tolstoy's *War and Peace*. This was the great age of debate between Pitt and Fox, between Burke and Sheridan, between "Jacobins and Anti-Jacobins," and between rival schools of poetry.[20] The very idea of opposition opened up new perspectives on society so that while the revolution was seen as a comprehensive process, it persistently produced varieties of political, social, and generational points of view.[21] In the words of James Chandler, contemporaries became adept in the construction of "comparative contemporanities."[22] Not only did "every reader" have "his own opinion and his prejudices," but the revolution had authorized those oppositionalities by authorizing the participation of ordinary people.[23] Any effort to comprehend the revolutionary era had to retrieve those parts and the partisanships that came with them.

Writing in 1799, the conservative observer Friedrich Gentz summarized the new situation expertly: "Never before in a period of ten years have such a large number of important and intertwined events, such a rapid sequence of extraordinary transformations and restless movement, and such piled-up revolutions taken place. Never before," Gentz caught his breath, "have changes of such astonishing variation and with such rich significance in all their social and political aspects occurred on a stage that was so open and accessible, and never have these changes repeated themselves in so many guises and been interpreted from such contradictory points of view."[24] What was astonishing to Gentz was not simply the events, but the accessibility of the stage to so many different kinds of people in so many various guises. The stage was there, sprawled out, filled to the wings, utterly enticing, but the proscenium had vanished along with the distinction of separation between actors and audiences.

Both the comprehensiveness of perceived historical forces, which pushed more and more people into the position of ordinary soldier or castaway émigré, and the admitted incomprehensibility of the compounded events spurred an intensified effort to figure out what was happening. In his 1998 study, *England in 1819*, James Chandler draws attention to the ways in which "the normative status of the period becomes a central and self-conscious aspect of historical reflection." This was the "age of the spirit of the age," in which the endeavor of representation had to be increasingly alert to context and to the particulars of time, place, and social position. Chandler goes on to argue that the "historical peculiarity of the age" was best represented by "individuality of character," which made Scott's middling hero Waverly the privileged witness.[25] Vividness and detail called for the vernacular character, just as empathy for the ordinary person relied on a good story and sufficient context.[26]

It was not simply that the French Revolution had weakened the foundations on which great men stood. The portraits of Wellington and Blücher, the celebrated victors at Waterloo, may have hung in the consulates and embassies with the inscription "To the Saviors of the World," as Alfred de Musset, the postwar French writer, imagined, but the suspicion persisted that such a safeguarded world had not found rest and would not find rest. For as Musset himself pointed out, when "a nobleman or a priest, or a sovereign passed," the people knew an older truth and perhaps smiled: "we have seen him before now in a different place; he looked very different then."[27] The "legend of Napoleon" persisted as a reminder of the world-altering capacities of contemporary history. But the portraits of Wellington and Blücher were themselves no longer adequate to the task of representing the open and accessible qualities of the modern stage and to the way history had taken possession of individual lives and revealed in its possession the particular force of events in every place. And thus Napoleon's status as a self-made man, the coarseness of his origins, the populist nature of his social conduct, the dramatic self-stylization of his gestures, and the tokens of possibility that continued to poke through his steady fall over the course of the years 1814–1815 turned out to be fitting elements in the new representation of historical potential. Napoleon stood for a kind of epistemological enfranchisement of new social and political elements.[28] History came to be understood in a Napoleon-like way in which the drama of ordinary, middling, and unlikely protagonists became poignant and telling.

In the first place, this meant that people could imaginatively place themselves into the theater of history. We often think that technical developments led to "flash-bulb" memories, such as the television era's shock upon hearing of the assassination of John F. Kennedy in 1963. But already in 1816, Rahel Varnhagen [or Rahel Varnhagen von Ense] reported on the shock of the new in an age when "everyone knows in fourteen days what has taken place."[29] In this way, the upset of the historical moment was based on understanding what the news meant to the recipient and the knowledge of what it has already meant or will mean to others. This knowledge of historical placement is precisely what Johann Wolfgang von Goethe reported when the revolutionaries beat back the forces of restoration at Valmy in 1792: that "from this place and from this day forth commences a new era in the world's history."[30] The shock—the instant—of recognition was evident when Germaine de Stäel could take the dread she felt about Napoleon's coup d'etat to be "the illness of a whole Continent."[31] The execution of the French king in 1793 or Napoleon's escape from Elba in 1815—news of the *"Evenement,"* as Rahel Varnhagen put it, moved extraordinarily quickly in March of that year—came as shocks illuminating with unusually bright clarity the historical consciousness and sense of contemporaneity that Europeans had come to share.[32] The stories of "where were you when" depended on a common historical stage and facilitated the development of minor celebrities as the individual refraction of the historical moment came to be passed on.

My argument here is not only could the historical moment be refracted through individuals, but also that this refraction through individuals was an appealing, attractive, compelling way to understand the historical moment, which is why the visitors to Waterloo saw the field whitened with the letters and notebooks of ordinary soldiers. The hundred years after Waterloo became the "century of memoirs," as Mme de Fars Fausselandry proclaimed already in 1830, on the first page of her own autobiography.[33] Foremost among these were the recollections of the émigrés, such as Fausselandry, whose fate seemed to resonate with the explicitly historical nature of readers' own displacements in a time of revolution and war, when lived family history appeared most imbricated in official national histories. Hundreds of memoirs of individuals high and low made popular history one of the most sought after genres in the nineteenth century. Indeed, contemporaries became increasingly aware of themselves as potential autobiographers and sought to archive their lives, which corresponded to the litter on the field at Waterloo. "Now I have to ask you one thing, dear Rahel!" pleaded her husband, Karl Varnhagen von Ense, from war-torn Hamburg in May 1813, *"don't* tear up and burn my letters. It is *these letters,* collected over many years, that will provide valuable details."[34]

So many personal accounts of the British campaign in Spain were published in newspapers that Wellington had to order the overseas correspondence stopped. Nonetheless, *Recollections of a Rifleman* or *Adventures in the Rifle Brigade* or *Letters from Portugal and Spain* found avid audiences. *The Journal of a Soldier of the 71st Regiment during the War in Spain* was published in 1815, went into a second edition in 1819, and was reprinted in 1822, 1828, and 1835.[35] "The common man's participation in war was recognized as important by him and by his readers," which is exactly what Scott made his literary business.[36] Much of the power of William Napier's acclaimed *History of the War in the*

Peninsula (1828–1840) was his attention to ordinary soldiers and their heroic achievements. In the nineteenth century, then, it was not at all unusual for contemporaries to construct their own, quite idiosyncratic syllabi of readings, choosing from any number of different sources that now included John Green's *The Vicissitudes of a Soldier's Life* as well as the great Wellington's memoirs and the historian's fat volume.[37] Old soldiers must have been asked to tell their stories, again and again: "in the graveyard at Tynemouth Priory there is a headstone to Corporal Rollo of the Royal Artillery, with the description: 'He held the lantern at the burial of Sir John Moore at Corunna.'"[38] To collect material for his own "epic-drama" of the Napoleonic period, for which he would "let Europe be the stage," the novelist Thomas Hardy repeatedly interviewed old veterans, many of them old men in London's Chelsea Hospital, as late as the 1870s.[39] Encountered in this way, veterans and other witnesses were actors, minor celebrities whose stories and embellishments gave them, when properly asked, a measure of fame.

On the stage of world history, open and accessible, historical actors appeared precisely at the moment when scripts and plots had lost their authority. They embellished their historical roles. Honoré de Balzac placed the most refractory émigrés in what he aptly named *The Gallery of Antiquities*, and he described one old-regime household in *Lily of the Valley* as follows: "family silver without uniformity, Dresden china which was not then in fashion, octagonal decanters, knives with agate handles, and lacquered trays." The narrator admits to his delight in these "quaint old things" but also in his agility to place characters historically in time and place.[40] The nobleman of the valley, the Comte de Mortsauf, is himself a wreck, inalterable in his opinions and old before his time. In Mortsauf, Balzac introduced a character readily identifiable in early nineteenth-century society: the man of the restoration dressed up in the court dress and fancy wiggery of the ancien regime.[41] Similarly anachronistic is the pharmacist Homais in Gustave Flaubert's *Madame Bovary*, who names one of his children "Napoleon." But, in fact, French republicans during the restoration quite deliberately put on their political costumes and wore the rosettes, caps, and colors of the revolutionary years.[42] From his childhood, Ernest Renan remembered an old man wrapped in a threadbare coat who died alone amid his books, among which was found "a packet containing some faded flowers tied up with a tri-colored ribbon. At first this was supposed to be some love-token, and several people built upon this foundation a romantic biography of the deceased recluse." But Renan's mother told him otherwise: "I am sure that he was one of the Terrorists. I sometimes fancy that I remember seeing him in 1793."[43]

The issue was whether these were relics or embers of something new, which made the whole business of collecting the bits and pieces of the battlefield so intriguing. Waterloo remained loquacious and mysterious. Thus, Stendhal choreographed the necessity of interpretation, pointing out the need for historians after the revolution, admonishing readers to look into the folds of everyday life. On the one hand, Lucien Leuwen, posted at Nancy, introduces the reader to a stagnant and corrupt life in which "Napoleon is gone and forgotten, or all but forgotten; his memory lingers as a vague nostalgia among the veterans gone cynical and corrupt in the service of the Restoration."[44] Everywhere veterans have made their peace, police are on the lookout and armed, and cloisters appear newly furbished. On the other hand, Nancy's monarchists constantly look over their shoulders, half-expecting another future to sweep them away: "And if it was suddenly announced that a Republic had been proclaimed in Paris, who would protect him against the local populace?"[45] When political bets in Paris are hedged, an observer exclaims: "Oh heavens ... do you think the republic so near?"[46] In *The Red and the Black*, Stendhal pokes fun at masters who pay their servants extra in case "the terror of '93 returns."[47] Julien himself, trying to make his way in the world, furtively reads the newly published histories of the revolution. Living in the shadows of 1789, 1793, and 1815, it was not clear whether current history taught the lesson of restoration or reversal or whether it advised young men to take up the priest's profession or the soldier's, to serve the Church or the nation.[48] But they were aware of the possibility of alternative futures, and posed and gestured in their name.

CHAPTER 9

Celebrity, Patriotism, and Sarah Bernhardt

KENNETH E. SILVER

After Queen Victoria, Sarah Bernhardt (1844–1923) was probably the most celebrated woman of the nineteenth century and certainly the most famous Frenchwoman. Apart from the drawing power of her obvious talent (the opinions of her theatrical detractors notwithstanding), Bernhardt's colossal celebrity was dependent upon and inextricably bound up with French prestige: its ancient and recent history, its real and imagined travails. The extent to which Bernhardt and France were the Gemini twins of the *fin-de-siècle* theatrical firmament became clear to me when Carol Ockman and I organized the exhibition, "Sarah Bernhardt: The Art of High Drama," for New York's Jewish Museum in 2005.[1] There I saw what amounted to a lifelong effort on the actress's part to fuse her persona to that of the nation. In this essay, I consider the roles Bernhardt chose for herself and when she chose to play them; her real life commitment to a variety of national causes; and how as a woman of Jewish descent and the daughter of a courtesan she managed to keep the "divine Sarah" a viable French "brand."

Bernhardt's avowed patriotism explains no small part of her appeal, both at home and abroad. This was especially evident during World War I, when by a strange twist of fate Bernhardt joined the ranks of the *mutilés de guerre*. On 22 February 1915, doctors amputated her right leg, owing to the onset of gangrene from an injury she had sustained years before. She was just over 70 years old. Within a year, Bernhardt had herself transported to the Front (to Rheims, along the Marne, to the Argonne, and close to Verdun), where she performed various patriotic pieces for the *poilus*. She was carried to the makeshift stages and jerry-built theaters on her specially designed sedan chair, and one can only imagine how moving it must have been for the soldiers to see *la Grande Sarah* share their ordeal, at least temporarily. Back in Paris, she performed in Eugène Morand's morale-boosting one-acter, *Les Cathédrales*, "in which various actresses, symbolizing the chief cathedrals of France, recited heroic couplets about the Patrie, La Gloire, [and] the recovery of Alsace-Lorraine."² Bernhardt played the role of Strasbourg Cathedral—a particular object of veneration, because it was in the "captured province" of Alsace—and brought the audience to its feet with her exhortation: "*Pleure, pleure, Allemagne! L'Aigle allemande est tombé dans le Rhin!*" (Weep, weep Germany! The German Eagle has fallen into the Rhine!).

Just before the United States entered the war in 1917, while on her farewell US tour in Nashville, Tennessee, the one-legged Bernhardt starred in *Du théâtre au champ d'honneur*. She played a twenty-two year old actor who enlists in the army and dies at the Front, while defending the French flag against the Germans. "No wonder France is giving her very heart in the struggle which she feels is for her honor and existence. For last night, Sarah Bernhardt, the divine, showed the spirit of France itself to an audience here which packed the Vendôme Theater to the walls," wrote the local drama critic, who continued,

> When as the dying soldier she clasped her tri-color about her form and the orchestra burst forth in the *Marseillaise* as the curtain fell, the audience rose to its feet and encored her in what was probably the greatest ovation ever given an actor or actress in this city. For it was France there before them. France, the youthful and joyous of old, now bleeding to death in No Man's Land, yet with the "drapeau" saved. Only one who has heard it on the field of battle could have put the expression that Bernhardt did into that dying invocation "Vive La France!" That was when the house rose to its feet and men shouted and men cried.³

Back home, at least one of her *fictive* countrymen felt quite differently about Bernhardt's national feeling and viability as a French spokesperson. "You haven't seen what Sarah Bernhardt said in the papers: 'France will go on to the end. If necessary the French will let themselves be killed to the last man,'" the Baron de Charlus says near the end of *Time Regained*, the culminating novel of *À la recherche du temps perdu*. "That I do not doubt," he temporizes, "but I ask myself to what extent Madame Sarah Bernhardt is qualified to speak in the name of France."⁴ It is the middle of *La Grande Guerre* and Charlus here seems to express the opinions of Marcel Proust who, several pages later, as Marcel-the-narrator, confides to the reader that, "The idea of a popular art, like that of a patriotic art, if not actually dangerous, seemed to me ridiculous."⁵ This, of course, is in striking contrast to the adoration that young Marcel expressed for the leading French actresses of the day—including Bernhardt, whom he names—in *Swann's Way*, the opening novel of the *Recherche*.

Needless to say, there is a great deal of history behind Proust's drastic change in attitude toward Bernhardt, including, one must suppose, jealousy of her celebrity and discomfort about their shared status as Frenchmen of mixed Jewish and Catholic descent and upbringing. As Susan Glenn notes of Bernhardt,

"While playing up her Frenchness at every opportunity, she managed the question of her Jewish background from a defensive posture that swung between denial and confession."[6] Such a modus operandi would have struck Proust as a disturbing alternative to his even less forthright way of dealing with his religious origins.[7] Moreover, as Proust knew full well, and as he let Charlus express at the conclusion of his great oeuvre, the question of whether Jews could be authentically French and patriotic, whether Bernhardt was "qualified" to speak for the nation, exemplified that age-old, anti-Jewish feeling all too common at the time. "Anti-Semites, in particular, were quick to deny [Bernhardt's] Frenchness, which they defined as a matter of race rather than cultural assimilation," writes Mary Louise Roberts. "But Bernhardt refused to be trapped by stereotypes and strongly asserted her own nationality."[8] As Roberts, Glenn, and Ockman all demonstrate, Bernhardt's myriad transgressions—confusing and confounding the rhetorical oppositions between male and female identity, high art and popular culture, art and business, local celebrity and foreign renown, Jews and Gentiles, among numerous others—gave her an almost unparalleled cultural power. Proust, in fact, points us toward another one of the actress's many transgressive zones: the overlap between art, politics, and popular culture, which, as Marcel says, he found either worrisome or laughable, but which defined Bernhardt's career.

Her first foray into the realm of legendary, national portrayal took place at the *Comédie Française*, in 1875, when she was cast in the title role of *La Fille de Roland* (*Roland's Daughter*) in Viscount Henri de Bornier's "sequel" to the Carolingian epic poem, *La Chanson de Roland*. As Berthe, she played the surviving daughter of Charlemagne's beloved nephew, the very model of a First Crusade knight who had fought and valiantly died in battle against the Saracens. Bernhardt found the versification somewhat flat, but the play bathed in a "great patriotic" atmosphere.[9] It was a huge suc-

Illustration 9.1. Sarah Bernhardt. (1844–1923). "*La fille de Roland*" (Self-portrait as Roland's daughter), 1876. Terracotta, 7¾″ x 6½″ x 5¼″. The Jewish Museum, New York, NY, US. Permission to reprint from the Jewish Museum, New York / Art Resource, NY ART385771.

cess and she knew why: "It was a short time after the terrible war of 1870. The play contained frequent allusions to it. And, thanks to the chauvinism of the public, it had a greater success than the work merited."[10] The "terrible" Franco-Prussian War, which ended in defeat and national humiliation, and the revolutionary Paris Commune (March–May 1871) take up several chapters of her autobiography, *Ma Double Vie* (*My Double Life*). Like many of her countrymen, Bernhardt was powerfully marked by the events of 1870–1871: "Ah! The horrible moment of awakening!" she exclaims, "The Emperor of France had to give his sword to the Emperor of Prussia. Nothing can wipe out the memory of that cry of pain and rage uttered by the whole nation!"[11]

When the war broke out, Bernhardt had just achieved her first great success, a breeches role in François Coppée's *Le Passant* at the Théâtre de l'Odéon. Almost immediately, she jumped into real, not fictive, action: during the German siege of Paris (November 1870–January 1871), Bernhardt established a military hospital—an *ambulance*—at the Odéon. She placed the soldiers' beds in the lobby and those of the officers in the theater buffet. When the bombardment became too intense, Bernhardt moved her sick and dying into the theater's basement, but rising water and rats forced her to find other quarters. As if a theatrical event, a poster announced that the Odéon hospital, "created and directed by Mlle Sarah Bernhardt," would move to the rue Taitbout. These efforts on behalf of France earned her a medal after the war.[12] This was her pattern, which she would repeat in World War I: stepping off the stage and becoming an actor in the real events of the nation.

Bernhardt's patriotic fervor was shaped by the particularities of her background. She was a centrist republican with leftist leanings and a fascination for charismatic leaders who take control in politically chaotic moments. Alongside the widespread and enduring French taste for a strong national leader in the anti-Bourbon, post-Revolutionary mold, Bernhardt also felt a direct attachment to Emperor Napoleon III, a man she knew personally and liked.[13] Bernhardt had performed at the Tuileries Palace for the Emperor and the Empress Eugénie with the Théâtre du Gymnase Company in 1864 and with the Odéon Company, in *Le Passant*, the year before the Prussian military victory forced Louis-Napoleon to abdicate his throne. But her connections went further back, to the salons of the van Hard sisters—Bernhardt's mother, Youle, and her aunt, Rosine—well-known and highly placed courtesans of the July Monarchy and Second Empire. Their guests included Napoleon III's doctor, Baron Hippolyte Larrey (whose father had been physician to Napoleon Bonaparte), and the illegitimate half-brother of Napoleon III, the rich and influential Duc de Morny, who facilitated young Sarah's entrance into the exclusive theater school, the Conservatoire, of the *Comédie Française*.[14]

Bernhardt's ties to the Bonapartes in no way restricted her sympathies to them alone, probably because her links were more sentimental than ideological. While her politics leaned more toward republicanism than Bonapartism, she espoused differing, yet ardent, views in response to changing political circumstances. She praised the conservative General MacMahon's "sublime but impotent struggle in the Franco-Prussian War."[15] But when this same general brutally put down the Commune uprising a year later, she sympathized with the Communards, justifying their violent acts—especially those of the women. As she wrote, "What suffering these desolate mothers, these frightened sisters, these worried fiancées endured! How excusable were their revolts in the Commune, even their murderous folly!"[16] All the same, she disliked war and violence, though without embracing pacifism: "And I hate war! It exasperates me; it makes me shudder all over ... Let everyone be a soldier in the moment of danger, yes, a thousand times yes! That everyone should arm himself for the defense of his country, and that one should kill to defend one-self and one's own, makes sense. But that there are still, in these modern times, young men whose only dream is to kill other people in order to make themselves a career—that passes the bounds of comprehension!"[17]

Her strong belief in the nation and its defense made certain of her onstage roles particularly compelling. She played Joan of Arc, the ultimate French heroine, twice: first in Jules Barbier's *Jeanne d'Arc* (1890), and almost two decades later, in Émile Moreau's *Le Procès de Jeanne d'Arc* (1909). As Venita Datta writes, "The staging of these two plays represented an attempt by republican authors and their famous actress collaborator to create an image of Joan, the 'patriotic saint,' 'above politics,' one that could be reconciled with both the Third Republic and the Catholic Church."[18] When novelist Anatole France saw Bernhardt as Joan of Arc, he wrote, "She bears upon her face that afterglow of stained glass which the visitations of the saints had left [on her]."[19] France added that Bernhardt's special capacity to embody myth made her at once "a vision of an ideal life and an exquisite archaism: she is the legend incarnated."[20] This was Bernhardt's intention—to bring myths to life and to present herself as a living myth. The public, she said, had taught her that it preferred mythmaking and storytelling to critical history:

> On occasion I have tried, along with the dramatist, to force the audience to return to the truth and to destroy the legendary aspect of certain characters whose true nature modern historians have revealed.

> But the audience has not followed me. I soon came to the realization that legend always triumphs over historical fact ... We do not want Joan of Arc to be a crude strapping peasant woman ... In legend she remains a frail being, led by a divine spirit. Her girl's arm, holding up the heavy standard, is supported by an invisible angel. The beyond is reflected in her child's eyes from which the warriors draw their strength and courage. It is thus that we wish her to be. And the legend remains triumphant.[21]

Early on, Bernhardt understood that her future lay not with the French elites, but with the public at large, and she remained attentive to what they cared about, and how passionately they felt about her and the roles she played. When she says "we" do not wish Joan to be a crude strapping peasant woman, "we" wish her to be a frail girl—she is speaking as one with her public.

Of course, to maintain popular appeal meant that one had to be adaptable. Hence, in 1902 and 1904, Bernhardt played in rapid succession the title role of the French revolutionary heroine in Hervieu's *Théroigne de Méricourt* and the role of Marie-Antoinette in Lavedan and Lenôtre's *Varennes*.[22] "If he is a republican, he must uphold with warmth and conviction royalist theories," Bernhardt wrote of the obligation of the actor to his métier, "and if he is a conservative, anarchist theories, if such is the wish of the playwright." This professional stance did not, however, negate her own personal sense of political responsibility. Bernhardt was a fervent supporter of Alfred Dreyfus, the Jewish army captain accused and convicted of treason on trumped-up evidence. In the famous *cause célèbre*, which lasted from Dreyfus's conviction in 1894 to his vindication more than a decade later, almost every issue of post-Revolution French national identity came into play: monarchy vs. republic, church vs. state, army vs. civil authority, aristocratic vs. bourgeois France, and, of course, Christian vs. Jew.

Interestingly, and unsurprising for a celebrity as huge as Bernhardt, even her real-life support for Dreyfus and his defender, Émile Zola, has been inflated and turned into legend. It has been claimed, for instance, that the actress was present at the *École Militaire* ceremony stripping Dreyfus of his rank on 5 January 1895: "Crowds had started to gather in the 'piercing cold' outside the ornate iron gates ... Nearby, undoubtedly attracting the most attention, Sarah Bernhardt waited with another group of notables under the elaborate stone reliefs of mythological figures that ran across the building's eighteenth-century walls."[23] There is no evidence of which I am aware for placing Bernhardt at the scene, aside from one unreliable source: Louis Verneuil, a Bernhardt fanatic, bad playwright, and briefly, Sarah's son-in-law.[24] This was the same Verneuil who contended that Zola owed his involvement in the Affair to the Divine One: "Zola had never paid any attention to the Dreyfus Case," Verneuil wrote, " [But] the clear, lucid, and irrefutable manner in which Sarah expounded the facts was a revelation to him. The very next day he saw [Senate Vice-President] Scheurer-Koestner, and three days later his mind was made up. Interrupting all other activities, he would now have only one object—to free the innocent man."[25] Not only did Verneuil claim that Bernhardt invented the Dreyfusard stance, but he likely launched the dubious idea, repeated so often that it passes for fact, that Bernhardt confronted a lynch mob alongside Zola the day after the publication of *J'Accuse*, his famous open letter to the President of France: "About six in the evening, a furious crowd marched up to the Rue de Bruxelles shouting 'Death to Zola!' and besieging the novelist's little house. The police had to be called in great haste. Suddenly a window opened on the second floor, and Sarah Bernhardt appeared. She had come to congratulate Zola on his courageous campaign, which she had initiated two months earlier."[26] There is no more evidence for Bernhardt's appearance in Zola's window than for her presence at the *École Militaire* at the time of Dreyfus's degradation.

It is probably fair to say that Bernhardt's greatest contribution to the Affair was as a moderating influence, specifically when, in 1900, she portrayed Franz, the Duke of Reichstadt, in *L'Aiglon* (*The Eaglet*). Playing a young man of seventeen as a fifty-six-year-old woman helped Bernhardt create a theatrical sensation, as did the play's author and its subject. *L'Aiglon* was Edmond Rostand's successor to his colossal triumph of 1897, *Cyrano de Bergerac*; now he had created a star-vehicle for his good friend Bernhardt. Drawn, like its predecessor, from French history, *L'Aiglon* is the story of the final days in the life of Napoleon Bonaparte's only surviving heir, his son Franz. It is set in the Viennese court, where after Napoleon's exile and death, Franz is held in luxurious, aristocratic captivity by his mother, the Archduchess Maria Louisa of Austria, his grandfather, the Emperor Francis, and Prince Metternich, the Austrian Chancellor. The theater historian Maurice Baring wrote that, "The first night of *L'Aiglon* ... was a battle ... because in that year, 1900, the Dreyfus case was raging, and the play, like everything else, had become a party question." Then he continued:

> That is to say, there was a party of Nationalists who were ready to praise or damn the play, and a party of Dreyfusards who were prepared to do the contrary to whatever the Nationalists did. Both parties were swept off their feet. Sarah conquered them in the first act. I never witnessed a more authentic triumph on the stage. Never before had I seen an audience fully prepared to be hostile so suddenly and completely vanquished.[27]

Rostand himself was a moderate Dreyfusard, but he insisted at every opportunity that *L'Aiglon* was not intended as a political statement: "Good God! It's not a cause/that I attack or defend ... and this is nothing other than the story of an unfortunate child."[28] Still, by mobilizing a national sentiment that most French people could share, *L'Aiglon* helped reconcile a France torn apart by the Affair. The plot, stretched extremely thin over the course of its six long acts in verse, involves the attempt on the part of the Eaglet's supporters—including one of his father's loyal old officers, Flambeau—to rally "Napoleon II" to return to France and seize the throne. Sensitive and weak, the Duke of Reichstadt is unequal to the task. The play's most famous scene has Franz at the battlefield of Wagram, impotently invoking the ghosts of his father's glorious and bloodied troops. But the Duke's predicament allowed the author—and thus his French audience—to wallow in hours' worth of Napoleon-worship, national pride, and self-pity. Partisans of both sides of the Dreyfus Affair could thereby unite in their lament, reaffirming their shared *francité* despite the celebrated case that had called into question nearly every tenet of French identity.

Bernhardt and Franz were tailor-made for each other, beginning with the costume that designer Paul Poiret may have had a hand in creating,[29] but which, judging from the sketches Rostand sent to Bernhardt, appears to have originated with *L'Aiglon*'s author. In this outfit, the once wraith-like star seemed to regain the svelte *ligne* for which she had long been known. An all-white uniform of cotton stretch-fabric, with bold, dark contrasting collar and sash, and a line of gold buttons running straight down the front provided a slenderizing contrast to the double row suggested in Rostand's sketch. But the role of Napoleon II suited Bernhardt in more important ways. It represented the culmination of the patriotic themes that had helped define her career from the beginning. Having already impersonated the trumped-up Carolingian heroine, Roland's daughter Berthe, as well as the legendary daughter of the nation, Joan of Arc, she could now resuscitate the short-lived, mostly forgotten son of France's greatest modern warrior. Bernhardt enjoyed the opportunity to "conquer," "vanquish," and "sweep" the audience off its feet with her lyrical tributes to Napoleon Bonaparte as the progeny of 1789. An interchange in Act III between Franz and the Austrian Chancellor sympathetically evokes Napoleon's seizure of power and the Revolution as spiritual grandparents—*grandsire* and *granddam*—of the Duke.

> Duke of Reichstadt: Upon my father's side
> I am related closely, Sire, to Freedom.
> Metternich: Yes, the Duke's grandsire was the eighteenth Brumaire!
> Duke of Reichstadt: Yes, and the Revolution was my granddam![30]

Buttressed by its star's evocative performance, *L'Aiglon* distracted its audience from France's current internecine strife. It also redirected national energies toward the memory of the Franco-Prussian War, the same defeat that, as Bernhardt knew so well, had meant the success of another less-than-scintillating verse drama, *La Fille de Roland*. Perhaps without realizing it, this is what critic Patrick Besnier means in saying, "*L'Aiglon* is in fact a long *lamento*, a meditation on defeat and death."[31] The "revenge" for 1870—both for the generalized national humiliation and the specific loss of the provinces of Alsace and Lorraine—reverberates throughout *L'Aiglon*. Not only is the enemy Germanic—surely the Austrian court is a none-too-subtle allusion to the Prussian one—but French taste is repeatedly lauded at the expense of the supposedly crude sensibility of Franz's captors. Flambeau tells the Duke that his brother is an upholsterer in Paris, so he knows of what he speaks: "They try to imitate us here; but Lord! They've got a curious kind of Louis-Quinze! … Just look how finicky this wood-work is." In comparison, he directs Franz's attention to the room's tapestry: "What taste! What mystery! It sings. It laughs ... Why? Don't you know? Why, these are Gobelins!" Then Flambeau brings home his point: "How plain it is that cunning craftsmen made them. This taste, this elegance swears with the rest—And you my Lord, were also made in France!"[32]

"Made in France," just like the star of *L'Aiglon*, the most celebrated actress in the world. What gave the role its special piquancy for the French was the superimposition of legendary performer and legendary character. Of course, the greatest stars always confront us with this epistemological problem: is it the actor or the acted that compels us? In the strange game of substitutions that characterizes all realist drama, *L'Aiglon* might be said to fetishize French national loss: instead of Napoleon, we get his son (instead of the Eagle we get the Eaglet); instead of the Dreyfus Affair, we get the story of Napoleon II's captivity and demise (itself a displacement of the Franco-Prussian defeat). And, of course, instead of the young male Franz, Duke of Reichstadt, we get the middle-aged woman, Sarah Bernhardt.

Rostand's play asserts both the futility and power of substitutions—of *fetishism*. And who better, amid the Dreyfus Affair, to embody the double-edged sword of make believe than the star who had burned bright for so long in the theatrical firmament, the Divine Sarah? Every time Franz asks about his father's legacy or his own potential for glory, it might as well be the aging Bernhardt inquiring about herself: "But where's the proof / That France still feels herself my Father's widow?" In Act II, the Duke asks about French national feeling for Napoleon, to which Flambeau replies: "Their love for you, my Lord? Why that's immortal!"[33] He proceeds to take from his person various articles—a pair of suspenders, snuff box, handkerchief, colored print, pipe, cockade, medal, egg cup, tumbler, plate, necktie, playing cards, almanac, knife, and a napkin ring—each of which bears a portrait of Franz. Flambeau wants the Duke to understand that it is these "trivial fancy goods" that prove, by their very ordinariness and ubiquity, the immortal love of France for the Bonapartes.

France, and the world, had offered just this sort of proof of their immortal love for Bernhardt—the endless photographs, pamphlets, posters, souvenir booklets, teacups, and dessert plates that bore her likeness. Indeed, with *L'Aiglon*, Bernhardt memorabilia achieved a spectacular new level of cultural penetration, as Ockman and I attempted to show in our exhibition. As if in uncanny imitation of the play itself, all of these objects featured the actress not in her real-life attire, but in her costume and makeup for the Duke of Reichstadt. They include photographs in which he/she is doubled, tripled, and even quintupled, advertisements, statuettes, buttons, and cufflinks (a pair, in the collection of the Museum of the City of New York, once belonged to playwright Moss Hart). Competing quinine aperitifs made use of the image of Bernhardt in the role of Reichstadt: a poster for L'Aiglon quinine shows Bernhardt as Franz with the improbable addition of Cyrano de Bergerac raising his sword behind a rock; a poster for Michaud quinine shows Bernhardt as Franz enjoying a drink amid a gaggle of contemporary celebrities.[34]

Since Rostand wrote the play expressly for Bernhardt, who was intimately involved in its creation, it seems likely that author and star had at least an inkling of the kinds of cultural displacements *L'Aiglon* might elicit. They must have sensed how charged the confusion between legendary star and star-crossed legend could be; indeed, they must have counted on it. Had this kind of substitution ever failed Bernhardt in the past? Once a skinny, Jewish, courtesan's daughter, she became an object of national veneration: school was closed in Paris on "Sarah Bernhardt Day," 9 December 1896; she was made Chevalier of the Legion of Honor in 1914. Born just five years after the beginnings of photography, that great new tool of reproduction, Bernhardt knew how much more powerful the surrogate was than the original. But she also knew, as she demonstrated by playing Napoleon's son, that not all substitutes are equally effective. Promoting herself, promoting France, promoting competing aperitifs: all were part of the great modern system of celebrity that on the stage as on the battlefield, on the boulevard as in the boardroom, belonged only to those who could act the part.

CHAPTER 10

Heroes, Celebrity, and the Theater in *Fin-de-Siècle* France
Cyrano de Bergerac

VENITA DATTA

> Why do they continuously raise that great red curtain? … Why these bravos, these encores, these cries? Why do all these faces seem transformed by tears and smiles? Why does this young name that a triumphant voice releases into the theater soar like a bird of glory passing from mouth to mouth, from evening to evening, from country to country? … Because this evening for the first time, *Cyrano de Bergerac* was staged at the Théâtre de la Porte Saint-Martin.

The author of these hyperbolic words is Rosemonde Rostand, describing the reactions to the dress rehearsal of her husband's play *Cyrano de Bergerac*.[1] First presented on the Parisian stage on 27 December 1897, just two weeks prior to the publication of Émile Zola's *J'Accuse*, Edmond Rostand's *Cyrano de Bergerac* has become one of the most beloved and most often staged plays in the history of the French theater.[2] Not only did the play mark the birth of Cyrano as a national figure, it also announced the arrival of Rostand as a worldwide celebrity. Almost immediately, Rostand received the Legion of Honor, and in May 1901, he was elected to the *Académie Française* at the ripe old age of thirty-three.

Since the *fin de siècle*, the play has been translated into countless foreign languages and adapted for the cinema, most recently in the 1990 Rappeneau film featuring the ubiquitous Gérard Depardieu. In 1997, the centennial of *Cyrano de Bergerac* inspired numerous festivities, among them two different revivals of the play, an exhibition organized in conjunction with the Bibliothèque historique de la Ville de Paris, and a great number of articles in the leading newspapers and weekly magazines. In 2006, Cyrano was revived at the *Comédie Française*.[3] US audiences perhaps know the Cyrano story best through its retelling by Steve Martin in the 1987 film *Roxanne*. In the original story,

Cyrano is not a fireman but rather a poet-soldier in love with his cousin, the *précieuse* Roxane. Unable to declare his love for her, he ends up wooing her for a handsome but inarticulate young nobleman named Christian, writing love letters to her in Christian's stead. When Christian dies in battle, Cyrano vows to keep his secret; it is only when Cyrano himself is dying that Roxane finally learns the true identity of the man she has loved all these years.

It is no exaggeration to state that *Cyrano de Bergerac* has become a *lieu de mémoire*, since both the play and its eponymous hero have been absorbed into French national memory.[4] Although a flawed hero, Cyrano corresponds to the image the French like to have of themselves. In fact, French commentators have compared Cyrano to historical figures from Vercingétorix to De Gaulle, all of whom have borne defeat with grace, or as Rostand would have put it, *panache*.[5] Although the play enjoys universal appeal and timelessness, it was also very much a product of its time and Cyrano a hero for the *fin de siècle*. An immediate critical and popular success, *Cyrano* played to full houses during the height of the Dreyfus Affair. Though Rostand himself was a Dreyfusard, Cyrano had admirers on both sides of the Affair. As many contemporaries noted, the French, divided by day, were reconciled at the theater by night, in great measure due to the talents of one of the leading actors of the day, Constant Coquelin, for whom Rostand had written the role. Cyrano became so much the quintessential French hero in a country wounded by the Franco-Prussian War and preparing already for the next battle, that his creators, skillful as they were, would forever be overshadowed by their creation.[6]

This essay examines the political, social, and cultural context in which *Cyrano* was presented and received in order, first, to explore the role of the theater in the construction of heroes and the forging of national identity, and, second, to examine one of the major themes of *Cyrano de Bergerac*: fame and success. In the play, Rostand decried both, instead exalting pure artistic values as incarnated by his hero. Yet *Cyrano's* phenomenal success—many critics called it an apotheosis—garnered the playwright the very fame he denounced. A study of *Cyrano de Bergerac* thus illuminates the role of mass culture in the construction of celebrity as well as the impact of both on writers at the *fin de siècle*.[7]

Heroes and French National Identity

In the years following defeat in the Franco-Prussian War, the cult of the hero gained great prominence in France, manifesting itself in all areas of national life, from primary school curricula to literature and the arts, and from the contemporary exaltation of the army to the popularity of both dueling and sports. Napoleon Bonaparte and Joan of Arc, along with Cyrano (Hercule Savinien de Bergerac, 1619–1655), the obscure seventeenth-century poet-soldier transformed by Rostand into a household name, figured among the most popular heroes of the era. The search for heroes was the consequence of a widespread sense of national inferiority vis-à-vis Germany as well as the product of collective guilt with regard to the egoism and selfishness of modern consumer culture.[8] Both of these fears fueled the contemporary crisis of masculinity in France, which some historians believe was exacerbated by a decline in the national birthrate and the emergence of the New Woman, who challenged traditional gender roles.[9]

Rostand set his play during the heroic seventeenth century, an age distant enough in time that most of his compatriots could accept it as part of a common national heritage. For the French of the *fin de siècle*, still smarting from the loss of the Franco-Prussian War and France's diminished international status, the swashbuckling age of Louis XIII represented national grandeur in an era when France dominated the European continent. Although the war with Spain depicted in the play nearly ended in defeat, the action described in its fourth act—the siege of Arras (1640)— represented an important turning point in the hostilities. Unlike the Franco-Prussian War two centuries later, the French averted defeat and then proceeded to victory.

In the late 1890s, contemporaries must have looked upon these seventeenth-century events with a certain amount of nostalgia, while many commentators heralded the play as the harbinger of a new era. Noted critic Emile Faguet declared in *Le Journal des débats* that *Cyrano de Bergerac* and its author announced the opening of the twentieth century in "a brilliant and triumphant manner" and that Europe would finally look upon France with envy.[10] *Le Journal's* ultrapatriotic critic Georges Thiébaud went even further, proclaiming that Cyrano announced the reawakening of nationalism in France.[11] Meanwhile, Jules Lemaître saw the play as the culmination of three centuries of French art, comparing Rostand to Pierre Corneille and Victor Hugo.[12] Whether viewed as part of a long French tradition or as the sign of a new French literature, the play enjoyed widespread acclaim as a source of French "pride," a word repeated so often in reviews that critics appeared to see in Rostand's work a redemption of France's lost honor.

Such views assumed particular importance amid the extraordinarily divisive Dreyfus Affair. Cyrano's verve in the face of adversity, his bravery, both physical and moral, comforted Dreyfusards and anti-Dreyfusards alike. His disdain of aristocratic privilege and patronage, his independence of thought, his wit and mastery of oratory also made him a quintessential French hero. Although he did not win the girl, he sacrificed all in the name of love, which is undoubtedly what made him appealing to the women in the audiences—by all accounts the play's popularity cut across gender lines.[13] Men, for their part, could admire his physical bravery and even his "disinterestedness," a heroic quality par excellence at this time.

Cyrano thus succeeded in uniting within the theater walls a public overtly divided along political lines outside. The most popular heroes of the era, Napoleon and Joan of Arc, along with Cyrano, were fictionalized by playwrights and represented by celebrated actors as incarnating a national unity "above politics." Thus, at the height of the Dreyfus Affair, *Cyrano de Bergerac* owed its huge popular success to a protagonist, at once swordsman and poet, military hero and intellectual hero, whose qualities attracted anti-Dreyfusards and Dreyfusards in equal measure.[14] Similarly, Sarah Bernhardt's Joan of Arc—in the 1890 revival of Jules Barbier's *Jeanne d'Arc* and Emile Moreau's 1909 *Le procès de Jeanne d'Arc*—succeeded in uniting audiences during a time when the Left and Right were grappling for control of Joan's legacy. Still, unity within the theater worked better in some cases than others. Despite calls for heroes "above politics," many of them remained embedded in the politics of the time; Napoleon, if not Cyrano and Joan, was more successfully co-opted by the nationalist Right.

Political, legendary, and heroic as these characters appeared, playwrights also depicted them as all too human, a quality that brought these transcendent figures down to earth for the *fin de siècle's* increasingly democratic audiences. When Félix Duquesne portrayed Napoleon in Victorien Sardou's 1893 production of *Mme Sans-Gêne*, he was dressed (or rather—undressed) in his dressing gown during much of the play and depicted not as the conquering military hero, but as a loving husband afraid he might be cuckolded. Similarly, Bernhardt represented Joan of Arc as a vulnerable young girl whose frailties made her destiny that much more remarkable.[15] The great poet and warrior Cyrano, completely in command in front of an audience, was tongue-tied and undone when he encountered the woman he loved, Roxane. Even as playwrights showed their characters' human side, they took pains to idealize, even sanitize, their lives. As Bernhardt herself noted, audiences did not want to see the sordid reality of historical figures but rather better versions of themselves, played by the most celebrated and charismatic actors of the age.[16]

The heroes of the theater, like the actors who portrayed them, thus became, with the help of the press, mass marketing, and publicity techniques, "intimate strangers" to an entire nation.[17] The public's fascination with the actors and their roles was facilitated in part by the literary culture in which theatrical conventions flourished. As Vanessa Schwartz, Dominique Kalifa, and others have shown, real-life events were transformed into spectacles in the press and other entertainment venues, as the line separating fiction from reality was increasingly blurred. James Lehning has equally noted that the melodramatic genre in France shaped the political culture of the nation.[18] Thus, as contemporaries were aware, political events of the *fin de siècle* took on a highly theatrical nature. In such an atmosphere, it is not surprising that the real-life, modest hero Alfred Dreyfus could not compete. He was neither "theatrical" nor "heroic" enough.[19]

The public's intimacy with the heroes of the stage also drew sustenance from the consumption of celebrity souvenirs.[20] To mark the one-hundredth performance of *Cyrano*, Raguneau pastries were passed out to audience members so that they could literally consume the play. Ironically, Cyrano, like Napoleon and Joan, became not only an object of commodification, but also an antidote to the burgeoning consumer culture of the age. Writing in *Les hommes d'aujourd'hui*, the critic Charles Donos exalted Rostand as an heroic example, calling him "a conqueror of popularity, who has understood during our contemporary period of money-worship, how to explain to the multitude sentiments of admiration and enthusiasm for a hero ... rich only in bravura, wit, love and abnegation."[21] Similarly, Emile Faguet wrote that this play was destined to "console us for all the industrial literature in which we are mired."[22]

Finally, the audience's identification with the actors and their heroic roles was also accomplished through self-conscious press techniques like the celebrity interview, which linked the actor's and the hero's charisma to accessible, human qualities in a symbiotic relationship. Like Bernhardt and other actors of the time, Coquelin was interviewed regularly and asked specifically about his humble origins as the son of a baker and pastrymaker. At the same time, actors imbued the characters they played with their celebrity, while the characters' heroic qualities were transferred onto the actors portraying the roles.[23] Thus, in interviews with Coquelin, journalists emphasized his strength and physical prowess, along with his prodigious memory. They spoke of the heroism of the actor learning his lines, as well as his "cerebral labor" and his "mission to incarnate" his role.[24] Similarly, the journalist Silvio depicted Rostand as "a young Bonaparte who wins his battles."[25]

The theater's ability to inspire intimacy and identification in its audience at a time of great political division thus illustrates the pivotal role the theater played in the cultural, social, and political life of *fin-de-siècle* France and suggests that we look beyond official celebrations, parliamentary debates, and school manuals for a complete understanding of discussions about national identity at this time. Premieres of important plays were feted in the press as events of national stature, while leading actors and actresses were hailed as celebrities, as well as symbols of the nation.

Fame and Success in *Fin-de-Siècle* France

Contemporary anxieties about modern consumer society manifested themselves not only in the debate concerning heroes, but also in discussions about the role of the writer in French society. Thus, another reason for *Cyrano's* triumph was its ambivalence toward fame and the commercialization of success. It played both to a popular audience fascinated with celebrity and to writers of the *fin de siècle* who lauded its overt rejection of facile fame in the name of freedom of thought and action.

Public debate about heroism and the commercialization of fame exploded onto the national scene during the Dreyfus Affair, as Dreyfusards and anti-Dreyfusards alike professed to value independence above the slavery of fame. Rostand captured this sentiment in Cyrano's famous *"non merci"* speech, in which he outlines his philosophy.[26] The Duc de Guiche, offering Cyrano his patronage, declares that a poet is a luxury (Act 2, scene 7). Cyrano counters with the following, which bears citing:

> What would you have me do?
> Seek out a powerful protector, pursue
> A potent patron? Cling like a leeching vine
> To a tree? *Crawl* my way up? Fawn, whine
> For all that sticky candy called success?
> No thank you. Be a sycophant and dress
> In sickly rhymes a prayer to a moneylender?
> Play the buffoon, desperate to engender
> A smirk on a refrigerated jowl? No thank you.[27]

Instead, a true poet and hero has to maintain his independence:

> But to go
> Free of the filthy world, to sing, to be
> Blessed with a voice vibrating virility,
> Blessed with an eye equipped for looking at
> Things as they really are, cocking my hat
> Where I please, at a word, at a deed, at a yes or no.
> Fighting or writing. This is the true life. So
> I go along any road under my moon,
> Careless of glory, indifferent to the boon
> Or bane of fortune, without hope, without fear,
> Writing only the words down that I hear...
> If fate succeeds
> In wresting some small triumph for me-well,
> I render nothing unto Caesar, sell
> No moiety of my merit to the world.
> I loathe the parasite liana, curled
> About the oak trunk. I myself am a tree,
> Not high perhaps, not beautiful, but free-

My flesh deciduous, but the enduring bone
Of spirit tough, indifferent, and alone!

In these lines, Rostand expressed his unease over a newly democratic society in which fame and celebrity often took precedence over real art. Like many other writers of his day, Rostand feared that the most celebrated artists were not necessarily the best. This was a common concern for writers from all ends of the political spectrum, from monarchist Charles Maurras and anti-Semite Edouard Drumont, to anarchists Paul Adam and Octave Mirbeau. They all blamed the "industrialization" of literature and the overproduction of materials for an insatiable but mediocre, undiscerning public, and the concomitant dominance of money for the decline of the writer's status. Deploring a society that valued industrialists and politicians over men of thought, avant-garde writers banded together in protest in the 1880s and 1890s. Defining themselves as an "intellectual aristocracy," they proposed to restore the grandeur and dignity French writers had lost to the marketplace. Some went on to become Dreyfusards, others anti-Dreyfusards, but all agreed on the right and the duty of the writer to pronounce on matters of national importance.[28] Cyrano's speech thus served as an apposite allegory for the *fin de siècle:* in Cyrano's time, writers had to flatter a wealthy protector; during the *fin de siècle,* that role now belonged to the mass public, on whom writers, especially those of the theater, depended for their success.[29] Rostand thus expressed his fear of the pedestrian tastes of the multitudes.

At the same time, however, Rostand rejected the isolation of the avant-garde. Although Cyrano rebuffed money, patronage, and protection in favor of destitution, danger, and independence in his *non merci* speech, he also eschewed retreat into the small coteries of the avant-garde and even referred disparagingly in the original French text to the illustrious predecessor of the avant-garde journal *Le Mercure de France.*[30] Small wonder then that most reservations regarding the play came from the avant-garde. *Le Mercure de France's* critic was downright insulting, claiming that Rostand had perfected the art of bad writing.[31] This cool reception was partly due to Rostand's jibe, but it was also linked to *Cyrano's* success with both the public and established critics, who claimed that it represented the revival of French youth and a welcome antidote to the avant-garde vogue of promoting foreign literatures.[32] Indeed, as Jules Lemaître noted in his review, unlike Hugo's *Hernani* and Corneille's *Le Cid* to which it was compared, *Cyrano* did not face the challenge of not being understood. *Cyrano's* accessibility underlay the avant-garde criticism of the play.[33]

Moreover, while the play decried material success and fame, it ironically earned its author those very same things. Avant-garde writers highlighted this tension, lashing out against the *"commerçants"* who made the play a huge success and against the self-congratulatory reactions of the established "bourgeois" critics. Still, many avant-gardists sought the very fame they denounced, and some of their reactions may be attributed to professional jealousy. And indeed, there was much to envy in Rostand's success. His induction into the *Académie Française* on 4 June 1903, two years after he was elected, was an event of national importance. When he arrived in Paris three weeks before the big day, reporters followed Rostand from the train station to his hotel. The induction ceremony itself was followed closely in the major newspapers, which reproduced Rostand's speech as well as that of the Vicomte de Vogüé, who received him into the academy.[34] Newspaper boys hawked the text of Rostand's speech before he actually delivered it, shamelessly doing so in the street in front of Rostand's hotel (bringing to mind the people who put spoilers of the last installment of J.K. Rowling's Harry Potter saga on the internet before the official publication date).[35]

Despite his profound unease with fame, Rostand became the great celebrity writer of the age, even buying a castle-like villa (Arnaga in Cambo-les Bains in the Pays basque) to which he retreated in order to "hide" from the public. In a sense, Rostand found himself trapped by his fame. In his speech welcoming the young author to the *Académie Française*, the Vicomte de Vogüé referred to the burden of fame Rostand had assumed.[36] Memoirs and newspaper accounts of the period also described Rostand as overwhelmed by the crowds of fans and reporters who assailed him when he was changing trains or cars for his journeys to Paris from Arnaga, and that Rostand was forced to adopt various subterfuges and disguises to escape the prying eyes of reporters.

Rostand's son Jean later insisted that his father did not welcome this media attention: "What I observed of my father is truly contrary to the legend. He fled publicity and the crowd. He was horrified by theater directors, *cabotins* [third-rate actors or those who prefer celebrity to their craft], and journalists. I knew him to be solitary, fond of the countryside, badly shaven."[37] Jean Rostand also claimed that his father resented the intrusion of his favorite actors, Coquelin and Bernhardt, because their arrival marred his solitude, bringing him the cares of the outside world and in particular their need for fame.[38]

Still, even though the Rostands, father and son, might have sought to distinguish the playwright from the vanity of actors and their need for adulation, Rostand himself most assuredly shared that need. In many ways, Rostand was like his hero, Cyrano de Bergerac. Both denounced fame, and both needed a public to survive. Cyrano could not "perform" the role of the hero without an audience; indeed, he literally stands on stage in the theater, when he takes the place of the actor Montfleury in Acts 1 and 2. Similarly, when he single-handedly fights off one hundred men, it is again a performance in front of witnesses. Yet he is unable to "perform" (that word can be interpreted in a number of ways) when he is alone with Roxane. Instead, he needs the conventions of the stage, notably the balcony, in the pivotal scene where he woos Roxane—ostensibly for Christian—in order to play the hero.

In the same way, Rostand himself seemed to need an audience, even though he claimed to prefer solitude. While the excesses of fame may have burdened him, he also fed the craze for information about him (like many celebrities of our own time), as an interview from the January 1913 issue of *Les Annales* suggests. The subtitle of the article, *"confidences recueillies"* (selected confidences), invites its readers' complicity in this so-called private conversation with a public figure, while the journalist's description of Rostand's home, in this case a rented apartment, heightened the impression of accessibility. This type of interview, conducted with actors and especially actresses of the day, anticipated the visits and tours of celebrities' homes in the 1950s that Edward R. Murrow found so painful to conduct.[39] From here, the reporter further invites his readers' collusion by telling them that as soon as the interview is over, the playwright will escape to the *loge* (box) of Jean Coquelin (the great actor's son—himself an actor), to elude the prying eyes of reporters. Yet the supposedly publicity-shy playwright has chosen to give this particular reporter an interview, recounting once again, for a public that has heard stories about the genesis of *Cyrano* many times before, how much of himself and his own life he put into the play.[40] This tension between coyness and revelation is typical of the celebrity interview, and Rostand continued to give such interviews over the years, to the point of backfiring: in his memoirs, Paul Faure attributed the collapse of Rostand's 1909 play *Chantecler* to overexposure.[41]

Despite his own success, Rostand was obviously fascinated with failure, since all of his heroes, Cyrano included, were *ratés* (failures) to some extent. Despite his bravery and heroism, Cyrano loses his love Roxane; despite his great talent, he gains no literary fame, but is surpassed by writers of lesser merit. This situation is exacerbated by his tragic flaw, his nose. Thus, his wit and bravery must compensate for his physical deformity. Yet Cyrano's wit and mastery of words were also a means of exacting revenge. Marc Lambron, writing in *Le Point* a few years ago, commented that Cyrano represented: "This national propensity to see a speech as an emblem of resistance."[42] Rostand himself saw Cyrano as an ideal, a symbol of purity, who battles the crass values of the marketplace represented by those who succeed in his place. Worldly failure thus became an emblem of purity or spiritual success.

Rostand's wavering attitude toward success reflects the ambivalence many celebrities have felt toward fame, simultaneously feeding on it for their egos and their creativity, while deploring its invasive aspects. Rostand's dismay over his media exposure has been magnified a hundred times over in our own twenty-first century culture, in which newshounds, professional or amateur, stalk their prey around the clock. But the case of Rostand and *Cyrano de Bergerac* also tells us something about the way celebrity was experienced and viewed in *fin-de-siècle* France. Members of the literary elite, to which Rostand belonged, were wary of fame and quick success, traits they associated with modern culture and designated as simultaneously "vulgar" and "American." They clearly feared being overrun by the "questionable" tastes of the masses. Rostand's supporters worked in vain to convince other literati that mass appeal and early success did not go hand in hand with superficiality and lack of artistic merit.

Popular audiences who flocked to *Cyrano de Bergerac*, however, did not share these views about celebrity, holding up famous actors such as Coquelin and Bernhardt as role models. Theatergoers of the *fin de siècle* reveled in the culture of celebrity and felt great sympathy for the new heroes of the democratic age, ones with whom they could identify. Not only were these heroes represented as better versions of the ordinary man or woman, but the success of the actors who portrayed them exemplified the meritocratic republic and its promise of social promotion.[43] While Rostand himself belonged to an elite, his actors Coquelin and Bernhardt came from the popular classes. As for Rostand, theatergoers and readers of the mass press, imbued with a national tradition that venerates writers, found themselves fascinated by the creator of their beloved Cyrano. Although they might not all have aspired to his fame and fortune, they could share it vicariously. Thus, Rostand's success was due in part to the complicity his audience felt with the great writer. Like his creator, Cyrano was an aristocratic hero with populist tendencies who appealed to the democratic masses of the *fin de siècle*. By literally and figuratively thumbing his nose at the rest of Europe, Cyrano became a conduit for national reconciliation, and even announced the nationalist revival that preceded the Great War. For Rostand himself, the success of *Cyrano de Bergerac* was at once his means to fame and cross to bear, a symbol of the *panache* he sought for the rest of his life.

Secular Anointings
Fame, Celebrity, and Charisma
in the First Century of Mass Culture

LEO BRAUDY

When I was somewhere in the middle of writing *The Frenzy of Renown*—which turned out to be a twelve-year project—my agent started getting anxious. "You'd better hurry up and finish," she said. "Soon, no one's going to be interested in fame any more." Yet today, more than twenty years later, US culture as well as global culture generally seems more flooded than ever before with the dissemination and merchandising of names and faces that are the hallmarks of modern fame.

To give her comment some credit, though, I must admit that fame is a somewhat odd subject to consider with any degree of intellectual and scholarly seriousness. We experience so many trivial and transient versions of it in our present celebrity-choked environment, that trying to stand back and understand the scope and nuances of its history may seem to be a fruitless academic exercise.

But I would argue that it is exactly our contemporary experience with what fame, celebrity, and even charisma have become that helps us to see more clearly what it has been and what evolving role it plays in the history of the last two or more centuries. Even while looking back on the nineteenth-century roots of fame, celebrity, and charisma, and at our own fascination with how they may be achieved and maintained, we are also unavoidably thinking about what is happening right in front of us.

In this book, our focus is on fame, celebrity, and charisma in the first century of mass culture. It is difficult to conceive of how any of the persons, places, and things that usually fit under those categories could have existed without the great expansion of media that began in the early nineteenth century. But the advent of photography, the flowering of popular journalism, the exploitation of more rapid and accurate printing resources, and the later rise of recording, radio, film, and television, hardly exhaust the question; there must be subject matter as well as the means to convey it and an audience to receive it. Jürgen Habermas designates the eighteenth century in England as the beginning of the bourgeois public sphere and sites its origins in the culture of the coffee house. But the coffee house, along with its equally stimulating associates in chocolate, tea, and tobacco, was a feature of Restoration England, a hundred years before, as a byproduct of an expanding international commerce. Some attention should be paid, in other words, to the prehistory of charisma as well as to its history.

In the same period, newspapers, satiric poems, and political engravings began appearing: some parroted the government line on the events of the day and others contradicted it. Not only was the concept of a loyal opposition being formed for the first time, but also the court, only recently returned from its exile in France during the Civil Wars, could not simply do what it wanted. Despite the honeymoon period of the first few years of the Restoration, when the wide sway of royal power over domestic and foreign affairs was more generally accepted, the royal government still had to persuade a wider and wider audience that its policies were right, and it had to use the resources of the current media to do it. Subjects, however hesitantly, were on the way to becoming citizens. With more media outlets and a freer press insured for a time by the lapse of the Licensing Act in the 1690s, by the end of the century an embryonic awareness that deserved the name of public opinion was gradually emerging.

But did celebrity or fame exist yet, let alone charisma? Celebrity in our contemporary meaning of someone of transient fame dates to the middle of the nineteenth century, at about the same time that, according to the *Oxford English Dictionary*, the word "soloist" first appears. Around that time, Matthew Arnold makes an already widespread distinction when he says that Spinoza has fame, whereas his successors have only celebrity. Fame, in other words, was still reserved for a substantial recognition that was much more lasting.[1]

But what of charisma? Max Weber introduces the term to sociology by 1920, lifting it from the language of Christianity. Chrism is the mixture of olive oil and balsam used as an anointment in various sacraments of both the Eastern and Western Churches, usually signifying grace and the possession of the Holy Spirit. The term appears most frequently in Weber's distinction between three types of authority: the dynastic and genealogical; the bureaucratic and rational; and the charismatic.[2]

Weber's argument also makes a transhistorical assertion—it is a useful way of looking at political figures across the centuries. His real focus, however, is the nineteenth century after the French and American revolutions, and especially after the triumphal rise of Napoleon, who himself used the word *prestige*, with its magical implications, for the sway that he held over hearts and minds across Europe.[3]

But the public attitude toward some earlier figures virtually shouts charisma, without acutally using the word. I think especially of Oliver Cromwell in the mid seventeenth century. Andrew Marvell's great poem on Cromwell describes him as a force of nature who somehow has managed to accomplish everything that the nominal monarch, Charles I, has not. Intriguingly, the distinction between Cromwell's charisma and Charles's traditional leadership mirrors the one Weber will make more than 250 years later, even while Marvell explicitly rejects a Christianized terminology to sanction supreme leadership. The English Civil Wars certainly had a strong religious component and ministers were attached to every unit in Cromwell's New Model Army. Yet Marvell calls his poem "An Horatian Ode." All talk of a monotheistic God is banished. Pagan heroism rather than Christian spirituality is the way to understand Cromwell's magic.[4]

Charles I, Marvell implies, is the mere "Royal Actor," admirably playing a part on the public stage but essentially a figurehead, while Cromwell can both "act and know." Then, after comparing Cromwell to a lightning bolt shattering the old order, Marvell says "much to the man is due." According to Marvell, Cromwell's unique power, what Weber will later call charisma, is the intersection of an individual with a historical moment; he is what Sidney Hook will later dub "an eventful man." As Marvell says in a later poem, written to celebrate Cromwell's first year as Lord Protector and head of the government, "If these the times, then this must be the man." It was a perception shared by many others, both those who supported Cromwell and those against him. After his death, Cromwell's sway was still so powerful that at the Restoration of Charles II, the Protector's body was dug up, decapitated, and the head stuck on a pike in front of Westminster Hall, to ensure that the spectral force of his nonmonarchical power would not continue to disturb the king's peace.[5]

Between Cromwell and Napoleon it is more difficult to find a European figure whose presence on the public scene might be called charismatic. The Duke of Marlborough, Frederick the Great, Catherine the Great, and George Washington might be worthy contenders. But the most interesting development is in the category of what I would call the international wise men—Voltaire, Jean-Jacques Rousseau, Benjamin Franklin, and Johann Wolfgang von Goethe—all of whom established reputations that drew admiring audiences across Europe for their work. I might even add Samuel Johnson to that list. Johnson, unlike the others, is for the most part a more locally English figure. But Johnson also is an intriguing linchpin between the sacred view of kingship and the new sacrament of charisma—and not just because he wrote *The Lives of the Poets*, the first work in English that concertedly argued that it was necessary to know the writer as well as his work. When he was three years old, Johnson was taken to London to be touched by Queen Anne to cure the scrofula he had contracted from a wet nurse. Scrofula was called "the King's evil," and Anne was in fact the last British monarch to hold periodic public audiences to cure the malady with the royal touch. In Johnson's case at least, it did not work and it may have later played a subconscious role in his denunciation of the system of aristo- cratic patronage, which helped mark the transition, for writers, from royalty to royalties.

In England and Germany particularly, ideas about originality were changing as well, and its double meaning of being unprecedented and reaching back to origins mirrors the desire to leap over the debased present and connect with the mythic past. In *The Frenzy of Renown*, a phrase I drew from this period, I hypothesize that there are three crucial factors that inflect the history of fame: the political system, the cultural definition of a perfect person, and the available media. In the late eighteenth and early nineteenth century, all of these factors were in flux. We might therefore expect and, in fact, we find a wealth of charis- matic figures beyond the political personalities on which Weber tends to focus. Many of them appeared within the context of the Romantic movement, itself an intriguing combination of the evocation of the distant past and the imme- diacy of personal self-display, a transnational cultural movement with national variation and specificity.

Stretching from the last third of the eighteenth century into the first third of the nineteenth century, Romanticism furnished a fertile seedbed for political and cultural change, especially in attitudes toward the individual, public and private. Language itself changed to record the new perception. A word like *virtuoso* in English, previously meaning a dilettante, shifted instead toward the description of unique ability, particularly in music, George Frideric Handel perhaps being the first to be so called in English.

Meanwhile, German aestheticians were hard at work distinguishing be- tween genius and talent, to the detriment of the latter. The Roman view that everyone *had* a genius was changing into the possibility that one could *be* a genius, the generic turned into the potentially unique. The new meaning of ge- nius swiftly found currency in England, France, and Germany, where another name for the period of *Sturm und Drang* of the 1770s was the *Geniezeit*. Just as the French Revolution found much of its imagery in the Roman world, English and German literature reached into the Middle Ages to find the authentic roots of poetic inspiration, the wellspring of genius.

But genius should be distinguished from charisma. Although in some peo- ple they might overlap, a genius then was recognizable primarily by youth, for example, Thomas Lawrence in painting, or Wolfgang Amadeus Mozart in mu- sic. It was a preternatural mastery of abilities, usually artistic, that would seem to be the province only of the most accomplished adult, or in some cases—the "Thresher Poet" Stephen Duck comes to mind—a lower-class mastery of abili- ties that would seem to be the province of the only upper classes.

Charisma by contrast was the overpowering allure to an audience of a figure on the public stage. Although Weber says that if the charismatic figure fails to deliver material benefit to his audience, they will begin to desert him, he nevertheless generally considers charisma to rest almost entirely in the person ("a certain quality of an individual personality") and tends to downplay or disregard the role of the audience in preparing the ground for both his accession to power and his continued possession of it.[6] But a prime characteristic of the visual culture of this period was the urge to be overwhelmed, the desire for ecstatic experience, whether it came from contemplating the deeds of Napoleon, the snowy peak of Mont Blanc in the Alps, or even a host of golden daffodils.

The role of the audience in the establishment of charisma and the designation of the charismatic person may suggest a potential analogy with Walter Benjamin's idea of aura in his 1936 essay "The Work of Art an Age of Mechanical Reproduction."[7] But, whether the audience is considered to be an active or passive participant in the creation of charisma, its response is generally defined by the present, while for Benjamin, aura requires a looking backward: we retrospectively invest objects with aura that may in their own time have seemed perfectly ordinary. Despite this difference, however, the exceptional quality of the charismatic individual and the aura of the art object before the age of mechanical reproduction transform an atmosphere of transcendence—previously confined to religion or monarchical divine right—into more secular conceptual realms.

Changes in the material culture of performance were also a part of the equation. The late eighteenth century was a time when the stage, thanks to the introduction of oil lamps, was becoming a more brilliantly lit place, while the audience sat watching in relative darkness. Innovations in scenic design by painters such as Philip de Loutherbourg created a more dramatic visual world on stage that highlighted the actor at the center of tumultuous events.

Despite the presence, then, of many late-eighteenth and early-nineteenth century figures from philosophy, literature, and the arts, whom we might appropriately call charismatic for their wide emblematic appeal to audiences in search of new meaning, Weber's view of charisma is focused almost exclusively on the realm of politics. Even though he makes frequent gestures at a longer historical sweep, his ideas inevitably reflect European politics in the upheaval of World War I and the dissolution of the German, Austro-Hungarian, and Russian empires. Even more crucially, he spends little time on the question of the relation of the charismatic individual to his audience and what needs such a figure serves in his admirers and followers. Political control and institutional change are his prime concern. Cultural figures like Rousseau or Goethe or Byron therefore play little role in his analysis.

But for the nineteenth century, the lengthening shadows of their artistic reputations helped shape and define how the extraordinary individual from any field presented himself and was seen in the public eye. As so often happens historically, cultural change preceded political and economic change in a manner at best occluded and at worst denied by the Marxist distinction between base and superstructure. It may be appropriate, though, that Weber should consider charisma as an issue in sociology, because in some sense it was a problem sociology had itself created by establishing the categories of normal and abnormal, by delineating insider and outside groups, and at its worst by turning these distinctions into hardened imperatives rather than fluid descriptions. Just as much of the analysis of nineteenth-century sociology diminished the variety of human nature by codifying its forms, so the concept of charisma attempts to restore something of its individual glory.

Artists and thinkers in fact have a somewhat different relation to charisma than do political figures. The international fame of the wise men, the rise of the charismatic writer, as well as the political and military ambitions of a Napoleon, also pose the larger question of whether charisma is more accurately an aspect of political nationalism as it developed in the nineteenth century or of internationalism—a question that seems to me to be a constant tension in the idea of charisma and a key to its complex usefulness as a historical divining rod.

Especially appropriate to a national and specifically a political context is Weber's concept of "routinizing charisma"—the way in which the changes wrought by the charismatic figure are absorbed into the day-to-day operations of the state after that figure has gone, or when the dust of his revolution has settled. But on the side of charisma as a force transcending locality and nation is the derivation of the term from saintly figures who were connected to a heavenly kingdom and to an international religion.[8] In their eighteenth-century secularized form, such individuals allowed their audiences to step outside the inherited localisms of their own culture and to protest against and even to oppose the hierarchies of the old monarchical system as well as the emerging new systems of national politics. This distinction might also be usefully phrased as the difference between *instrumental charisma*, whose persuasiveness translates into actions, especially political and military; and *intrinsic charisma*, which confers a nonstructural and ahistorical authority, embodied in performance and display, and focusing primarily on the self-enhancement of the audience.

Crucial to the changes that brought about this charismatic era were the US and French revolutions. They dethroned the central and almost exclusive ability of the hereditary monarch to promulgate and embody images of authority within the state, and replaced them with new images, often derived from a distant, romanticized past, where heroes and heroines walked the earth. In the French Revolution particularly, the idea of the republic of virtue and the attack on royal power contradicted the traditional ways of depicting authority.

An intriguing set of examples of the overlap between national and international charisma, as well as the interplay between its instrumental and intrinsic phases, can be found in Jacques-Louis David's portraits of Napoleon over the period of a decade or so at the start of the nineteenth century. In the first, *Napoleon Crossing the Alps*, painted in 1801, a young Napoleon sits astride a rearing horse.[9] Without actually holding the reins, in the midst of a driving wind, he is calm and in control. On the rocks beneath the horse's hooves are inscribed the names of previous great men who trod this path, like Charlemagne and Hannibal. David painted this work a year after the establishment of the Consulate—again the Roman analogy—and Napoleon's 1799 election as First Consul for ten years. Two years later, the Constitution confirmed Napoleon's political position for life, essentially establishing the right of one man to rule in the name of all—the emblematic figure who summarizes the aspirations of the nation, the megaself who rules for the multitude.

As it had with Cromwell, charisma entered history in a time of monarchical deflation and defeat. But notice as well how important nostalgia was in this construction of charisma, reaching over the immediate past to a host of ancient and canonized forerunners. When Cromwell came to power, his court painter was instructed to depict him "warts and all," not as a prettified ruler with a long genealogy but as he really was. As Marvell commented in his poem on the first year of Cromwell's rule, "to be Cromwell was a greater thing, / Than ought below, or yet above a king." Similarly, in the time of the French revolution, the idealized form of courtly painting was replaced with different ideals, drawn especially, as in the early paintings of David, from Roman history. Napoleon himself invoked both Roman figures and Joan of Arc as his forerunners, while toward the middle of the century, Napoleon III vainly attempted to duplicate his uncle's charisma by including the relics of Charlemagne in his throne, among other attempts to legitimize his power.

Five years or so after the first David painting of Napoleon rampant, grandly leading his troops in the footsteps of Hannibal and Charlemagne, came another, much larger and grander painting of a public event, *Napoleon's Coronation*, an occasion notorious for Napoleon's self-crowning, albeit in the presence of an acquiescent Pius VII. In the painting, however, David has downplayed Napoleon's explicit rejection of papal authority to choose instead the moment when he serenely confers the crown on Josephine.

So far, then, we have seen through the eyes of David: Napoleon as the young hero, calm before the elements, and Napoleon as the enthroned Emperor, as replete as any traditional monarch with the gold and jewels of office. But in 1812, a decade after *Napoleon Crossing the Alps*, David paints a still different Napoleon. This is not the hero or the general or the emperor, but the civil servant, the statesman, the lawgiver. Napoleon is in his study. Beside him is a guttering candle and a clock indicating a time after 4 AM. How hard at work he is for the benefit of the French nation! Considering a piece of paper in his hand labeled "Code," we can assume that work is on the Code Napoleon, in other words, not the work of revolution but the establishment of order and the continuity of law. Not quite routine, but certainly part of a process of codification and institutionalization.

* * *

In contrast to Marvell's jaundiced view of Charles I as a mere actor, the Napoleonic model of grand performance pervaded the atmosphere in the early nineteenth century.[10] Part of Napoleon's lesson, I would say, was to mix a transnational form of epic self-presentation with a dramatization of essential national character. It was a concoction that suited the times. In an analogous example from the visual arts, the English painter John Constable, from 1819 to 1825, painted six monumental landscapes of the Stour river area where he grew up. His critics and audiences praised him, especially for his ability to get at the essence of the English landscape and assert the Englishness of English art. From 1830 to 1832, five volumes of mezzotints based on Constable's paintings appeared that helped establish the area as a tourist mecca in a process that would be further helped by direct train access from London.[11] Meanwhile, in Germany Karl Baedeker launched his pioneering travel books, the first ones celebrating the Rhine landscape as the embodiment of the German "soul."[12] As sacred chrism would turn into secular charisma, pilgrimage was turning into tourism.

Once again, we should not miss the practical context that, together with the Romantic atmosphere, helped create many of these opportunities. Constable decided to paint such large paintings because in Royal Academy exhibitions, paintings covered the wall, around the room and from top to bottom. If you were not favored, you could be stuck below eye level or near the ceiling. The only exception was for a large painting, which had to be hung above a baseline in full view. Before these showings, Constable was over forty and had yet to make more than a marginal career from his painting. But when he showed what he called his "six-footers," he became famous. It was the atmosphere of the times. By a grand gesture, he had taken the public stage.

The style of the unique was in the air, especially in the arts. But although David's painting of Napoleon burning the midnight oil might be considered the routinizing of charisma, the more accurate formulation for his influence on personal assertions like Constable's might be making charisma into a routine, a vaudeville turn, which others could learn. Perhaps in public life, the routinizing of charisma is an obvious indication of progress, as disruption gives way to institutionalization. But what of the charisma that is created through art? Napoleon might be one benchmark of charisma, but he had to share the world with others who had, with a similar blend of instinct and premeditation, made themselves into household names. Byron especially was one whose achievements and personal story retained their grip on the European imagination. In 1855, thirty years after Byron's death, Matthew Arnold mourned him as one of the great figures of the early part of the century whose powers the present could not match. Byron, writes Arnold, bore "the pageant of his bleeding heart" from

England to Greece, while "thousands counted every groan, / And Europe made his woe her own." Even when seemingly defeated in their national aspirations—Byron wandering through Europe, Napoleon on Elba and St. Helena—each in exile further ensured his ethereal presence on an international stage as a consummate outsider. David may have portrayed the late Napoleon as the earnest civil servant burning the midnight oil, but one of Byron's favorite portraits was by Thomas Philips. Painted in 1813, it showed Byron dressed as an Albanian, looking away from the viewer, in a self-conscious embrace of the exotic.[13]

Illustration 11.1. In one of the frequent reproductions of Thomas Philips's portrait, Lord Byron, dressed in Albanian costume—although not in Albania—looks away from the viewer, into some visionary realm of personal transcendence.

Despite Weber's general lack of interest in the degree to which charisma might be constructed by its spectators, this pose of inspired separateness while in front of an audience was widespread in the attention-seeking performers in all spheres during the early nineteenth century, and with particular force and nuance in the great musical virtuosi. Interestingly enough in the history of the arts, it was painting that first separated from religious justifications for creativity to assert the individual artist's special relation to artistic truth. Literature followed not long after, while music, because of its expense and its more collective enterprise, lagged behind. But paradoxically, it was exactly the performance aspect of music, along with its greater portability across political and linguistic borders, which allowed it to surge ahead in the charisma races of the nineteenth century.

As one of the earliest freelance composer/performers, Ludwig van Beethoven stood athwart the change from a musical culture primarily fostered by court and clergy patronage to a more secular musical culture, no doubt favored and cosseted by the patrons of old, but hardly so exclusively. Franz Liszt, of course, was the great figure in this new world of charismatic performance. He was the virtuoso whose rapt audience clamored for rumors about his private life and collected his green silk gloves and his cigar butts as avidly as any religious devotee saves the relics of martyrdom. It was a frenzy Heinrich Heine called "Lisztomania," one of the earliest examples of the audience's desire to know more and more about the private life of the charismatic figure in an effort to ground his overwhelming appeal in some kind of common human nature.

But Liszt also emerged within a context of others, like Frédéric Chopin and Hector Berlioz, whose performing personas similarly mingled aspects of the great artist with backstage tales of private life. And let us not forget Niccolò Paganini, twenty to thirty years the elder of this group, who stressed the personal and improvisatory in his performances, even to the extent of keeping the violin parts secret from his accompanying orchestra until the moment of performance, much as Chuck Berry has spent a career going from town to town, picking up local backup bands, and laying on them the burden of keeping up with him no matter what he did.

Paganini did not invent the violin as a solo rather than a continuo instrument, but he certainly hammered the lesson home. And conducting existed before Berlioz, but he decisively helped to make it an authoritative interpretive technique. Liszt, although he performed often with orchestras, was the great forerunner of the piano recital, another example of the growing taste for individual self-display among artists and audiences alike.

But whether solo or in concert, some credit for what Liszt was able to do in dazzling his audiences should go to the advances in piano-making techniques that were the material setting for his virtuosity. The piano for which Haydn, Mozart, and for the most part Beethoven wrote was different from what might be called the Romantic piano. Haydn and Mozart, for example, used a five-octave piano. By 1821, seven-octave pianos were being made. Thicker strings, higher tension, and stronger construction helped set the stage for a more commanding sound to fill larger concert halls and appeal to larger audiences. At the same time, the demands of virtuosi for greater control and volume inspired new methods of construction. One technical innovation particularly intrigues me: the invention in 1821 by Sébastien Érard of what was called the "double escapement," which allowed a key to be played repeatedly even though it had not yet returned to an entirely vertical position. This was a quantum leap forward, one that permitted longer cantabile runs, lyrical legato lines, and complex fingerings that were part of the new performance style. Even so, the "new piano" was sometimes no match for the exalted ambitions of the rampant virtuoso. In a famous caricature of the 1840s, Liszt is depicted with four pianos on stage. As strings and pieces of wood fly into the air, he successively demolishes each piano in its turn as those that remain try to slink off the stage while still in one piece.[14]

* * *

What might be called the politics of charisma was especially notable in those countries—France and the United States—that the eighteenth-century democratic revolutions affected most directly and where the possibility of appealing to public opinion for cultural sanction and success, as well as the opportunity for joining the exalted ranks of the heroic, were most on the surface. Unencumbered by the overbearing mountain of monarchical fame, in which it was difficult to climb above your particular ledge, democratic and even semi-democratic societies promised the potential of upward movement, even to the summit. Once Napoleon and others had raised the banners of romantic heroism, however, the lure of greatness knew no political boundaries. As Henry Wadsworth Longfellow wrote in 1838 ("A Psalm of Life"),

> Lives of great men all remind us,
> we can make our lives sublime,
> and, departing, leave behind us,
> footprints on the sands of time.

Not long after, Thomas Carlyle, with his book *On Heroes, Hero-Worship, and the Heroic in History* (1840), and Ralph Waldo Emerson, in *Representative Men* (1850), tried to define some of the new possibilities by focusing on such figures as Napoleon and Cromwell, Dante and Shakespeare, Jesus and Mohammed. Similarly at mid century, a little over ten years after the invention of photography, Mathew Brady's *Gallery of Illustrious Americans* (1850) applied the new technology to what would become its prime journalistic use—the depiction of individuals. If Napoleon and Byron are the avatars of modern charisma, embodying on earth a heaven-sent aura of greatness, Carlyle and

Emerson are two of charisma's prime theorists and publicists. By attempting to codify the types of representative greatness, they struggle to revamp the older religious and monarchical charisma for a more democratic, constitutional, and secular society.

Despite their similar approaches to the question of the individual in history, the typologies of Carlyle and Emerson are somewhat different. Carlyle still emphasizes the charisma of political and military power, with an almost Hobbesian—and perhaps Weberian—sense of the need for a central figure of authority in the state. Emerson, by contrast, is more interested in the spiritual sanction charisma brings and is more sensitive to the tension between the individualist and the general side of the hero. Even more than Carlyle, he emphasizes the great man's lack of originality: "Great men are more distinguished by range and extent, than by originality ... The greatest genius is the most indebted man ... all originality is relative. Every thinker is retrospective."[15]

Essayists like Carlyle and Emerson, like the writers of multi-volume biographies, focused on the emblematic man, the embodiment of the general will, or the world soul on horseback (as Hegel called Napoleon at Jena). But it was nineteenth-century journalism that incessantly tallied the myriad celebrities of daily life, the minor league charismas of the moment. Not only generals, politicos, and actors, but also engineers, mathematicians, and inventors became emblematic—if not quite charismatic—figures of national aspiration in the nineteenth-century redefinition of greatness and recognition. In the United States, such figures often absorbed the imagery of the frontiersman, working at the edge of human knowledge and experience, but the explorer and adventurer were European fascinations as well. Nineteenth-century journalism was filled with such figures and their doings because of the narrowing communications gap between events and their reception. The War of 1812 was over for two weeks when the Battle of New Orleans was fought, a fact that did nothing to undermine Andrew Jackson's reputation. But with such advances as the uses of photography in the Crimean War (1854–1856) and the laying of the Atlantic Cable in the late 1850s, events and prominent individuals moved closer and closer to their audiences, and the construction of charisma became a more explicit undertaking. For all its seeming detachment from the norm, charisma in a thousand instances was shown to be a creation as well, and journalists in particular became adept at its manipulation as the century proceeded. Even more decisively, journalism became aware of its own role in conferring recognition, and journalists joined the celebrity throng as the anointed intermediaries between the famous and their audience, skilled in the arts of virtual presence.[16]

The many caricatured images of Liszt, like similar ones of other artists and public figures, emanating from the lower circles of charisma and self-display, emphasize as well the increasing nineteenth-century vogue for visually conveying and commenting upon public presence. In the eighteenth century, William

Hogarth had been instrumental in getting prints protected by copyright, but their cost still kept circulation down. As printing and papermaking techniques improved, however, the politics of popular portraiture became a crucial element in the dissemination of renown or, more often, notoriety. Hogarth is of course a forerunner of this style, but by the early decades of the nineteenth century, political satire and caricature by artists like James Gillray and George Cruikshank were reaching a larger and larger audience. New magazines and journals featuring such work became widely popular: in Paris, there were Charles Philipon's *La Caricature* in 1829 and *Le Charivari* in 1832, for which Honoré Daumier did most of his work. Its imitator in London was Henry Mayhew's *Punch, or the London Charivari* in 1841. Some years later, Thomas Nast began drawing for *Harper's Weekly* in 1862, while *Vanity Fair* began publishing in 1868.[17] Although unmentioned by Weber, both visual and verbal caricature were styles of constructing and critiquing charisma that intriguingly embody his formula that the charismatic figure "bypass[es] traditional routes of authority." Satire and panegyric often march together in the politics of visual culture, idealizing your political and cultural friends while caricaturing your enemies. Napoleon's grandiose propaganda and Gillray's caricatures of Napo-

Illustration 11.2. One of James Gillray's many satiric political prints, "The Plum-Pudding in Danger" (1805), shows the two "state epicures"—Napoleon, usually referred to by British satirists as "Boney" and William Pitt—dividing the world after Napoleon's recent political overtures toward detente.

leon were contemporaneous. But the agency here was in the audience, not the individual, and monarchical power was not exempt from its critique, as shown by Philipon's famous 1831 caricature of the four steps needed to turn Louis-Philippe into a pear. This image aptly demonstrated the pseudo-charisma of the "bourgeois monarch" as well as the emptiness of all inherited power.[18]

I certainly do not want to underplay the important role of photography in the creation and dissemination of public recognition, but I pause for a moment on the significance of graphic caricature because it will not be until much later in the century that printing processes will have advanced enough that photographs will be a common element in newspapers and magazines. For most of the century, wood engravings and drawings were the illustrations that accompanied news articles, even when the source was a photograph, as in the coverage of the Crimean War and the US Civil War.[19]

After the photographic carte de visite helped promote such figures as Jenny Lind, Lola Montez, and Abraham Lincoln to a wider public, caricature still played a crucial role in the establishment of a visual presence for both the transient and the more long-lasting of celebrities, as it continues to do today through such venues as editorial cartoons and *Mad* magazine. Caricature, with its bias toward mockery, in fact makes an intriguing complement to photography, with its implicit claim to represent reality itself. The common element in both, however, is the emphasis on the visible self as a central element in recognition and fame.[20]

All of this brings me back to charisma proper. In speaking of the power of exile to enhance the figures of Byron and Napoleon, I allude to another significant strand in the construction of charisma in this first century of mass culture—and that is the stress of many artists (in contrast with most politicians or other public men) on the element of reticence or resistance in their self-presentations. Already in his portrait of Napoleon, Carlyle warns against what he calls "lionism," the turning of an authentic hero into a mere celebrity, the excessive playing to the crowds, the possibility of being ensnared and distorted by one's own audience. The tension between assertion and evasion is therefore a nineteenth-century constant, especially for artists; for every Byron there is a Keats, for every George Sand or Sarah Bernhardt, an Emily Dickinson or a Charlotte Brontë.

Both reticence and resistance are therefore explicit responses to the onrushing commercial culture of the nineteenth century, with its emphasis on the commodification of practically everything, in particular, the human image. Unlike the assertive monarchical object that stares back at you, subordinating the viewer to its presence, the charismatic figure often looks away toward another reality, inviting the viewer to follow in the quest. Whether it is John Keats saying that he wishes his tombstone to read, "Here lies one whose name is writ on water," whether it is the urge to anonymity and detachment in a figure

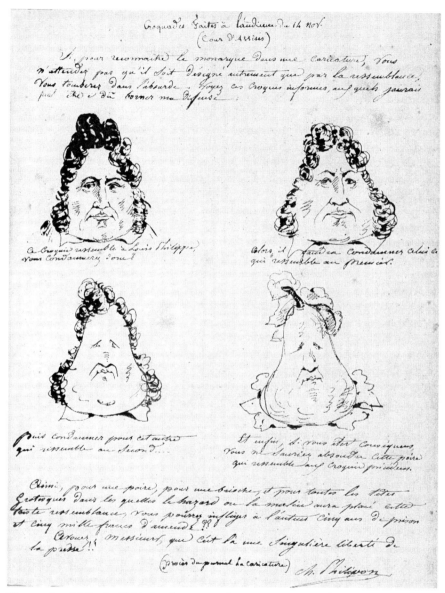

Illustration 11.3. In 1831, *La Caricature*, the pioneering French satiric journal, published its editor Charles Philipon's image of the new King Louis-Philippe as a pear—an image that became widespread shorthand for the inadequacies of his reign. After being imprisoned for his transgression, Philipon wrote: "Nous avons le droit de personnifer le pouvoir! ... [T]outes les ressemblances nous appartiennent!" (I have every right to give political power a human face. All these likenesses belong to me!)

like Charles Baudelaire's "painter of modern life," or the starving, unappreciated artist of *la vie bohème*—each of these poses, sincere or artificial, in their different ways both reject and are shaped by the juggernaut of nineteenth-century commercial culture.

All types of public recognition hold out the promise of freedom and an enhanced sense of identity. The growing consumer society of the nineteenth century, I would argue, was the crucible within which the classical idea of fame before an immediate audience merged with the spiritual idea of fame before God, posterity, or some other invisible audience. The more stress the nineteenth century placed on rational and legal authority, the more charisma and fame, along with their stepchild celebrity, became critical elements in politics and culture. As a complex, urbanized world of increasing numbers of other people simultaneously widened the opportunity for making your mark and narrowed it by dint of sheer numbers, individuals in varying ways exploited the new media resources on the way to their goals. Celebrity embraces immediacy; fame climbs to the less time-bound realms of honor and glory; charisma, most paradoxically, often seems to look away from the audience, defining itself as a rejection or transcendence of the norms that characterize mass society, even while it seeks to carry that audience along with it.

In this account of the central place of the audience for public performance, the rise of advertising also plays a crucial role in the metamorphoses of charisma, especially when disposable income began to rise in Europe and the US in the late nineteenth century. Testimonials had been used for two hundred years and more, particularly in the promotion of patent medicines. In the early days, the endorser was an (supposedly) ordinary person who had been helped by the product, while later advertisers introduced the upper-class endorser, whose social status presumably implied greater sway and perhaps even truth.[21] But with the more extensive ad space allowed by half-tone engraving, the images of people who might lend their prestige to a product began to populate the pages of magazines and newspapers. Sometimes the approach was direct: in 1884, the popular US minister Henry Ward Beecher made a ringing endorsement of Pears soap (a pioneer in the endorsement field), by playing on the proverbial connection between cleanliness and godliness. Sometimes the endorsement was more demure or oblique, as when Sarah Bernhardt appeared costumed in a famous role within an ad for face powder or tea. Sometimes the nominal endorser made no overt connection with the product at all, as in the torrent of ads for a variety of products during the Jubilee year of 1887 that featured Queen Victoria.[22]

With varying elements of assertion and denial, the commodity took on the allure of the charismatic person, while the famous but perhaps not so charismatic person began to absorb an aura from the familiar product. The symbolic allure of the solitary poet in the garret turning away from the present and writing for posterity, as well as that of the nineteenth-century Great Man and (occasional) Great Woman grandly posing in front of an audience, then, were parallel responses to the flattening effect of mass society on individual aspiration, in a world where traditional definitions of hierarchy were under constant threat. The Europe-wide cult of the medieval in the nineteenth century similarly shows this double aspect: on the one hand, it admires the deeds and characters of the great knights of the past, Lancelot, Gawain, and others; on the other hand, as in the work of William Morris, it emphasizes the collective arts to counterbalance the cult of the individual artist.

One result of this conflict or interplay between the grand public figure and the adoring but fickle audience, which we can still see plainly in our own day, is the diluting of charisma into celebrity. As journalism and the media generally widen the occasion to admire the charismatic, they also promise a vicarious participation in the processes of charisma creation: buy the product, read the magazine, and you too can absorb some scrap of charisma into yourself. In the modern age, Walter Benjamin argues, the aura of the object withers when it can be reproduced in an endless series of simulacra—a process he applauds because it opens the sacred object to critique and democratic access. Benjamin's view—that photography and cinema are the prime agents of this draining of unique meaning in the art object—accords nicely with the way the technology of image-making simultaneously allows a greater scope for charisma to impose upon its audience, even while it dilutes the essence of what it means to be charismatic. For Weber as well, the deterioration and routinizing of charisma is somewhat of a relief, since it is regularized in the necessary process of institution building—a welcome return to normality after an era of disruption.

Terms like charisma and aura themselves have a kind of instrumental vagueness. Historians of ideas can argue what Weber or Benjamin meant by them, but their utility is in their sweep and how they are applied, not necessarily in what their originators may have meant by them. Cultural historians try to bridge a relation between the facts of a situation and the less tangible and less quantifiable emotional currents of their world. On one side are the archives, the magazines, the constructors of charisma who could sense the new moment and tried to meet it as best they could. On the other are the emotions of the situations—why audiences responded to such figures.[23]

We usually think of facts as being inert without interpretation. But they are also inert without some sense of the cultural and emotional atmosphere in which they appear. I have suggested here a relationship between charisma and a nineteenth-century nationalism that stressed its own ethnocentric and affective roots. Such a national political charisma might be said to have ended with Hitler and Mussolini, at least in Europe. But of course there are other versions.

Roosevelt and Churchill had charisma—and what of the charisma of the ordinary, like that supposedly embodied by George W. Bush, the guy you could sit down with and have a beer?

With the collapse of the studio system and the end of the European totalitarian regimes, along with the rise of television and the Internet, we are awash in petty charismas of all sorts. I would hesitate to call the present moment post-charismatic. That seems impossible in a media world where charisma or its simulation plays such a central part in politics and culture. But we may be in a neocharismatic phase. The public confrontation a few years ago between Sumner Redstone, the owner of Viacom, and the mega-movie star Tom Cruise is intriguing in this way. The ostensible reason for Redstone's canceling a fourteen-year-old contract with Cruise's production company was the actor's antics on Oprah Winfrey's television show, which Redstone claimed to have resulted in a loss of between $100 and $150 million worldwide for the movie *Mission Impossible 3*. But Redstone also invoked a larger reason: stars do not open films the way they used to. In other words, their charisma does not directly translate into dollars in the old way, just as George W. Bush with a beer did not translate into military or political effectiveness for a growing majority of his audience.[24]

Charisma began as a protest against business (and power) as usual. It was an anti-commodity that invoked more spiritual and less tangible standards of value that nevertheless quickly became a commodity itself. Perhaps, in some Gresham's law of culture, bad charisma, perfunctory charisma, always drives out good. To entitle a book *Constructing Charisma* deftly exposes these and other paradoxes with an oxymoronic scalpel.

❧ NOTES ☙

Introduction

1. This book stems from a conference jointly sponsored by NYU's Institute of French Studies and Rutgers University Newark's Department of History. Leo Braudy, whose contribution serves as the volume's conclusion, gave the keynote address. Our authors represent five academic disciplines: art history, English (2), French (2), history (5), and musicology.
2. On hero worship in the nineteenth century, see Geoffrey Cubitt and Allen Warren, *Heroic Reputations and Exemplary Lives* (Manchester: Manchester University Press, 2000).
3. Paul Starr, *The Creation of the Media. Political Origins of Modern Communications* (New York, 2004), 35–41.
4. See Wolfgang J. Mommsen, "Max Weber's 'Grand Sociology.' The Origins and Composition of *Wirtschaft und Gesellschaft Soziologie,*" in *Max Weber's Economy and Society: A Critical Companion*, ed. Charles Camic, Philip S. Gorski, and David M. Trubek (Stanford, CA, 2005), 86–92 (70–97).
5. Max Weber, *Economy and Society: an Outline of Interpretive Sociology*, ed. Guenther Roth and Claus Wittich, 2 vols. (Berkeley and Los Angeles, 1978), 1:241.
6. Weber, *Economy and Society*, 1:242.
7. William H. Friedland, "For a Sociological Concept of Charisma," *Social Forces* 43, no. 1 (Oct., 1964): 18–26.
8. Charles Camic, "Charisma, Its Varieties, Preconditions, and Consequences," *Sociological Inquiry* 50, no. 1 (1980): 7–8.
9. Weber, *Economy and Society*, 1:399–401.
10. Weber, *Economy and Society*, 2:1116, 1:245.
11. Weber, *Economy and Society*, 1:242.
12. The most recent biography, Tim Jeal's, *Stanley. The Impossible Life of Africa's Greatest Explorer* (New Haven, 2007), argues, among other things, that Stanley did not actually utter the words, "Dr. Livingstone, I presume?"
13. Leo Braudy, *The Frenzy of Renown. Fame and its History* (New York, 1986), 32–40.
14. Braudy, *Frenzy*, 56.
15. Braudy, *Frenzy*, 117.
16. Braudy, *Frenzy*, 121.
17. Weber, *Economy and Society*, 2:1135–1141.
18. Weber, *Economy and Society*, 2:1146.
19. Weber, *Economy and Society*, 2:1148. Weber adds, "In times of great public excitement, charismatic leaders may emerge even in solidly bureaucratized situations ... [but] only

extraordinary conditions can bring about the triumph of charisma over the organization." (2:1132).

20. John B. Thompson, *The Media and Modernity: A Social Theory of the Media* (Stanford, 1995), examines the "intimacy at a distance" created by mass media, as does Richard Schickel, *Intimate Strangers: The Culture of Celebrity* (New York, 1985).

21. Braudy, *Frenzy*, part V.

22. On Lueger as charismatic figure, see Carl E. Schorske, *Fin-de-Siècle Vienna: Politics and Culture* (New York: Knopf, 1980), ch. 3. "*Der schöne Karl*," Schorske writes, "commanded that fine, almost dandyish presence which, as Baudelaire observed, arises as an effective attribute of political leadership in 'periods of transition when democracy is not yet all-powerful and aristocracy is only partially tottering.' His elegant, almost cool manner demanded deference from the masses, while his capacity to speak to them in Vienna's warm folk dialect won their hearts."

23. Paul Gerbod, "L'éthique héroïque en France (1870–1914)," *La Revue historique* 268 (1982): 409–429; Christian Amalvi, *Les héros de l'histoire de France* (Paris, 1979); Jean-François Chanet, "La Fabrique des héros: Pédagogie républicaine et culte des grands hommes de Sedan à Vichy," *Vingtième Siècle* 65 (January–March 2000): 13–34.

24. Dana Gooley, *The Virtuoso Liszt* (Cambridge, UK, 2004), ch. 3.

25. Gooley, *Virtuoso Liszt*, 133.

26. David S. Meyer and Joshua Gamson, "The Challenge of Cultural Elites: Celebrities and Social Movements," *Sociological Inquiry* 65, no. 2 (May 1995): 181–206.

27. Braudy, *Frenzy*, 381.

28. On hot and cool, see Marshall McLuhan, *Understanding Media* (New York, 1966).

29. Braudy, *Frenzy*, 380–382. For Braudy's comparison of Franklin and Rousseau, see 371–380. See also, "Reading Rousseau," in Robert Darnton, *The Great Cat Massacre and Other Episodes in French Cultural History* (New York, 1983).

30. Braudy, *Frenzy*, 371–380.

31. Weber, *Economy and Society*, 1:242.

32. Schorske, *Fin-de-Siècle Vienna*, ch. 3.

33. Weber's most prominent US commentator, Edward Shils, took this point to its ultimate conclusion, namely, that celebrated, charismatic people embody collective goals and norms. Charisma thus stems from an individual's ability to exemplify the aspirations and beliefs already held by his or her audience. The anthropologist James Scott gives another twist to this idea, arguing that subjected populations possess "hidden transcripts" not readily audible to elites. For Scott, the charismatic leader arises out of this context, verbalizing openly, and apparently radically, what the disenfranchised are already saying in their hidden transcripts. In each of these cases, the charismatic figure is persuasive precisely because he or she manages to perceive an existing *Zeitgeist* awaiting form and expression. See Edward Shils, *Center and Periphery. Essays in Macrosociology* (Chicago, 1975), 6, 7, 15, and 21; James C. Scott, *Domination and the Arts of Resistance: Hidden transcripts* (New Haven, 1990).

34. Thompson, *Media and Modernity*, 197, 207–208, 219–225.

35. Eric Hobsbawm and Terence Ranger, ed., *The Invention of Tradition* (Cambridge, UK, 1992), esp. ch. 4.

36. Leonore Davidoff and Catherine Hall, *Family Fortunes: Men and Women of the English Middle Class, 1780–1850* (Chicago, 1987); Philippe Ariès and Georges Duby, ed., *A History of Private Life*, vol. 4 (Cambridge, MA, 1987); Bonnie G. Smith, *Ladies of the*

Leisure Class: The Bourgeoises of Northern France in the Nineteenth Century (Princeton, 1981).

37. Mary Louise Roberts, *Disruptive Acts. The New Woman in Fin-de-Siècle France* (Chicago, 2002); Lenard R. Berlanstein, *Daughters of Eve: a Cultural History of French Theater Women from the Old Regime to the Fin de Siècle* (Cambridge, MA, 2001).
38. See Susan A. Glenn, *The Female Spectacle: The Theatrical Roots of Modern Feminism* (Cambridge, MA, 2000).
39. Susan Grogan, "'Playing the Princess': Flora Tristan, Performance, and Female Moral Authority during the July Monarchy," in *The New Biography: Performing Femininity in Nineteenth-Century France,* ed. Jo Burr Margadant (Berkeley and Los Angeles, 2000); Flora Tristan, *Le tour de France: état actuel de la classe ouvrière sous l'aspect moral, intellectuel et matériel* (Paris, 1980); Margaret Talbot, "An Emancipated Voice: Flora Tristan and Utopian Allegory," *Feminist Studies* 17, no. 2 (Summer 1991).
40. Elaine Showalter, *Sexual Anarchy: Gender and Culture at the Fin-de-siècle* (New York, 1990); Judith Surkis, *Sexing the citizen: Morality and Masculinity in France, 1870–1920* (Ithaca, NY, 2006); Annelise Maugue, *L'identité masculine en crise au tournant du siècle, 1871–1914* (Paris, 1987).
41. Daniel Boorstein famously described celebrities as people "known for [their] well-knownness." See Boorstein, *The Image. A Guide to Pseudo-Events in America* (New York, 1961), 57.

Chapter 1

1. Adam Hochschild, *King Leopold's Ghost* (New York, 1998).
2. The philosopher Stephen Turner recently noted the use of "charisma" as the stage name of a movie star (Charisma Carpenter), and on the doorplates of a German modeling agency, a British record company, and a Florida hairdressing salon. See Stephen Turner, "Charisma Reconsidered," *Journal of Classical Sociology* 3, no. 1 (2003): 6.
3. Stephen Turner, "Charisma and Obedience: A Risk Cognition Approach," *Leadership Quarterly* 4, no. 3–4 (1993): 237–240. See also Philip Reiff, *Charisma: The Gift of Grace and How It has Been Taken Away from Us* (New York, 2007).
4. Max Weber, *Economy and Society: an Outline of Interpretive Sociology,* ed. Guenther Roth and Claus Wittich, 2 vols. (Berkeley and Los Angeles, 1978), 1:244.
5. For a skeptical view of the term, see K.J. Ratman, "Charisma and Political Leadership," *Political Studies* 12: 341–354.
6. Charles Camic, "Charisma: Its Varieties, Preconditions, and Consequences." *Sociological Inquiry* 50 (1980): 12–13; David Rapaport, *The Collected Papers of David Rapaport* (New York, 1967).
7. Turner, "Charisma and Obedience," 245.
8. Turner, "Charisma and Obedience," 246–247.
9. David S. Meyer and Joshua Gamson, "The Challenge of Cultural Elites: Celebrities and Social Movements," *Sociological Inquiry* 65, no. 2 (May 1995): 181–206.
10. Weber, *Economy and Society,* 2:1117.
11. This and the following paragraphs summarize Jaak Panksepp, *Affective Neuroscience: The Foundations of Human and Animal Emotions* (New York, 2004), 51–55 and passim.
12. Panksepp, *Affective Neuroscience,* 52.

13. Panksepp, *Affective Neuroscience*, 53.
14. Weber appears to have developed his ideas about charisma during the second decade of the twentieth century, perhaps between 1912 and 1914. The chapters in which he elaborates them constitute one of the few fully completed sections of his great post-humously published work, *Economy and Society*. See Wolfgang J. Mommsen, "Max Weber's 'Grand Sociology.' The Origins and Composition of *Wirtschaft und Gesellschaft Soziologie*," in *Max Weber's Economy and Society: A Critical Companion*, ed. Charles Camic, Philip S. Gorski, and David M Trubek (Stanford, CA, 2005), 86–92 (70–97).
15. On the "new journalism" and the mass press, see John B. Thompson, *The Media and Modernity. A Social Theory of the Media* (Stanford, 1995); Jean-Pierre Rioux and Jean-François Sirinelli, *La culture de masse en France de la Belle Epoque à aujourd'hui* (Paris, 2002); Mark Hampton, *Visions of the Press in Britain, 1850–1950* (Urbana and Chicago, 2004); Aled Jones, *Powers of the Press: Newspapers, Power and the Public in Nineteenth-Century England* (Aldershot, UK, 1996); C. John Sommerville, *The News Revolution in England* (New York, 1996); George Boyce, James Curran, and Pauline Wingate, *Newspaper History. From the seventeenth Century to the Present Day* (London, 1978); Joel H. Wiener, ed., *Papers for the Millions. The New Journalism in Britain, 1850s to 1914* (New York, 1988); Alan J. Lee, *The Origins of the Popular Press in England, 1855–1914* (London, 1976); Lucy Brown, *Victorian News and Newspapers* (Oxford, 1985); Claude Bellanger, et al, *Histoire générale de la presse française*, 3 vols. (Paris, 1969); Thomas Ferenczi, *L'Invention du journalism en France* (Paris, 1993); Bernard Voyenne, *Les Journalistes français* (Paris, 1985); Marc Martin, *Médias et journalistes de la République* (Paris, 1997); Jean-Yves Mollier, *La lecture et ses publics à l'époque contemporaine* (Paris, 2001); Dominique Kalifa, *L'Encre et le sang: Récits de crimes et société à la Belle Epoque* (Paris, 1995); Michael B. Palmer, *Des petits journaux aux grandes agences* (Paris, 1983); Vanessa R. Schwartz, *Spectacular Realities. Early Mass Culture in Fin-de-Siècle Paris* (Berkeley, 1998), ch. 1; For the United States, see Michael Schudson, *Discovering the News. A Social History of American Newspapers* (New York, 1978); Dan Schiller, *Objectivity and the News. The Public and the Rise of Commercial Journalism* (Philadelphia, 1981).
16. James Gordon Bennett, the *New York Herald's* founding editor, is credited with conducting the first interview in the 1840s. The British journalist and editor of the *Pall Mall Gazette*, William T. Stead, popularized the interview in the 1880s, and Emile Zola, among others, complained of its effects. "Whenever the smallest event occurs," he said, "dozens of interviewers congregate at my door … and I can't get anything done." ("Zola interviewé sur l'interview," *Le Figaro*, 12 January 1893).
17. Anne-Marie Thiesse, *Le Roman du quotidien. Lecteurs et lectures populaires à la Belle Epoque* (Paris, 1984).
18. Daniel J. Boorstein, *The Image. A Guide to Pseudo-Events in America* (New York, 1961), 57. Joshua Gamson, *Claims to Fame. Celebrity in Contemporary America* (Berkeley and Los Angeles, 1994), rightly argues that analysts of celebrity have generally made too much of this distinction.
19. Weber, *Economy and Society*, 2:1116, 1134.
20. Though Brazza published far less than either Stanley or Lyautey, the media trumpeted his trials and tribulations and framed his work as wondrous, meaningful, and great.
21. On this crowd phenomenon, see Gregory Shaya, "The *Flâneur*, the *Badaud*, and the Making of a Mass Public in France, circa 1860–1910," *American Historical Review* 109, no. 1 (February 2004): 41–77.

22. Weber discusses the appropriation of charisma by traditional and bureaucratic leaders in a section of *Economy and Society* entitled, "The Charismatic Legitimation of the Existing Order."
23. Elaine Showalter, *Sexual Anarchy. Gender and Culture at the Fin-de-Siècle* (New York, 1990); Leo Braudy, *From Chivalry to Terrorism. War and the Changing Nature of Masculinity* (New York, 2003); George L. Mosse, *The Image of Man. The Creation of Modern Masculinity* (New York, 1996), 78–82; John Tosh, *Manliness and Masculinities in Nineteenth-Century Britain. Essays on Gender, Family and Empire* (London, 2005).
24. Anne-Emmanuelle Demartini and Dominique Kalifa, *Imaginaire et sensibilités au XIXe siècle: études pour Alain Corbin* (Paris, 2005).
25. Sylvain Venayre, *La gloire de l'aventure* (Paris, 2002); Showalter, *Sexual Anarchy*, 79ff.; Tosh, *Manliness*, 199–201.
26. John M. MacKenzie, "Heroic Myths of Empire," in *Popular Imperialism and the Military*, ed. John M. MacKenzie (Manchester, 1992); Allen J. Frantzen, *Bloody Good. Chivalry, Sacrifice, and the Great War* (Chicago, 2004).
27. Quoted in John Bierman, *Dark Safari. The Life Behind the Legend of Henry Morton Stanley* (New York, 1990), 127.
28. Jean Stengers, "L'Impérialisme colonial de la fin du xix siècle: Mythe ou réalité," *Journal of African History* 3, no. 3 (1962): 489.
29. *Illustrated London News*, 10 May 1890.
30. Felix Driver, "Stanley and His Critics: Geography, Exploration, and Empire," *Past & Present* 133 (1991): 134.
31. Frank McLynn, *Stanley, Sorcerer's Apprentice* (London, 1991), 319.
32. Musée Royale de l'Afrique Centrale, Tervuren, Belgium. (Hereafter MRAC, SA) Stanley Archives, 2264–2452, Momt to Stanley, 25 March 1890.
33. MRAC, SA, 2264-2452, Burcombe to Stanley, 3 July 1890.
34. Quoted in Edward Marston, *How Stanley Wrote In Darkest Africa*, (London, 1890), 53.
35. On this point and the question of "sub-imperialism" in general, see John Darwin, "Imperialism and the Victorians: The Dynamics of Territorial Expansion," *English Historical Review* 112, no. 447 (June, 1997): 638. See also, J.S. Galbraith, *Mackinnon and East Africa* (Cambridge, 1976).
36. Catherine Hall and Leonore Davidoff, *Family Fortunes: Men and Women of the English Middle Class, 1780–1850* (Chicago, 1987); John Tosh, *A Man's Place. Masculinity and the Middle-Class Home in Victorian England* (New Haven, 1999).
37. Christopher Lasch, *Haven in a Heartless World* (New York, 1977).
38. Duncan Bell, *The Idea of Greater Britain: Empire and Future of World Order, 1860–1900* (Princeton, 2007), 35.
39. Bell, *Idea of Greater Britain*, 37. Labillière was Honorary Secretary of the Imperial Federation League.
40. J.A. Mangan, *The Games Ethic and Imperialism* (London, 1998), 18.
41. *Edinburgh Review*, October 1890, 372.
42. *Queen, the Lady's Newspaper*, 8 February 1890.
43. Driver, "Stanley and His Critics," 138.
44. Tosh, *Manliness*, 112–113.
45. Tim Jeal's recent biography, *Stanley. The Impossible Life of Africa's Greatest Explorer* (New Haven, 2007), argues that Stanley exaggerated the violence of his voyages of exploration to satisfy readers eager for blood and gore. In reality, Jeal says, Stanley was no more violent than most other explorers.

46. Driver, "Stanley and His Critics," 150.

47. Bierman, *Dark Safari,* ch. 26.

48. G. Froment-Guieysse, *Brazza* (Paris, 1945), 90.

49. Schwartz, *Spectacular Realities,* 133–134.

50. Schwartz, *Spectacular Realities,* ch. 3.

51. Richard West, *Brazza of the Congo. European Exploration and Exploitation in French Equatorial Africa* (Newton Abbot, 1973), 124.

52. West, *Brazza.*

53. Charles de Chavannes, *Avec Brazza* (Paris, 1935), 14–15.

54. Centre d'Archives d'Outre-Mer, Aix-en-Provence (CAOM), Fonds Brazza PA 16/VII, Carton 12. Brazza scrupulously saved his correspondence, which, until the 1960s, the family kept in a private archive.

55. A. Berthet, CAOM, Fonds Brazza PA 16/VII, Carton 12.

56. Thompson, *Media and Modernity,* 219.

57. Ferry to G. de Courcel, 1 Dec 1884, quoted in Andrew, "Centre and Periphery," 20.

58. 4 October 1905.

59. *Le Figaro,* 18 December 1907.

60. 22 July 1906.

61. 19 May 1904.

62. Thompson, *Media and Modernity,* 219.

63. 475 AP/110. Lyautey had his secretary number most letters.

64. Ibid., G. Vallières to Lyautey, 29 April 1912, letter 438.

65. Ibid. See, for example, letters 13 and 167.

66. Ibid., letter 63. Roger Lusanne, 28 April 1912.

67. Ibid., letters 62, 63, and an unnumbered letter of 28 April 1912, whose signature is illegible.

68. Ibid., Roger de Salvery to Lyautey, 28 April 1912, unnumbered.

69. Ibid., letter 450, Charles Hollot to Lyautey, 2 May 1912. Or letter 218, 5 May 1912.

70. Ibid., letter 23. P. Michel to Lyautey, 30 April 1912.

71. Eugen Weber, *The Nationalist Revival in France* (Berkeley, 1959).

72. 18 October 1912.

73. Marshall McLuhan, *Understanding Media: The Extensions of Man* (New York, 1964).

74. Edward Shils, "Charisma, Order, and Status," *American Sociological Review* 30, no. 2 (April 1965): 201 (199–213).

Chapter 2

1. Geheimes Staatsarchiv Preussischer Kulturbesitz (hereafter GStA PK), I HA Rep. 89 Nr. 2318, Nicolaas K. v. Cammenga to Wilhelm I, 13 June 1876, Blatt 172. See a similar sentiment expressed in: GStA PK, I HA Rep. 89 Nr. 2319, Christian Zwingauer to Wilhelm I, 29 May 1884, Blatt 94-95.

2. I borrow the phrase from Leo Braudy, *The Frenzy of Renown: Fame and its History* (Oxford, 1986).

3. Max Weber, *Economy and Society: an Outline of Interpretive Sociology,* ed. Guenther Roth and Claus Wittich, 2 vols. (Berkeley and Los Angeles, 1978), 2:1133–1141, 1146–1148, and more generally "Chapter XIV: Charisma and its Transformation," 2:1111–1157.

4. David Cannadine, "The Context, Performance and Meaning of Ritual: The British Monarchy and the 'Invention of Tradition,' c. 1820–1977," in *The Invention of Tradition*, ed. Eric Hobsbawm and Terence Ranger (Cambridge, 1983).

5. See, for instance: Klaus-D. Pohl, "Der Kaiser im Zeitalter seiner technischen Reproduzierbarkeit: Wilhelm II. in Fotographie und Film," in *Der Letzte Kaiser: Wilhelm II im Exil*, ed. Hans Wilderotter und Klaus-D. Pohl (Gütersloh/Munich, 1991), 10; Ursula Peters, "Aufklärung, Volksbildung oder Herrschaftsstrategie? Die Prominenz im Sammelfoto," *Fotogeschichte* 3, no. 9 (1983): 21–40. For Benjamin's original formulation, see Walter Benjamin, "The Work of Art in the Age of Mechanical Reproduction," in *Iluminations: Essays and Reflections*, ed. Harry Zohn (New York, 1968).

6. See the pathbreaking work of Norbert Elias, *The Court Society*, trans. Edmund Jephcott (Oxford, 1983). For the German states in particular, see Andreas Gestrich, *Absolutismus und Öffentlichkeit. Politische Kommunikation in Deutschland zu Beginn des 18. Jahrhunderts* (Göttingen, 1994).

7. See, among others: letter number 104, to Luise's mother-in-law, Königinwitwe Friederike, 9 June 1798, and letter number 103, to her brother Georg, 4 June 1798, in Luise, Königin von Preussen, *Briefe und Aufzeichnungen, 1786–1810*, ed. Malve Gräfin Rothkirch (München, 1985), 137–138.

8. Robert Dohme, *Unter fünf preussischen Königen: Lebenserinnerungen*, ed. Paul Lindenberg (Berlin, 1901), 39–41; Louis Schneider, *Aus meinem Leben*, 3 vols. (Berlin, 1879–1880), 3:112–120.

9. Emil Frommel, "Erinnerungen an Kaiser Wilhelm I. und Gastein," *Der Bär* 17 (1890–1891): 392, 404.

10. Paul Lindenberg, *Berlin*, 5 vols. (Leipzig, 1886), 5:35.

11. See the section on "Der Kaiser in Berlin," in *Berlin und die Berliner: Leute, Dinge, Sitten, Winke* (Karlsruhe, 1905), 293–302.

12. GStA PK, I HA Rep. 89 Nr. 2792, Präsident des Reichskanzleramts to Wilmowski, 3 September 1878, Blatt 31a.

13. Adolf Streckfuß, *Berlin im 19. Jahrhundert*, 3 vols. (Berlin, 1868), 1:30–31; Adolf Streckfuß, *Vom Fischerdorf zur Weltstadt. Berlin seit 500 Jahren, Geschichte und Sage*, 4 vols. (Berlin, 1864), 4:168.

14. For two recent contributions to the field of consumer culture in Wilhelmine Germany, see Dirk Reinhardt, *Von der Reklame zum Marketing: Geschichte der Wirtschaftswerbung in Deutschland* (Berlin, 1993); David D. Hamlin, *Work and Play: the Production and Consumption of Toys in Germany, 1870–1914* (Ann Arbor, 2007).

15. The topic of royal relics and manuscripts on the collectibles market will be treated in depth in the author's forthcoming book, *Monarchy, Myth, and Material Culture in Germany 1750–1950* (Cambridge, forthcoming 2010).

16. See the prices of such objects in the trade journal *Der Sammler*, 1879–1914.

17. Jules Laforgue, *Berlin: the City and the Court*, trans. William Jay Smith (New York, 1996), 49–50, 166, 190; Julius Aufseesser, *Aus meinem Sammlerleben* (Berlin, 1926), 14–15; Hans Wachenhusen, *Berliner Photographien*, 2 vols. (Berlin, 1867), 2:106–112.

18. M.A.E. Nickson, *Early Autograph Albums in the British Museum* (London, 1970); Günther Mecklenburg, *Vom Autographensammeln. Versuch einer Darstellung seines Wesens und seiner Geschichte im deutschen Sprachgebiet* (Marburg, 1963); Alfred Fiedler, *Vom Stammbuch zum Poesiealbum: eine volkstümliche Studie* (Weimar, 1960).

19. For Longfellow, Poe, and others, see A.M. Broadley, *Chats on Autographs* (New York, 1910), 40.

20. Brandenburgisches-Preussisches Hausarchiv (hereafter BPH), Rep. 113, Nr. 1170, correspondence between Hermann Zeiner and Eulenburg, January 1907, Blatt 223–224; GStA PK, I HA Rep. 81, Gesandtschaft München, Nr. 11, Bülow to the königliche Gesandtschaft zu München, 24 February 1879, section 1 (unpaginated).
21. Schneider, *Aus meinem Leben*, 1:134–136.
22. GStA PK, I HA Rep. 89 Nr. 2792, Bülow to Wilhelm I, 31 March 1878, Blatt 29–30.
23. GStA PK, I HA Rep. 89 Nr. 2792, correspondence between Wilmowski and Wesdehlen, 21 February to 1 March 1883, Blatt 46–47. Eugen Ritter von Mor, "Das Autographensammeln," *Der Sammler* 9 (1887): 128–133.
24. Mecklenburg, *Autographensammeln*, 14; Broadley, *Chats*, 62.
25. M.M., "Kaiser und Gratulant," *Der Bär* 20 (1893–1894): 51.
26. This was true regarding other famous statesmen as well. Bismarck felt plagued by the "massive numbers" of autograph requests he had to field, inducing him to develop a "hatred" for autograph seekers and the "modern sickness" of autograph hunting. Adolph Kohut, *Bismarck als Mensch* (Berlin, 1899), 166.
27. See examples in: GStA PK, I HA Rep. 89 Nr. 2792, Bülow to Wilhelm I, 31 March 1878, Blatt 29–30; Wilmowski to Wesdehlen, 21 February 1883, Blatt 46; GStA PK, I HA Rep. 89 Nr. 2792, Anders to unknown recipient, 17 December 1878, Blatt 32. The marginalia on the last item shows that the photograph was sent back the following day, on December 18.
28. See, for example: GStA PK, I HA Rep. 89 Nr. 2319, correspondence between Anders, Gossler, and Wilhelm I, 26 June to 23 August 1884, Blatt 98–101.
29. John B. Thompson, *The Media and Modernity: a Social Theory of the Media* (Stanford, 1995), 208.
30. For a history of the carte-de-visite, and its career in Germany in particular, see James E. Cornwall, "Die Geschichte der Photographie in Berlin," *Mitteilungen des Vereins für die Geschichte Berlins* 72 (Berlin, 1976); William C. Darrah, *Cartes de Visite in Nineteenth Century Photography* (Gettysburg, 1981); Gisèle Freund, *Photographie und Gesellschaft* (München, 1974); Helmut Gernsheim and Alison Gernsheim, *The History of Photography: from the Camera Obscura to the beginning of the modern era* (New York, 1969); Ursula Peters, *Stilgeschichte der Fotografie in Deutschland 1839–1900* (Köln, 1979); Hela Zettler and Horst Mauter, *Berlin in frühen Photographien 1844–1900* (Berlin, 1994).
31. For a history of the photoalbum, see Ellen Maas, *Das Photoalbum 1858–1918: Eine Dokumentation zur Kultur- und Sozialgeschichte* (München, 1975); and Ellen Maas, *Die goldenen Jahre der Photoalben: Fundgrube und Spiegel von gestern* (Köln, 1977).
32. Franziska Windt, "Majestätische Bilderflut. Die Kaiser in der Photographie," in *Die Kaiser und die Macht der Medien*, ed. Generaldirektion der Stiftung Preussischer Schlösser und Gärten Berlin-Brandenburg (Berlin, 2005), 67. For parallels in iconography between photography and painting more generally, see Peters, *Stilgeschichte*. For developments in painted royal portraiture in the nineteenth century, see Rainer Schoch, *Das Herrscherbild in der Malerei des 19. Jahrhunderts* (München, 1975).
33. Examples cited in Maas, *goldene Jahre*, 114, 142.
34. Pohl, "Kaiser," 10.
35. For examples, see the Photographische Sammlung, Stiftung Stadtmuseum Berlin, inventory items: I 52, 108 for an image at the front; and GE 2005/316 VF; GE 2005/319 VF; XI 28983 b; GE 2005/337 VF; GE 2005/304 VF; XI 28903 for images dispersed variously throughout.

36. Laforgue, *Berlin*, 206; Hans Brendicke, "Kuriosität, Rarität, Antiquität," *Der Sammler* 12 (1890): 223–224, 235–236.
37. Alexa Geisthövel, "Den Monarchen im Blick: Wilhelm I. in der illustrierten Familien-presse," in *Kommunikation als Beobachtung. Medienwandel und Gesellschaftsbilder 1880–1960*, ed. Habbo Knoch and Daniel Morat (München, 2003), 76. Geisthövel makes this observation regarding a xylographic reproduction of a photograph portrait of Wilhelm I. The observation works equally well, however, for the original photograph.
38. Thompson, *Media*, 219–220.
39. Quoted in Alessandra Comini, *The Changing Image of Beethoven: A Study in Myth-making* (New York, 1987), 22. See also Rellstab's original memoirs, reprinted in Alfr. Chr. Kalischer, "Ludwig Rellstab in seinem persönlichen Verkehre mit Ludwig von Beethoven," *Der Bär* 12 (1885–1886): esp. 537.
40. Karl Müller, "Vom Porträt-Sammeln," *Der Sammler* 7 (1885): 178–179; G.L., "Ueber eine Sammlung sächsischer Fürsten-Porträts," *Der Sammler* 8 (1886): 65.
41. Bernd Weise, "Pressefotografie III. Das Geschäft mit dem aktuellen Foto: Fotografen, Bildagenturen, Interessenverbände, Arbeitstechnik. Die Entwicklung in Deutschland bis zum Ersten Weltkrieg," *Fotogeschichte* 10, no. 37 (1990): 13–36.
42. Windt, "Majestätische Bilderflut," 69.
43. It is for this reason that photojournalists were not able to capture political or military action before the 1880s; such "action" images had to be produced through lithographic means for newspapers. Bernd Weise, "Pressefotografie II. Fortschritte der Fotografie- und Drucktechnik und Veränderungen des Pressemarktes im Deutschen Kaiserreich," *Fotogeschichte* 9, no. 33 (1989): 27–62. Likewise, workers were rarely photographed at their workplaces or in the process of work, at least until the turn of the century. Peter Kühnel, "Fotografishe Berufsdarstellungen im 19. Jahrhundert," *Fotogeschichte* 2, no. 4 (1982): 3–14.
44. It is interesting to speculate whether Wilhelm II, with his far more theatrical person-ality, would have deigned to hold such poses for the camera. It is a moot point, how-ever, as snapshot photography, developed by the beginning of his reign, made such measures unnecessary. For restaged theater scenes, see Timm Starl, "'Mosaik,' Stereo und Serienbild: Anmerkungen zur Vorgeschichte des Films," *Fotogeschichte* 2, no. 3 (1982): 43–52. For the difficulties that even actors encountered in creating such posed, pseudo-action shots—in particular preventing the blurring of facial expressions—see Susanne Holschbach, "*Phädra* im Fotoatelier: Fotografische Rollenporträts im 19. Jahrhundert," and Petra Löffler, "Das Schauspiel der Fotografie: Posieren vor der Ka-mera—die Lehrbücher von Carl Michel und Albert Borée," both in *Fotogeschichte* 26, no. 101 (2006): 3–15 and 17–30, respectively.
45. Again, this was different for Wilhelm II, as the fixidity of the carte-de-visite was lifted by the invention of reproductive techniques that enabled seriality and motion: snap-shot photography (mid 1880s) and film (mid 1890s). Instead, people frequently com-plained about the insufficiency of any one image to capture Wilhelm II's many moods. For the similarity of descriptions of Wilhelm I's countenance, see Laforgue, *Berlin*, 49–50, 166, 190; Untitled, *Neue Preußische Zeitung (Kreuzzeitung)*, Nr. 68, 22 March 1877 (unpaginated); Helge Evers-Milner, *Ein Frauenbild aus der Menzelzeit. Berliner Erinnerungen* (Berlin, 1944), 90–92; Felix Philippi, *Alt-Berlin. Erinnerungen aus der Jugendzeit*, ed. Mario Krammer (Berlin, 1950), 51–52, 96.
46. For the aesthetic critique of photography as lifeless, see Gerhard Plumpe, *Der tote Blick. Zum Diskurs der Photographie in der Zeit des Realismus* (München, 1990).

47. Untitled, *Neue Preußische Zeitung (Kreuzzeitung)*, Nr. 68, 22 March 1877, unpaginated.
48. GStA PK, I HA Rep. 89 Nr. 2792, correspondence between Braunstein and Wilmowski, 18 to 28 June 1879, Blatt 33–35.
49. GStA PK, I HA Rep. 89 Nr. 2792, correspondence between Karl Friedrich Gok, Wilhelm I, Wilmowski, and Magnus, 7 to 20 June, 1876, Blatt 1–2, 9.

Chapter 3

1. If the topic was addressed, it was only to discuss whether Wilhelm II saw himself as a charismatic leader or exhibited any charismatic character traits, matters that interested Weber little, and for good reason. See Ulrich Sieg, "Wilhelm II.—Ein leutseliger Charismatiker," in *Charismatische Führer der deutschen Nation*, ed. Frank Möller (Munich, 2004), 85–108. For the most reliable biographical source on Wilhelm II, see John C.G. Röhl, *Wilhelm II. Der Aufbau der persönlichen Monarchie* (Munich, 2001), esp. 137ff.
2. This, of course, does not mean that Weber regarded Wilhelm II as a full-fledged charismatic ruler. See Wolfgang Mommsen, *Max Weber und die deutsche Politik. 1890–1920* (Tübingen, 1959), 155, 286.
3. Walther Rathenau, *Der Kaiser. Eine Betrachtung* (Berlin, 1919), 30. Max Weber discusses the term "Caesaropapism" in *Economy and Society: an Outline of Interpretive Sociology*, ed. Guenther Roth and Claus Wittich, 2 vols. (Berkeley and Los Angeles, 1978), 2:1159–1177.
4. See Jan Rüger, *The Great Naval Game: Britain and Germany in the Age of Empire* (Oxford, 2007), 50–57.
5. See John Plunkett, *Queen Victoria: First Media Monarch* (Oxford, 2003), 199–238; Richard Williams, *The Contentious Crown: Public Discussion of the British Monarchy in the Reign of Queen Victoria* (Aldershot, 1997), 190–229. See also the classic account: Walter Bagehot, *The English Constitution* (Ithaca, 1966) [first published 1867], 82–98.
6. This holds true, at least, for the press; less so, however, for films. See Richard S. Wortman, *Scenarios of Power: Myth and Ceremony in Russian Monarchy II: From Alexander II to the Abdication of Nicholas II* (Princeton, 1995), 485ff.
7. Hans Boldt, "Deutscher Konstitutionalismus und Bismarckreich," in *Das kaiserliche Deutschland. Politik und Gesellschaft 1870–1918*, ed. Michael Stürmer (Berlin, 1970), 119–142, 130ff.
8. Theodor Eschenburg, "Die improvisierte Demokratie. Ein Beitrag zur Geschichte der Weimarer Republik," in *Die improvisierte Demokratie. Gesammelte Aufsätze zur Weimarer Republik*, ed. Theodor Eschenburg (Munich, 1964), 15. Christoph Schönberger, *Das Parlament im Anstaltsstaat. Zur Theorie parlamentarischer Repräsentation in der Staatsrechtslehre des Kaiserreichs (1871–1918)* (Frankfurt a.M., 1997), 27.
9. Schönberger, *Parlament*, 179ff., 230, 290f. See also Elisabeth Fehrenbach, *Wandlungen des deutschen Kaisergedankens 1871–1918* (Munich, 1969), 179ff.
10. See Martin Kohlrausch, *Der Monarch im Skandal. Die Logik der Massenmedien und die Transformation der wilhelminischen Monarchie* (Berlin, 2005), 84–102.
11. Friedrich Naumann, *Demokratie und Kaisertum. Ein Handbuch für die innere Politik* (Berlin, 1900), 173.

12. Fehrenbach, *Wandlungen*, 203.
13. Gabriele Brude-Firnau, *Die literarische Deutung Kaiser Wilhelms II. zwischen 1889 und 1989* (Heidelberg, 1997), 20f.
14. Hermann Oncken, *Der Kaiser und die Nation. Rede bei dem Festakt der Universität Heidelberg zur Erinnerung an die Befreiungskriege und zur Feier des 25jährigen Regierungsjubiläums Kaiser Wilhelms II.* (Heidelberg, 1913), 16.
15. See Jeremy Paxman, *On Royalty* (London, 2006), 263–293.
16. Tellingly, Victoria was fiercely criticized when she no longer appeared in public after the death of Albert. Antony Taylor, *'Down with the Crown'. British Anti-monarchism and Debates about Royalty since 1790* (London, 1999), 80–85.
17. Quoted in John C.G. Röhl, "The Kaiser's court," in *The Kaiser and his Court: Wilhelm II and the Government of Germany*, ed. John C.G. Röhl (Cambridge, 1994), 70–106, 104.
18. For an overview of the media landscape in Wilhelmine Germany, see Kohlrausch, *Skandal*, 48–52; Dominik Geppert, *Öffentlichkeit und Diplomatie in den deutsch-britischen Beziehungen 1896–1912* (Munich, 2007), 38–47.
19. Andreas Schulz, "Der Aufstieg der 'vierten Gewalt:' Medien, Politik und Öffentlichkeit im Zeitalter der Massenkommunikation," *Historische Zeitschrift* 270 (2000): 65–97; Axel Schildt, "Das Jahrhundert der Massenmedien:Ansichten zu einer künftigen Geschichte der Öffentlichkeit," *Geschichte und Gesellschaft* 27 (2001): 177–206.
20. Jörg Requate, "Öffentlichkeit und Medien als Gegenstände historischer Analyse," *Geschichte und Gesellschaft* 25 (1999): 5–33; Peter Fritzsche, *Reading Berlin 1900* (Cambridge, MA, 1996), 51ff.
21. Robert G.L. Waite, "Leadership Pathologies: The Kaiser and the Führer and the Decisions for War in 1914 and 1939," in Betty Glad, *Psychological Dimensions of War* (London, 1990), 143–168, 145; Saskia Asser and Liesbeth Ruitenberg, "Der Kaiser im Bild—Wilhelm II. und die Fotografie als PR-Instrument," in *Der Kaiser im Bild. Wilhelm II. und die Fotografie als PR-Instrument. Der fotografische Nachlaß des letzten deutschen Kaisers*, ed. Huis Marseille (Zaltbommel, 2002), 46, 32. See Franziska Windt, Jürgen Luh, and Carsten Dilba, ed., *Die Kaiser und die Macht der Medien* (Berlin, 2005), 67–76.
22. Gerhard Voigt, "Goebbels als Markentechniker," in *Warenästhetik. Beiträge zur Diskussion, Weiterentwicklung und Vermittlung ihrer Kritik*, ed. Fritz Haug (Frankfurt a.M., 1975), 231–260.
23. This occurred in a film by the British pioneer Birt Acres, financed through the Chocolate-Company Stollwerck. Martin Loiperdinger, "Kaiser Wilhelm II: Der erste deutsche Filmstar," in *Idole des deutschen Films*, ed. Thomas Koebner (Munich, 1997), 41–53. See also Klaus-Dieter Pohl, "Der Kaiser im Zeitalter seiner technischen Reproduzierbarkeit: Wilhelm II. in Fotografie und Film," in *Der letzte Kaiser. Wilhelm II. im Exil*, ed. Klaus-Dieter Pohl and Hans Wilderotter (Gütersloh/Munich, 1991), 9–18.
24. Paul Klebinder, *Der Kaiser im Film* (Berlin, 1912), 16.
25. On the specific conditions of the visibility of the monarch see Alexa Geisthövel, "Wilhelm I. am 'historischen Eckfenster': Zur Sichtbarkeit des Monarchen in der zweiten Hälfte des 19. Jahrhunderts," in *Die Sinnlichkeit der Macht. Herrschaft und Repräsentation seit der Frühen Neuzeit*, ed. Jan Andres, Alexa Geisthövel, and Matthias Schwengelbeck (Frankfurt a.M., 2005), 170–185.
26. Eric Hobsbawm, "Mass-Producing Traditions: Europe 1870–1914," in *The Invention of Tradition*, ed. Hobsbawm and Terence Ranger (Cambridge, 1996), 263–308.

27. See Philip Mansel, *Dressed to Rule: Royal and Court Costume from Louis XIV to Elisabeth II* (New Haven, 2005), 124–128.
28. See Jost Rebentisch, *Die vielen Gesichter des Kaisers. Wilhelm II. in der deutschen und britischen Karikatur* (Berlin, 2000), 62, 289, 310.
29. Siegfried A. Kaehler, *Vier quellenkritische Untersuchungen zum Kriegsende 1918*, in Siegfried A. Kaehler, *Studien zur deutschen Geschichte des 19. und 20. Jahrhunderts, Aufsätze und Vorträge* (Göttingen, 1961), 301.
30. Kari Palonen, "Herrschaft und Rhetorik bei Max Weber," *vorgänge* 160 (2002): 59–67, 61. Friedrich Wilhelm IV used speeches, but rarely in the political way that Wilhelm II did. See Volker Wittenauer, *Im Dienste der Macht: Kultur und Sprache am Hof der Hohenzollern. Vom Großen Kurfürst bis zu Wilhelm II.* (Paderborn 2007), 180–186. Tellingly, it was not the Queen but Gladstone who first used public speeches in a modern sense in England. See Joseph S. Meisel, *Public Speech and the Cutlrue of Public Life in the Age of Gladstone* (New York, 2001), 277ff.
31. Gisela Brude-Firnau, "Preußische Predigt: Die Reden Wilhelms II," in *The Turn of the Century: German Literature and Art. 1890–1915*, ed. Gerald Chapple and Hans H. Schulte (Bonn, 1981), 149–170.
32. James Retallack, "Ideas into Politics: Meanings of 'Stasis' in Wilhelmine Germany," in *Wilhelminism and Its Legacies: German Modernities, Imperialism and the Meanings of Reform. 1890–1930*, ed. Geoff Eley and James Retallack (New York, 2003), 235–252.
33. Alfred Hermann Fried, *Kaiser werde modern!* (Berlin, 1905), 5.
34. Alfred Kerr, *Wo liegt Berlin? Briefe aus der Reichshauptstadt* (Berlin, 1997), 496.
35. See Mark Hewitson, "The Kaiserreich in Question: Constitutional Crisis in Germany before the First World War," *Journal of Modern History* 73 (2001): 725–780.
36. Otto Julius Bierbaum, *Prinz Kuckuck. Leben, Taten, Meinungen und Höllenfahrt eines Wollüstlings* (Munich, 1907), 590, 595. Thomas Mann, *Königliche Hoheit* (Berlin, 1909), 258; Rudolf Borchardt, "Der Kaiser," *Süddeutsche Monatshefte* 5 (1908): 237–252, 240, 247.
37. Jens Ivo Engels, *Königsbilder. Sprechen, Singen und Schreiben über den französischen König in der ersten Hälfte des 18. Jahrhunderts* (Bonn, 2000), 232; Monika Wienfort, *Monarchie in der bürgerlichen Gesellschaft. Deutschland und England von 1640 bis 1848* (Göttingen, 1993), 137.
38. Kohlrausch, *Monarch*, 88–94.
39. Hermann Conradi, "Wilhelm II. und die junge Generation. Eine zeitpsychologische Betrachtung," in Hermann Conradi, *Gesammelte Schriften III*, ed. Gustav Werner Peters (Munich, 1911), 311.
40. Georg E. Hinzpeter, *Kaiser Wilhelm II. Eine Skizze nach der Natur gezeichnet* (Bielefeld, 1888), 7.
41. "Das psychologische Moment," *Hannoverscher Courier*, 10 July 1908, No. 273.
42. Bülow actually used the German term "Philister," with its negative connotation as conformist. See Martin Kohlrausch, "Wilhelm II and the Fragility of the Royal Individual," in *The Body of the Queen. Gender and Rule in the Courtly World 1500–2000*, ed. Regina Schulte (New York, 2006), 259.
43. Gustav Adolf Erdmann, *Der deutsche Kaiser und sein Volk* (Leipzig, 1901), 7–8.
44. Ernst Johann, ed., *Reden des Kaisers. Ansprachen, Predigten und Trinksprüche Wilhelms II.* (Munich, 1966), 116ff.
45. See Friedrich Zipfel, *Kritik der Öffentlichkeit an der Person und an der Monarchie Wilhelms II. bis zum Ausbruch des Weltkrieges* (Ph.D. diss., Freie Universität Berlin 1952), 114.

46. R. Falke, "Der religiöse Standpunkt unseres Kaisers," *Der Tag,* 6 September 1907.
47. "Kurze Meldung," *Berliner Lokal-Anzeiger,* 25 August 1908 (Nr. 431).
48. See Juliane Vogel, *Elisabeth von Österreich. Momente aus dem Leben einer Kunstfigur* (Frankfurt a.M., 1998), 33ff., 88ff.
49. Jörg Michael Henneberg, *Das Sanssouci Kaiser Wilhelms II. Der letzte Deutsche Kaiser, das Achilleion und Korfu* (Oldenburg, 2004), 79–88.
50. Asser and Ruitenberg, *Kaiser im Bild,* 16–77, 55, 53. Birgit Marschall, *Reisen und Regieren. Die Nordlandfahrten Kaiser Wilhelms II.* (Hamburg, 1991), 34ff.; Thomas A. Kohut, *Wilhelm II and the Germans: A Study in Leadership* (New York, 1991), 164f.; 235–267.
51. On the interdependence of royal ceremonial and the media see Johannes Paulmann, *Pomp und Politik. Monarchenbegegnungen in Europa zwischen Ancien Régime und Erstem Weltkrieg* (Paderborn, 2000), 337ff.
52. Lothar Reinermann speaks of a "charismatization" in this context. Lothar Reinermann, *Der Kaiser in England. Wilhelm II. und die britische Öffentlichkeit* (London, 2000), 110ff.
53. Thomas Lindenberger, *Straßenpolitik. Zur Sozialgeschichte der öffentlichen Ordnung in Berlin 1900 bis 1914* (Bonn, 1995), 61f.
54. Rathenau, *Kaiser,* 18.
55. John B. Thompson, *Political Scandal. Power and Visibility in the Media Age* (Cambridge, 2000), 40ff.
56. Kohlrausch, *Monarch,* 186–228; Isabel V. Hull, *The Entourage of Kaiser Wilhelm II. 1888–1918* (Cambridge, 1982), 109–145.
57. *Vossische Zeitung,* 23 October 1907 (no. 498).
58. On 7 July 1907, the tabloid paper *B.Z. am Mittag* for the last time featured a headline on the trials on its front page: "Eulenburg vor den Geschworenen. Der Prozeß auf unbestimmte Zeit vertagt."
59. Jllo, "Die Sensation," *Berliner Tageblatt,* 11 November 1907, (No. 574). On sexuality and the press, see Frank Bösch, "Das Private wird politisch: Die Sexualität des Politikers und die Massenmedien des ausgehenden 19. Jahrhunderts," *Zeitschrift für Geschichtswissenschaft* 52 (2004): 781–801.
60. Peter Winzen, *Das Kaiserreich am Abgrund. Die Daily-Telegraph-Affäre und das Hale-Interview von 1908* (Stuttgart, 2002), 37–67.
61. Ludwig Thoma, "Der große Skandal," *März* 1 (1907): 269–273.

Chapter 4

I would like to thank Edward Berenson, Eva Giloi, and Kenneth Hamilton for their expert comments on this chapter.

1. "The state, that's me." "The concert, that's me."
2. Eduard Hanslick, *Musikalisches Skizzenbuch* (Berlin, 1888), 167.
3. Robert Walser, *Running with the Devil: Power, Gender, and Madness in Heavy Metal Music* (Middletown, 1993), 57 and 76–77.
4. Richard Leppert, "Cultural Contradiction, Idolatry, and the Piano Virtuoso: Franz Liszt," in *Piano Roles: Three Hundred Years of Life with the Piano,* ed. James Parakilas (New Haven, 1999), 273–275.
5. Lawrence Kramer, *Musical Meaning: Toward a Critical History* (Berkeley and Los Angeles, 2002), 70.

6. See chapter 2, "Inventing the Recital," in Kenneth Hamilton, *After the Golden Age: Romantic Music and Modern Performance* (Oxford, 2007).

7. Leon Botstein, "Reflections on Franz Liszt: Mirror to the Nineteenth Century," in *Franz Liszt and his World*, ed. Christopher H. Gibbs and Dana Gooley (Princeton, 2006).

8. Detlef Altenburg, "Franz Liszt and the legacy of the classical era," *19th Century Music* 18, no. 1 (1994): 46–63.

9. For a fuller picture of Liszt's interaction with audiences and its relationship to charisma, see chapter 7 in Hamilton, *After the Golden Age.*

10. See, for example, Tia di Nora's revisionist view of Beethoven's career in *Beethoven and the Construction of Genius: Music and Politics in Vienna, 1792–1803* (Berkeley and Los Angeles, 1995).

11. Heinrich Schwab, "Formen der Virtuosenehrung und ihr sozialgeschichtlicher Hintergrund," in *International Musicological Society, Report of the Eleventh Congress, Copenhagen 1972*, ed. Henrik Glahn, Søren Sørensen, and Peter Ryom (Copenhagen, 1974), 637ff.

12. Habermas's term *bürgerliche Öffentlichkeit* is normally translated as "bourgeois public sphere." My alternate translation is intended to avoid the economic and social connotations that the word "bourgeois" carries in English.

13. Jürgen Habermas, *The Structural Transformation of the Public Sphere*, trans. Thomas Burger (Cambridge, MA, 1991), 7.

14. Habermas, *Structural Transformation*, 16.

15. Angus Heriot's book, *The Castrati in Opera* (New York, 1975), is breezy but remains the only overview of the castrati in English. On opera seria as ritual of social and political authority, see Martha Feldman's "Magic Mirrors and the Seria Stage: Thoughts Toward a Ritual View," *Journal of the American Musicological Society* 48, no. 3 (1995): 423–484. Feldman has developed the argument of this article in her book *Opera and Sovereignty: Transforming Myths in Eighteenth-Century Italy* (Chicago, 2007). The castrato is discussed on pages 69–82.

16. Simon McVeigh, *Concert Life in London from Mozart to Haydn* (Cambridge, 1993), 19–20.

17. Chopin wrote to his family on 13 August 1829: "It's said everywhere here that the local nobility likes me. The Schwartezenbergs, the Wobrzes, etc. all speak in high terms of the delicacy and elegance of my playing; Count Dietrichstein, who came on to the stage, is an example." *Chopin's Letters*, ed. Henryk Opienski, trans. E.L. Voynich (New York, 1988), 55.

18. Max Maratzek, *Crotchets and Quavers: or, Revelations of an Opera Manager in America* (New York, 1855), 121–122.

19. John Dizikes, *Opera in America: a Cultural History* (New Haven, 1993), 129–130.

20. Joseph Horowitz, *Understanding Toscanini* (New York: 1987), 25.

21. Ludwig Rellstab, "Life Sketch," (1842), as translated in *Franz Liszt and his World*, 345.

22. Joseph d'Ortigue, "Frantz Liszt," *Gazette musicale de Paris* (1835), as translated in *Franz Liszt and his World*, 314.

23. For a selection of contemporary reports on the young Liszt in Paris, see Adrian Williams, *Portrait of Liszt: By Himself and his Contemporaries* (Oxford, 1990), 13–30.

24. Anne-Martin Fugier, *La vie élégante, ou la formation du Tout-Paris, 1815–1848* (Paris, 1990), 107–108. Thomas Carlyle, writing in 1841, saw the eighteenth-century "man

of letters" as the modern secular incarnation of previously numinous figures: "Intrinsically it is the same function which the old generations named a man Prophet, Priest, Divinity for doing." *On Heroes, Hero-Worship, and the Heroic in History,* ed. Michael K. Goldberg (Berkeley, 1993), 134.

25. For a brief discussion of the hatred of the bourgeoisie in Parisian artistic circles, particularly that of Victor Hugo, see Anne Martin-Fugier, *Les Romantiques: Figures de l'artiste 1820–1848* (Paris, 1998), 140–143.

26. See Angela Esterhammer, "The Cosmopolitan *improvvisatore:* Spontaneity and Performance in Romantic Aesthetics," *European Romantic Review* 16, no. 2 (2005): 153–165.

27. An excerpt of this essay translated into English, and introduced by Ralph Locke, is found in *Franz Liszt and his World,* 291–302. The original French text can be found in R. Strecker, ed., *Franz Liszt: artiste et société* (Paris, 1995).

28. The core of Weber's theory is in *Economy and Society: An Outline of Interpretive Sociology,* ed. Guenther Roth and Claus Wittich, 2 vols. (Berkeley and Los Angeles, 1978), 2:1111–1157. On the revolutionary character of charisma, see 2:1115–1117.

29. Weber, *Economy and Society,* 2:1117.

30. Kramer, *Musical meaning,* 91.

31. Two representative pamphlets are Joseph Duverger, *Notice biographique sur Franz Liszt* (Paris, 1843), and J.W. Christern, *Franz Liszt: nach seinem Leben und Wirken* (Hamburg/Leipzig, 1841).

32. Such coordinated efforts are treated in detail in James Deaville, "Publishing paraphrases and creating collectors," in *Franz Liszt and his World,* 255–290.

33. Liszt also demonstrated his anti-commercialism by publishing very few pieces or arrangements that the general public could play, at a time when most virtuoso pianists produced such pieces in large numbers. His Schubert transcriptions, many of them playable by amateurs, may be the most significant exception to this rule.

34. Alan Walker, *Franz Liszt: the Virtuoso Years 1811–1847* (New York, 1983), 289.

35. *Correspondance de Liszt et de Mme. d'Agoult,* 2 vols., ed. E. Ollivier (Paris, 1935), 1:227–228.

36. *Humorist,* 7 December 1839.

37. *Correspondance de Liszt,* 582 (13 May 1840).

38. Ibid., 588 (15 May 1840).

39. Ibid., 596 (19 May 1840). For a discussion of Liszt and changes in male fashion see Botstein, "Mirror to the Nineteenth Century," 541–544. For images of Liszt, see Ernst Burger, ed., *Franz Liszt: A Life in Pictures and Documents* (Princeton, 1989).

40. Jacqueline Bellas and Serge Gut, ed., *Correspondance Franz Liszt/Marie d'Agoult* (Paris, 2001), 610 (29 May 1840).

41. For contemporary reactions to Liszt's hands, see Leppert, "Cultural contradiction," 276–277.

42. See Mendelssohn's letters to his mother of 27 October 1840 (*Letters of Felix Mendelssohn Bartholdy,* ed. Julius Rietz, trans. Lady Wallace [Boston, 1863], 192–193) and 19 July 1842 (*Felix Mendelssohn: Letters,* ed. G. Selden-Goth [London, 1946], 306–309).

43. Liszt was strongly opposed to the mass education of musicians in conservatories, preferring to teach by force of charismatic example in the master class format. Ironically, he became the pivotal figure in the establishment of a conservatory in Budapest in the later nineteenth century, a classic example of "routinized" charisma.

44. Peter Gay, *The Bourgeois Experience: Victoria to Freud,* 5 vols. (New York, 1984–98).

45. Len Platt, *Aristocracies of Fiction: The Idea of Aristocracy in Late-Nineteenth-Century and Early-Twentieth-Century Literary Culture* (Westport, CT, 2001).
46. On Liszt as military hero, see Dana Gooley, *The Virtuoso Liszt* (Cambridge, UK, 2004), 78–116, and Leppert, "Cultural contradiction," 278–280.
47. Richard Sennett, *The Fall of Public Man* (New York, 1974), 199–203.

Chapter 5

1. Mary Ann Caws, *Surprised in Translation* (Chicago, 2006), 30.
2. Ibid.
3. Stéphane Mallarmé, "Edgar Poe," in *Oeuvres complètes* II, ed. Bertrand Marchal (Paris, 2003), 145. Further references to this volume will appear in the text as OC II.
4. T.J. Clark, *The Absolute Bourgeois: Artists and Politics in France 1848–1851* (London, 1973).
5. Jean-Claude Bonnet, *Naissance du Panthéon: essai sur le culte des grands hommes* (Paris, 1998).
6. Leo Braudy, *The World in a Frame: What We See in Films* (Garden City, NY, 1976), and *The Frenzy of Renown: Fame and its History* (New York, 1986). Richard Dyer, *Stars* (London, 1998) and *Heavenly Bodies: Film Stars and Society* (New York, 2004 [1986]).
7. Braudy, *Frenzy*, 15.
8. Emily Apter, *Continental Drift: From National Characters to Virtual Subjects* (Chicago, 1999), see chapter 8, "Cleopatra's Nose: Characterology and the Modern Subject in Belle Epoque Paris," 149–163.
9. Marcel Proust, *Swann's Way*, in *Remembrance of Things Past*, trans. C.K. Scott Montcrieff and Terence Kilmartin, vol. 1 (New York, 1982), 80.
10. Stéphane Mallarmé, "Vers de circonstances," in *Oeuvres complètes* I, ed. Bertrand Marchal (Paris, 1998), 284. Further references to this volume will appear in the text as OC I.
11. Roger Pearson, *Mallarmé and Circumstance: The Translation of Silence* (Oxford, 2004), 169–170.
12. Jean-Luc Steinmetz, *Mallarmé: L'absolu au jour le jour* (Paris, 1998). Steinmetz citing a letter from Mallarmé to Verlaine, 10 Nov. 1885.
13. Ibid., 19–20. Steinmetz suggests that Mallarmé was highly selective when answering for his ancestors. When, in 1885, Verlaine queried him about a family link to François René Auguste Mallarmé, Mallarmé refused to acknowledge him. This particular Mallarmé was a president of the revolutionary Convention, who voted to execute the King as well as thirty-two "Virgins of Verdun" "guilty of having offered flowers and fruit to the King of Prussia when he entered their city" (19).
14. See, Jacques Scherer, *Le "Livre" de Stéphane Mallarmé* (Paris, 1957). See also additional text and variations published as "Notes en vue du 'Livre'" in Mallarmé, OC I.
15. Barbara Johnson, "Erasing Panama: Mallarmé and the Text of History," *A World of Difference* (Baltimore, 1987), 59.
16. Fredric Jameson, "Mallarmé Materialist," in *The Modernist Papers* (London, 2007), 316.
17. Ibid., 314–315.
18. Georg Simmel, "The Secret in Secret Society" in *The Sociology of Georg Simmel*, ed. Kurt H. Wolff (New York, 1950 [1908–1917]), 307–338.

19. E.S. Burt, *Poetry's Appeal: Nineteenth-Century Lyric and the Political Space* (Stanford, CA, 1999), 94.

20. Tamara Chaplin, *Turning on the Mind: French Philosophers on Television* (Chicago, 2007), 80 and 144. Chaplin is citing Jeannette Colombel, who is quoting Foucault on "Spécial: Michel Foucault," 22 June 1994.

21. Ibid., 105.

22. Marshall McLuhan, *The Interior Landscape: The Literary Criticism of Marshall McLuhan 1943–1962*, ed. Eugene McNamara (New York, 1969), 11.

23. Robert Greer Cohn, "Mallarmé's Wake," *New Literary History* 26, no. 4 (Autumn 1995): 885–901.

24. McKenzie Wark, *Gamer Theory* (Cambridge, MA, 2007)

25. Roger Ansell Pearson, *Unfolding Mallarmé: The Development of a Poetic Art* (Oxford, 1996), 251.

26. Burt astutely reads the problem of constraint and restraint in Mallarmé's aesthetics. Representational constraints apply to such cases as when "the poet's reverie around a meaningless signifier can find an exact translation in a commercial landscape of everyday, nineteenth century Parisian life." Burt contrasts this representationally constrained language with Mallarmé's commitment to "representing without a represented." See her chapter, "Mallarmé's 'Bound Action.' The Orders of the Garter," in *Poetry's Appeal*, 119.

27. Alain Badiou, *Le Siècle* (Paris, 2005).

28. Jeffrey Mehlman, "Ad Centrum?" in *Literary Debate: Texts and Contexts: Postwar French Thought, Vol. II.*, ed. Jeffrey Mehlman and Denis Hollier (New York, 1999), 169.

29. Ibid., 177.

30. Svetlana Boym, *Death in Quotation Marks: Cultural Myths of the Modern Poet* (Cambridge, 1991), 40.

31. Roland Barthes, "The Death of the Author," in *The Rustle of Language*, trans. Richard Howard (Berkeley and Los Angeles, 1989), 50.

32. Ibid., 52.

33. Richard Sieburth, *Times Literary Supplement*, 15 Oct. 1999, "The Master's Testament."

34. Wayne Koestenbaum, "Party of None," *Bookforum* 14, no. 1 (April/May 2007): 50.

35. Leo Bersani, *The Death of Stéphane Mallarmé* (Cambridge, 1982), 33.

36. Work on the social Mallarmé was inaugurated by Roger Dragonetti and Marcel Raymond, and further advanced by Marian Zwerling Sugano, Antoine Compagnon, Eric Benoît, Bertrand Marchal, Roger Pearson, Jean-Luc Steinmetz, Rosemary Lloyd, and Damian Catani. On this particular approach, see Steinmetz, *Mallarmé*, 165.

37. In an appendix to *Les Mots anglais*, Mallarmé accorded the proper name considerable attention. Proper names are characterized as archaic survivals of primitivist linguistic techne. Intermixed with speech, they reveal the imagination in a state of its incipient awakening to meaning; as such, they are stamped with alterity, the incomprehensible, the ancient, the bizarre. Mallarmé, Appendice, *Les Mots anglais* (OC II, 1087).

38. Damian Catani, *The Poet in Society: Art, Consumerism and Politics in Stéphane Mallarmé* (New York, 2002), 57.

39. Fritz Gutbrodt, "Poedelaire: Translation and the Volatility of the Letter," *Diacritics* 22, no. 3–4 (fall–winter 1992): 49–68.

40. Thomas Hanson, "Mallarmé's Hat," *Yale French Studies* 54 (1977): 222–23.

41. Ibid., 223.

42. Aristotle, *Nicomachean Ethics*, 1177b, 31.

43. David Harvey, *A Brief History of Neoliberalism* (Oxford, 2005), 166.

Chapter 6

The author would like to thank Edward Berenson and Eva Giloi for their generous invitation to participate in the "Constructing Charisma" conference, as well as their diligent criticism and editing of this chapter. She is also grateful to Andrew Aisenberg, Camille Robcis, Vanessa Schwartz, and Susan Zaeske for their very helpful readings of earlier drafts.

1. Lenard Berlanstein, "Historicizing and Gendering Celebrity Culture: Famous Women in Nineteenth-Century France," *Journal of Women's History* 16, no. 4 (2004): 66.
2. Bonheur received the *Légion d'honneur* in 1865. Whitney Chadwick called her the "most admired woman painter of the nineteenth century." See "'The Fine Art of Gentling': Horses, Women and Rosa Bonheur in Victorian England," in *The Body Imaged: The Human Form and Visual Culture since the Renaissance*, ed. Kathleen Adler and Marcia Pointon (Cambridge, 1993), 90. See also Albert Boime, who calls her "the best known woman artist of the nineteenth century," in "The Case of Rosa Bonheur: Why Should a Woman Want to be More like a Man?" *Art History* 4, no. 4 (1981): 384–406.
3. See Theodore Stanton, *Reminiscences of Rosa Bonheur* (New York, 1910), 24.
4. *Le Gaulois*, 11 April 1882, Caricatures, Opuscules, Presse satirique, illustrée, Sarah Bernhardt, (hereafter COPSI), Séries 30, Bibliothèque historique de la ville de Paris (hereafter BHVP).
5. Sarcey is quoted in Henry Lapauze, "Sarah Bernhardt," *La Revue Littéraire, Beaux Arts, Sciences*, 15 December 1893, Boîte Sarah Bernhardt (hereafter BSB), Collection de l'Association des régisseurs de théâtres (hereafter CART), BHVP.
6. For other references mentioning Bernhardt's "eccentricities," see Marie Colombier, *Le Voyage de Sarah Bernhardt en Amérique* (Paris, 1881), 315–316; Albert Wolff, "Courrier de Paris: Sarah Bernhardt," *Le Figaro*, 7 February 1883, in Recueil factice de coupures de presse Sarah Bernhardt (hereafter RFCPSB), Vol. 1, Collection Rondel (hereafter CR), Bibliothèque nationale, Département des arts du spectacle (hereafter BNDAS); "Le Lion de Sarah Bernhardt," n.p, 15 July 1895, Coupures de presse jusqu'à 1900 sur Sarah Bernhardt (hereafter CPSB), Séries 30, BHVP; n.t., *La Vie parisienne*, 25 November 1893, RFCPSB, Vol. 3, CR, BNDAS; Mario Bertaux, "Sarah Bernhardt," n.p., n.d., Dossier Sarah Bernhardt (hereafter DSB), Bibliothèque Marguerite Durand, (hereafter BMD).
7. "Lettre de Mme. Sarah Bernhardt," *La France*, 14 November 1890, RFCPSB, Vol. 2, CR, BNDAS. See also Jules Huret, *Sarah Bernhardt* (Paris, 1899), 42; Fernand Goupillé, *La Presse*, 18 March 1891, RFCPSB, Vol. 2, CR, BNDAS.
8. Sarah Bernhardt, *Ma double vie: Mémoires de Sarah Bernhardt* (Paris, 1907), 210.
9. Tamar Garb, *Sisters of the Brush: Women's Artistic Culture in Late Nineteenth-Century Paris* (New Haven, 1994), 120; and "L'Art Féminin: The Formation of a Critical Category in Late Nineteenth-Century France," in *The Expanding Discourse: Feminism and Art History*, ed. Norma Broude and Mary D. Garrard (New York, 1992), 192.
10. Historians have paid attention to various eccentrics, but not much to the phenomenon itself. In "Art Matronage in Post-Victorian America," *Cultural Leadership in America: Art Matronage and Patronage* (Boston: Trustees of the Isabella Stuart Gardner Museum, 1997), 9–24, Wanda Corn deals in passing with Isabella Stuart Gardner as an eccentric. Brian Cowlishaw's *A Geneaology of Eccentricity* (Ph.D. thesis, University of Oklahoma, 1998) is a more systematic study of eccentricity in the nineteenth century, but his focus is primarily on such literature as *Don Quixote*.

11. Particularly helpful to me in thinking through the norm here was Georges Canguil-hem, *The Normal and the Pathological* (New York: Zone Books, 1989), esp. 51, 178.

12. James Kendall, *Eccentricity; or a Check to Censoriousness with Chapters on Other Subjects* (London: Simpkin, Marshall & Co., 1859), 27.

13. See entry for "eccentric" in *Oxford English Dictionary*, 2nd ed., 20 vols. (Oxford, 1989), 5:720. Hereafter *OED*.

14. *Trésor de la langue française, Dictionnaire de la langue du XIXe et du XXe siècle, Dictionnaire de la langue française; Dictionnaire historique de la langue française, Deutsches Wörterbuch*.

15. This statement is based on word counts collected in the ARTFL (American and French Research on the Treasury of the French Language) database. According to the ARTFL website (http://humanities.uchicago.edu/orgs/ARTFL/artl.flyer.html), the database contains nearly 2,000 texts, "ranging from classic works of French literature to various kinds of non-fiction prose and technical writing. The eighteenth, nineteenth and twentieth centuries are about equally represented." According to ARTFL, the use of the words "excentrique," "excentriques," "excentricité," and "excentriquement" for the modern period are as follows: 1810: 1; 1820: 5; 1830:7; 1840: 17; 1850: 26; 1860: 17; 1870: 20; 1880: 10, 1890: 12; 1900: 11; 1910: 6; 1920: 12; 1930: 23; 1940: 14; 1950: 5; 1960: 1.

16. See ARTFL "excentricité, " citation 51; "excentriques," citation 30; "excentricité," citations 62–64; "excentrique," citations 44–46.

17. Jerrold Seigel, *Bohemian Paris: Culture, Politics and the Boundaries of Bourgeois Life, 1830–1930* (New York, 1986). See also Elizabeth Wilson, *Bohemians: The Glamorous Outcasts* (New Brunswick, NJ, 2000); Mary Gluck, *Popular Bohemia: Modernism and Urban Culture in Nineteenth-Century Paris* (Cambridge, 2005).

18. See entry for "star" in *OED*, 16:525; *Trésor de la langue française*. Neither "etoile" nor "star" have this metaphorical meaning in the *Dictionnaire de l'Académie française*, 1832–1835.

19. "Soleils couchants," *La Vie en rose*, 26 October 1902, RCPSB, CR, BNDAS.

20. Sartorys, "Le Roman comique," n.p., April 1882, COPSI, Séries 30, BHVP.

21. See J.M. "Sarah Bernhardt," in *Les Contemporains célèbres*, 1890, RFCPSB, Vol. 2, CF, BNDAS.

22. Mince, "Les Étoiles des théâtres de Paris: Sarah Bernhardt," n.p., 14 May 1898, Fol. SW 208, RFCPSB, CF, BNDAS.

23. "Sarah Bernhardt," n.p., December 1896, RFCPSB, Vol. 6, CR, BNDAS

24. Danielle Digne, *Rosa Bonheur ou l'insolence: l'histoire d'une vie, 1822–1899* (Paris, 1980), 102.

25. Gabriel Weisberg, "Rosa Bonheur's Reception in England and America: The Popularization of a Legend and the Celebration of a Myth" in Dahesh Museum, *Rosa Bonheur: All Nature's Children* (New York, 1998), 3–5.

26. Weisberg, "Rosa Bonheur's Reception in England and America," 3.

27. Judy Grainger, "Buffalo Bill, Boulanger and Bonheur: Trans-Atlantic Cultural Exchanges in the Fin-de-Siècle," *Proceedings of the Western Society for French History* 26 (1999): 248.

28. "Sarah Bernhardt: Artiste dramatique," *L'Eclair*, 25 October 1890, RFCPSB, Vol. 2, CR, BNDAS; Enrico Ferri, "Physionomie nerveuse des femmes artistes," *La Revue*, 15 December 1896.

29. Claude-Roger Marx, "Sarah Bernhardt," *Comoedia illustrée*, n.d., RT 5943, CR, BNDAS.

30. Mario Bertaux, "Sarah Bernhardt."
31. Martha Vicinus, "Fin-de-Siècle Theatrics: Male Impersonation and Lesbian Desire," in *Borderlines: Genders and Identities in War and Peace, 1870–1930*, ed. Billie Melman (New York, 1998), 172.
32. Ernest Lys, "Sarah Bernhardt dans Jeanne d'Arc," *Gil Blas*, 6 December 1889, RCPSB, Vol. 1, CR, BNDAS. See also Marie Colombier, *Mémoires de Sarah Barnum* (Paris, 1883), 195–196, 209.
33. Edward Said, *Orientalism* (New York, 1978), 102–104.
34. Vanessa Schwartz, *Spectacular Realities: Early Mass Culture in Fin-de-Siècle Paris* (Berkeley, 1998), 16.
35. See entry for "eccentricity" in *OED*, 5: 721, meaning #6.
36. Lewis Carroll and Edward Lear are two who come to mind.
37. See entry for "therianthropic" in *OED*, 17: 913, as "combining the form of a beast with that of a man; of or pertaining to deities represented in the combined forms of man and beast, as dog- or eagle-headed divinities."
38. Gretchen Van Slyke, "The Sexual and Textual Politics of Dress: Rosa Bonheur and Her Cross-dressing Permits," *Nineteenth-Century French Studies* 26, no. 3–4 (1998): 321–335.
39. Stanton, *Reminiscences*, 365–366.
40. Dore Ashton with Denise Browne Hare, *Rosa Bonheur: A Life and a Legend* (New York, 1981), 109–110.
41. Eugène de Mirecourt, *Les Contemporains: Rosa Bonheur* (Paris, 1856), 54.
42. Ashton with Hare, *Rosa Bonheur*, 163. For Bonheur's gender ambivalence, see also "L'Oeuvre de Rosa Bonheur," *La Fronde*, n.d. [May 1899], Dossier Rosa Bonheur, BMD.
43. See the words of Robert David d'Angers in Stanton, *Reminiscences*, 24. Bonheur's clothing was deemed important enough to be talked about in her obituaries. See "La Vie à Paris: Rosa Bonheur," *Le Petit Niçois*, 30 May 1899; "Rosa Bonheur," *La Fronde*, 27 May 1899, all Dossier Rosa Bonheur, BMD.
44. "Les Travestis de Sarah," *Illustré théâtral*, 12 December 1895, Fol. SW, 252. RFCPSB, Sarah Bernhardt, CR, BNDAS.
45. Lenard Berlanstein, "Breeches and Breaches: Cross-Dress Theater and the Culture of Gender Ambiguity in Modern France," *Comparative Studies in Society and History* 38 (1996): 338–369.
46. Elaine Aston, *Sarah Bernhardt: A French Actress on the English Stage* (Oxford, 1989), 123–124, 126.
47. Related in August Germain, "L'Aiglon," *Echo de Paris*, 15 March 1900. For other reviews of Bernhardt's performance, see *Le Gaulois*, 16 March 1900; *Echo de Paris*, 17 March 1900; *La Fronde*, 16 March 1900.
48. A. Fabrèque, "Chez Edmond Rostand," *Le Journal*, 7 March 1900, RFCPSB, Vol. 5, CR, BNDAS. See also Ruth Brandon, *Being Divine* (London, 1991), 339–343; Jill Edmonds, "Princess Hamlet," in *The New Woman and Her Sisters: Feminism and Theatre, 1850–1914*, ed. Viv Gardner and Susan Rutherford (New York, 1992), 59–76. For Bernhardt's own views on cross-dressing, see her *L'Art du théâtre* (Paris, 1993), 139–146; "Les Travestis de Sarah," *Illustré théâtral*, 12 December 1895, Fol. SW, 252. RCPSB, CR, BNDAS; René d'Armand, "Les Travestis de Sarah," *La Rampe*, 16 June 1899; G. Geller, *Sarah Bernhardt* (Paris, 1931), 221; "Life as I see it: A few Fancies and some stories," *Pearson's Magazine*, November 1912 in CART, BHVP.

49. Robert Darnton, *The Great Cat Massacre and Other Episodes in French Cultural History* (New York, 1983), 92–94; Kathleen Kete, *The Beast in the Boudoir: Petkeeping in Nineteenth-Century Paris* (Berkeley, 1994), 115.
50. Katharine Briggs, *Nine Lives: The Folklore of Cats* (New York, 1980), 83.
51. David Weeks and Jamie James, *Eccentrics: A Study of Sanity and Strangeness* (New York, 1995).
52. Ashton with Hare, *Rosa Bonheur*, 97. Bonheur's menagerie was a topic of discussion in her obituaries. See "Rosa Bonheur," *Petit bleu*, 27 May 1899, Dossier Rosa Bonheur, BMD.
53. Joanna Richardson, *Sarah Bernhardt* (London, 1959), 113–114.
54. "Le Lion de Sarah Bernhardt"; Jules Huret, *Sarah Bernhardt* (Paris, 1899), 41; Colombier, *Le Voyage de Sarah Bernhardt*, 243–244; Cornelia Otis Skinner, *Madame Sarah* (Cambridge, MA, 1967), 134, 189–190, 239; Alberty, "Sarah Bernhardt: La Veille d'une première," *Le Figaro*, October 1894, RT 5881, Recueil factice de diverses interviews de Sarah Bernhardt, 1890–1920, CR, BNDAS.
55. Skinner, *Madame Sarah*, 136.
56. G. Geller, *Sarah Bernhardt: Divine Eccentric*, trans. E.S.G. Potter (New York, Frederick A. Stokes Company, 1933), 151.
57. According to the French *Littré* dictionary, a cat can refer to "*tout animal du même genre que le chat*" ("any animal belonging to the same species as the cat"), including the lion, tiger, lynx, etc.
58. Boime, "The Case of Rosa Bonheur," 399.
59. Ashton with Hare, *Rosa Bonheur*, 135; Anna Klumpke, *Rosa Bonheur, Sa vie, son oeuvre* (Paris, 1908), 278–280.
60. I am grateful to Vanessa Schwartz for this insight about wild animals, danger, and Bohemia.
61. Norman B. Spector, ed. and trans, *The Complete Fables of Jean de la Fontaine* (Evanston, IL, 1988), 130.
62. Klumpke, *Rosa Bonheur*, 282.
63. Jules Claretie, "Rosa Bonheur—An Appreciation with Some Hitherto Unpublished Studies," *Harpers's Magazine* 104 (1901–2): 139.
64. Jean Lorrain, "Une Visite chez Sarah," *Événement*, 3 November 1887, RFCPSB, Vol. 1, CR, BNDAS.
65. Skinner, *Madame Sarah*, xviii, 16–17, 93–94, 135.
66. Ashton with Hare, *Rosa Bonheur*, 139. See the letters by Bonheur quoted in Stanton, *Reminiscences*, 166–168, 179, 252–254, 279.
67. Arsène Alexandre, "Rosa Bonheur," *Le Figaro*, 27 May 1899.
68. Klumpke, *Rosa Bonheur*, 310.
69. Klumpke, *Rosa Bonheur*, 311; Mirecourt, *Rosa Bonheur*, 53.
70. Quoted in Stanton, *Reminiscences*, 338.
71. See Alex Potts, "Natural Order and the Call of the Wild: The Politics of Animal Picturing," *Oxford Art Journal* 13, no. 1 (1990): 20.
72. Ruskin is quoted in Ashton with Hare, *Rosa Bonheur*, 112. See also Boime, "The Case of Rosa Bonheur," 397. James M. Saslow revises this view by arguing that Bonheur skillfully hid faces in such paintings as "The Horse Fair," in order to present her own image there. See "Disagreeably Hidden: Construction and Constriction of the Lesbian Body in Rosa Bonheur's *Horse Fair*," in *Expanding Discourse*, Broude and Garrard, 189.
73. Berlanstein, "Historicizing and Gendering Celebrity Culture," 80–81.

Chapter 7

1. "When we heard of the death of Byron, it seemed to us that a part of our future was being taken away." Quoted in Gabriel Matzneff, "Byron et ses fils spirituels," *L'Humanité*, 7 April 2007.
2. In Fiona MacCarthy, *Byron: Life and Legend* (London, 2002), 555.
3. Lamartine, 'L'Homme,' from *Méditations poétiques* (1820), lines 2, 27.
4. Homer, *Odyssey*, 2 vols, 2ⁿᵈ edition revised by George E. Dimock, trans. A.T. Murray (Cambridge, MA, 1995), 2: 237.
5. Hesiod, "Works and Days," in *Hesiod*, ed. and trans. Glenn W. Most, 2 vols. (Cambridge, MA, 2006-2007), 1:760–764.
6. The word reached the French language much later, perhaps only in the 1960s. Paul Robert's dictionary of 1965 does not pick up any secular usage of the word.
7. In a review (*New York Times*, Sunday Book Review, 4 March 2007) of Philip Rieff's last book entitled *Charisma: The Gift and How it Has Been Taken Away From Us*. According to Rieff, the word charisma has "been battered to death."
8. Roland Barthes, *Mythologies* (Paris, 1957), 70.
9. Leslie Alexis Marchand, *Byron: A Biography*, 3 vols. (London, 1957), 2:692.
10. Marchand, *Byron*, 3:963.
11. Entry for 19 October 1822, in *The Journals of Mary Shelley, 1814–1844*, ed. Paula R. Feldman and Diana Scott-Kilvert (Baltimore, 1995).
12. Lord Byron, "Childe Harold's Pilgrimage," in *The Complete Poetical Works*, 7 vols., ed. Jerome J. McGann (Oxford, New York, 1980–1993), 2: canto III, 1045. Hereafter *CHP*.
13. Lord Byron, *Selected Poems*, ed. Susan J. Wolfson and Peter J. Manning (London, 1996), 786–787.
14. Leslie Alexis Marchand, ed., *Byron's Letters and Journals*, 13 vols. (London, 1973–1994), 1:237. Hereafter *BLJ*.
15. *CHP*, canto II, 339.
16. *CHP*, canto II, 553.
17. *CHP*, canto II, 545–547.
18. *CHP*, canto II, 541–549. Compare the revision to *CHP*, canto II, 559–561. The published version, talking of Ali Pasha, reads: "It is not that yon hoary lengthening beard/ Ill suits the passions which belong to youth;/Love conquers age..." An earlier version of line 560 reads: "Delights to mingle with the lip of youth."
19. See his remarks to Byron on receiving three cantos of *Don Juan* (numbers 6–8): "I declare to you they were so outrageously shocking that I would not publish them if you were to give me your Estate—Title—and Genius" (letter of 29 October 1822, quoted in Marchand, *Byron*, 3:1040).
20. *CHP*, canto I, 35, 37, 46, 52, 73-74.
21. See, for example, Lamartine's passionate identification with the *Childe*: "Mystérieux héros! c'était moi, j'étais lui ... Nos deux coeurs, nos deux voix, sentaient, chantaient ensemble" (Mysterious hero! it was I, I was he ... Our two hearts, our two voices, felt, sang together), in "Le Dernier chant du pèlerinage d'Harold," IV (1825).
22. Jerome J. McGann, "Milton and Byron," in *Byron and Romanticism*, ed. James Soderholm (Cambridge, 2002), 19–35.
23. Marchand, *Byron*, 1:335.
24. *CHP*, canto I, 865–872.

25. Marchand, *Byron*, 1:313.
26. His attitude in 1817 was unchanged. To Thomas Moore, he wrote: "If I live ten years longer, you will see … that it is not over with me—I don't mean in literature, for that is nothing; and it may seem odd enough to say, I do not think it my vocation" (Letter of 28 February 1817, *BLJ*, 5:177).
27. Letter to Robert Charles Dallas, 31 October 1811 (*BLJ*, 2:122). Marchand comments perceptively on Byron's ability to "shut off one side of his divided self from the other" (*BLJ*, 1:1).
28. Letter to John Murray, 7 June 1819 (*BLJ*, 6:149).
29. Letter to Thomas Love Peacock, [17 or 18] December 1818, *The Letters of Percy Bysshe Shelley*, 2 vols., ed. Frederick L. Jones (Oxford, 1964), 2: 58.
30. Marchand, *Byron*, 3:1259.
31. Quoted in Ibid., 2:746.
32. Ibid., 3:1239.
33. Letter to John Hunt, 10 March 1823 (*BLJ*, 10:120).
34. F. Rosen, *Bentham, Byron, and Greece: Constitutionalism, Nationalism, and Early Liberal Political Thought* (Oxford, 1992), 193.
35. Of the published, or partially published, archives of this period, the following are particularly valuable for Byron: those of Mavrokordatos, the Metropolitan Ignatios, and the Koundouriotis brothers. *Ιστορικόν Αρχείον Αλεξάνδρου Μαυροκορδάτου*, five parts, ed. E.G. Protopsaltis (Athens: Akadimia Athinon, 1963-1978) [hereafter *IAM*]; *Ιγνάτιος μητροπολίτης Ουγγροβλαχίας (1766–1828)*, two parts, ed. E.G. Protopsaltis (Athens: Akadimia Athinon, 1959–1961) [hereafter *IMO*]; *Αρχεία Λαζάρου και Γεωργίου Κουντουριώτου (1821–1832)*, 10 vols., ed. A. Lignos (Athens: Vivliothiki Yenikon Archion tou Kratous, 1920–1969). See also *Αρχεία της ελληνικής παλιγγενεσίας 1821–1832*, 10 vols. (Athens: Vivliothiki tis Voulis ton Ellinon, 1971–1978 and 1979–) [hereafter *AEP*]. I have explored the broader issues raised by this material in "Lord Byron and Mavrokordatos," *Romanticism* 12, no. 2 (December 2006): 126–142; "Letters to Lord Byron," *Romanticism on the Net* 45 (February 2007); "Byron and Mesolongi," *Literature Compass*, 4, no. 4 (July 2007).
36. *AEP*, 1, no. 344.
37. *AEP*, 1, no. 344.
38. Pietro Gamba, *A Narrative of Lord Byron's Last Journey to Greece* (Paris, 1825), 215.
39. *IMO*, 2:164.
40. See his letters of 29 June 1823 and 29 July 1823 to Mavrokordatos (*IAM*, 3, no. 704 and *IMO*, 2:162).
41. Gamba, *Narrative*, 207–209.

Chapter 8

1. Philip Shaw, *Waterloo and the Romantic Imagination* (London, 2002), 67; Georgy Capel, accessed in http://homepages.ihug.co.nz/~awoodley/waterlooseries/archives.html.
2. Annette Wieviorka, *The Era of the Witness* (Ithaca, 2006). See also Marilyn Yalom, *Blood Sisters: The French Revolution in Women's Memory* (New York, 1995).
3. David Bell, *The First Total War: Napoelon's Europe and the Birth of Warfare as We Know It* (Boston, 2007).

4. Here, I appreciate the helpful formulation of Edward Berenson.

5. Entries for 5, 11, and 27 September, "Diary of a Journey to Paris in 1802," in Sir Samuel Romilly, *Memoirs of the Life of Sir Samuel Romilly, Written by Himself; with a Selection from his Correspondence, Edited by his Sons* (London, 1840), 78–79, 84–85, 92. In general, *A Practical Guide to a Journey from London to Paris* (London, 1803), and *Galigarni's New Paris Guide* (Paris, 1827).

6. Quoted in J.R. Watson, *Romanticism and War: A Study of British Romantic Period Writers and the Napoleonic Wars* (London, 2003), 85–86.

7. On spectatorship and history, Peter Fritzsche, *Stranded in the Present: Modern Time and the Melancholy of History* (Cambridge, 2004); Pamela Pilbeam, *Madame Tussaud and the History of Waxworks* (London, 2003); and Maurice Samuels, *The Spectacular Past: Popular History and the Novel in Nineteenth-Century France* (Ithaca, 2004).

8. Jerome Christensen, *Romanticism and the End of History* (Baltimore, 2000).

9. Pilbeam, *Madame Tussaud*, 66.

10. Gentz to Adam Müller, 23 Oct. 1802, in *Briefe von und an Friedrich von Gentz*, ed. F.C. Wittichen and Ernst Salzer, 3 vols. (Munich, 1909–1913), 2:383.

11. Gentz to Brinkmann, 8 Nov. 1824, in Gentz, *Briefe*, 2:341.

12. François-René de Chateaubriand, *The Memoirs of François René Vicomte de Chateaubriand*, trans. Alexander Teixeira de Mattos, 6 vols. (London, 1902), 6:255.

13. Seamus Deane, *The French Revolution and Enlightenment in England, 1789–1832* (Cambridge, 1988), 41.

14. Linda Orr, *Headless History: Nineteenth-Century French Historiography of the Revolution* (Ithaca, 1990), 21.

15. Dorothea Schlegel to Sulpiz Boisserée, 4 Aug. 1808, in Mathilde Boisserée, ed., *Sulpiz Boisserée*, 2 vols. (Stuttgart, 1862), 1:53.

16. Agnes von Gerlach to Marie von Raumer, 30 Oct. 1806 and 23 Dec. 1808, in Hans Joachim Schoeps, ed., *Aus den Jahren Preussicher Not und Erneuerung. Tagebücher und Briefe der Gebrüder Gerlach und ihres Kreises, 1805–1820* (Berlin, 1963), 359, 368–369.

17. Yalom, *Blood Sisters*, 1, 10–11. For examples of the genre, see Adélaide Sousa Botelho Mouraoe Vasconelles, *Emilie et Alphonse* (Paris, 1799), *Eugénie et Mathilde* (Paris, 1811), and *Adèle de Selange* (Paris, 1821); as well as August Heinrich Julius Lafontaine, *Clara du Plessis und Clairant. Eine Familiengeschichte französischer Emigranten* (Berlin, 1795).

18. *Politisches Journal*, December 1794: 1266–1267.

19 Charlotte von Stein to Charlotte Schiller, 6 Mar. 1790, in Günter Jäckel, ed., *Das Volk braucht Licht: Frauen zur Zeit des Aufbruchs 1790–1848 in ihren Briefen* (Darmstadt, 1970), 82; Anne-Charlott Trepp, *Sanfte Männlichkeit und selbständige Weiblichkeit: Frauen und Männer in Hamburger Bürgertum zwischen 1770 und 1840* (Göttingen, 1996), 271–272.

20. Watson, *Romanticism and War*, 22.

21. Reinhart Koselleck, *Futures Past: On the Semantics of Historical Time* (Cambridge, 1985), 282.

22. James Chandler, *England in 1819: The Politics of Literary Culture and the Case of Romantic Historicism* (Chicago, 1998), 107.

23. *Politisches Journal*, November 1800: 1095–1096.

24. Gentz quoted in Ernst Wolfgang Becker, *Zeit der Revolution!—Revolution der Zeit?*

Zeiterfahrungen in Deutschland in der Ära der Revolutionen 1789–1848/49 (Göttingen, 1999), 59.

25. Chandler, *England in 1819*, 78, 149.
26. Thomas W. Laqueur, "Bodies, Details, and the Humanitarian Narrative," in *The New Cultural History*, ed. Lynn Hunt (Berkeley, 1989).
27. Alfred de Musset, *A Modern Man's Confession*, trans. G.F. Monkshood (London, 1908), 6, 10.
28. Ralph Waldo Emerson, *Representative Men* (Boston, 1850), 221.
29. Rahel Varnhagen to Ludwig Robert, 5 Feb. 1816, in Rahel Varnhagen, *Briefwechsel* (Munich, 1979), 4:101.
30. Ibid., and Nicolas Boyle, *Goethe: The Poet and the Age, Volume II* (New York, 2000).
31. Quoted in Golo Mann, *Secretary of Europe: The Life of Friedrich Gentz, Enemy of Napoleon*, trans. William H. Woglom (New Haven, 1946), 154.
32. Rahel to Markus Levin, 29 Mar. 1815, in Varnhagen, *Briefwechsel*, 4:79.
33. Fars de Fausselandry quoted in Yalom, *Blood Sisters*, 1.
34. Varnhagen to Rahel, 21 May 1813, in Varnhagen, *Briefwechsel*, 2:214.
35. Watson, *Romanticism and War*, 118, 197.
36. Clive Emsley, *British Society and the French Wars, 1793–1815* (London, 1979), 172–173. See also Gustav René Hocke, *Das europäische Tagebuch* (Wiesbaden, 1963), 67, 201–202; and Peter Gay, *The Naked Heart* (New York, 1995), 109.
37. See, for example, Edward Costello, *The Peninsular and Waterloo Campaigns*, ed. Antony Brett-James (London, 1967 [1839]); Emile Erckmann and Alexandre Chatrian, *The Conscript: A Story of the French War of 1813* (New York, 1912); John Green, *The Vicissitudes of a Soldier's Life* (Louth, 1827); *Memorials of the Late War*, 2 vols. (Edinburgh, 1828); E. Gridel and Richard, ed., *Cahiers de vieux soldats de la Révolution et de l'Empire* (Paris, 1902); B.H. Liddell Hart, ed., *The Letters of Private Wheeler* (Boston, 1952).
38. Watson, *Romanticism and War*, 197.
39. Ibid., 223–224.
40. Honoré de Balzac, *Lily of the Valley*, trans. Katherine Prescott Wormeley (Boston, 1901), 49–50. See also Balzac, *The Gallery of Antiquities*, trans. Katherine Prescott Wormeley (Boston, 1901).
41. See also Hugh Honour, *Romanticism* (New York, 1979), 196.
42. Sudhir Hazareesingh, "Memory and Political Imagination: The Legend of Napoleon Revisited," *French History* 18 (2004): 463–483.
43. Ernest Renan, *Recollections of My Youth*, trans. C.B. Pitman (London, 1883), 25, 82–83, 97, 100. See also the letters and revolutionary mementos in Adolf von Knigge, *Aus einer alten Kiste. Originalbriefe, Handschriften und Dokumente aus dem Nachlasse eines bekannten Mannes* (Leipzig, 1853), 21; and Knigge's letter to his daughter, 15 July 1790, in Claus Träger, ed., *Die französische Revolution im Spiegel der deutschen Literatur* (Leipzig and Frankfurt, 1975), as well as Gustave Flaubert, "A Simple Heart," *Three Tales* (London, 1961), 43.
44. Robert M. Adams, *Stendhal: Notes on a Novelist* (New York, 1959), 152.
45. *Lucien Leuwen*, trans. H.L.R. Edwards (London, 1991), 143.
46. Ibid., 440.
47. Cited in Stendhal, *The Red and the Black*, trans. Robert M. Adams (New York, 1969), 76.
48. Ibid., 58.

Chapter 9

1. Carol Ockman and Kenneth E. Silver, *Sarah Bernhardt: The Art of High Drama*, exh. cat. (New York, 2005).
2. Cornelia Otis Skinner, *Madame Sarah* (Cambridge, MA, 1967), 320.
3. "Bernhardt Has Spirit of France / Noted Actress Receives Ovation at Vendome / Her Greatness Undiminished / Audience Aroused to Unbounded Enthusiasm by War Playlet," *Nashville Tennessean* (9 February 1917). Julia Rather, State of Tennessee Archives, Nashville, communicated this anonymous article to Danielle Chamaillard, Department of the Arts du Spectacle, Bibliothèque nationale de France, Paris, who passed in on to me.
4. Marcel Proust, *Time Regained* (*Le Temps retrouvé*), trans. C.K. Scott Moncrieff and Terence Kilmartin; and by Andreas Mayor (New York, 1982), 854–855.
5. Proust, *Time Regained*, 917.
6. Susan A. Glenn, *Female Spectacle: The Theatrical Roots of Modern Feminism* (Cambridge, MA and London, 2000), 31.
7. See my discussion of Proust and Bernhardt in "Sarah Bernhardt and the Theatrics of French Nationalism: From Roland's Daughter to Napoléon's Son," in Ockman and Silver, *Sarah Bernhardt*, 84–88.
8. Mary Louise Roberts, *Disruptive Acts: The New Woman in Fin-de-Siècle France* (Chicago and London, 2002), 210.
9. "On nous fit la lecture de la nouvelle pièce de Bornier, *La Fille de Roland*. Le rôle de Berthe me fut confié, et nous commençâmes de suite les répétitions de cette belle pièce, aux vers un peu plats, mais enveloppée d'un grand souffle patriotique," in Sarah Bernhardt, *Ma double vie: Memoires de Sarah Bernhardt* (Paris, 1907), 351.
10. "La pièce eut un gros succès… C'était peu de temps après la terrible guerre de 1870. La pièce contenait de fréquentes allusions. Et, grâce au chauvinisme du public, elle eut une carrière plus belle que ne le méritait l'oeuvre en elle-même." Bernhardt, *Double vie*, 353.
11. Sarah Bernhardt, *My Double Life: The Memoirs of Sarah Bernhardt*, trans. Victoria Tietze Larson (Albany, 1999), 101.
12. See Bernhardt's letter to the journalist Jouvin, of *Le Figaro*, translated in Skinner, *Madame Sarah*, 99.
13. "… Emperor Napoléon III whom I very much liked," in Bernhardt, *My Double Life*, 192.
14. Arthur Gold and Robert Fizdale, *The Divine Sarah: A Life of Sarah Bernhardt* (New York, 1991), 13.
15. Bernhardt, *My Double Life*, 101: "Then there was MacMahon's sublime but impotent struggle as he was pushed back to Sedan."
16. Bernhardt, *My Double Life*, 113.
17. Bernhardt, *My Double Life*, 99–100.
18. Venita Datta, "On the Boulevards: Representations of Joan of Arc in the Popular Theater," Chapter 4 of her forthcoming study. I am grateful to Datta for sharing portions of this recent work with me.
19. "Elle porte sur elle ce reflet de vitrail que les apparitions de saints ont laissé sur la belle illuminée de Domrémy," cited in Noëlle Guibert, ed., *Portrait(s) de Sarah Bernhardt* (Paris, 2000), 44. This English translation from Gold and Fizdale, *Divine Sarah*, 244.
20. Stuart Jeffries, "Desperately Seeking Sarah," *The Guardian*, 25 October 2000, UK, [n.p., Guardian Unlimited website]. Bernhardt would play the great French heroine in

another production, many years later, in 1909, in Émile Moreau's *Le Procès de Jeanne d'Arc*.

21. Bernhardt, *My Double Life*, 59.

22. See Elisabeth Roudinesco, *Théroigne de Méricourt: A Melancholic Woman during the French Revolution*, trans. Martin Thom (London and New York, 1991), 225–227.

23. Michael Burns, *Dreyfus: A Family Affair* (New York 1991), 150.

24. Burns, *Dreyfus*, 516n29. Louis Verneuil, in *The Fabulous Life of Sarah Bernhardt*, trans. Ernest Boyd (New York and London: Harper and Brothers, 1942), 207, says that Bernhardt was among the "few privileged persons who had been present at the degradation of Captain Dreyfus."

25. Verneuil, *The Fabulous Life*, 221.

26. Verneuil, *The Fabulous Life*, 222–223.

27. Maurice Baring, *Sarah Bernhardt* (NY and London, 1940), 138–139.

28. "Grand Dieu! Ce n'est pas une cause/Que j'attaque ou que je défends … /Et ceci n'est pas autre chose/Que l'histoire d'un pauvre enfant": these lines, which Rostand placed at the front of his published version of *L'Aiglon*, were added at the suggestion of Jean Jaurès to avoid the play's political appropriation by the French right, according to Patrick Besnier, ed., *Edmond Rostand, L'Aiglon* (Paris, 1986), 414. See also Venita Datta's excellent discussion of the political implications of the play in "'L'appel au soldat': Visions of the Napoleonic Legend in Popular Culture of the Belle Epoque," *French Historical Studies* 28, no. 1 (Winter 2005): 1–30.

29. The drawing for Franz's costume is contained in a letter Rostand wrote to Bernhardt in late 1899 and is now in the collection of the Département des Arts du Spectacle, Bibliothèque nationale de France, Paris. It is unclear to what extent Poiret contributed to the costume design for the Duc de Reichstadt in *L'Aiglon*. Palmer White says that Poiret designed the famous white uniform, but that a rude remark Poiret made during a rehearsal led Bernhardt to demand that his employer, Jacques Doucet, fire him, which White says he did (see *Poiret le Magnifique* (Paris, 1986), 47). Yvonne Deslandres says he was "charged with creating the costumes for Sarah Bernhardt in *L'Aiglon*," but dismissed because of an arrogant remark. See *Paul Poiret* (New York, 1986), 36.

30. Edmond Rostand, *L'Aiglon*, trans. Louis N. Parker (New York and London:, 1900), act 3, 136.

31. Patrick Besnier, ed. *Edmond Rostand, L'Aiglon* (Paris, 1986), 12.

32. Rostand, *L'Aiglon*, act 2, 113.

33. Rostand, *L'Aiglon*, act 2, 117.

34. Both of these posters are in the collection of the Bibliothèque Forney, Paris.

Chapter 10

1. Rosemonde Rostand, *Edmond Rostand* (Paris, 1935), 5–7.

2. Much has been written about Rostand, especially since the centenary of *Cyrano*. Among the numerous books, see Sue Lloyd, *The Man who was Cyrano* (Bloomington, 2002); Jacques Lorcey: *Edmond Rostand*, 3 vols. (Paris, 2004); Jean-Baptiste Manuel, *Edmond Rostand, écrivain imaginaire* (Paris, 2003); Marc Landry, *Edmond Rostand: le panache et la gloire* (Paris, 1986); Caroline de Margerie, *Edmond Rostand ou le baiser de la gloire* (Paris, 1997). The work closest resembling my own is that of Jean-Marie Apostolidès, *Cyrano: Qui fut tout et qui ne fut rien* (Paris, 2006).

3. As I write, Kevin Kline's Cyrano is playing to full houses on Broadway.
4. The expression *les lieux de mémoire* has been translated into English as "realms of memory" and refers to people, places, and events that have marked national memory in France. See Pierre Nora, ed., *Les Lieux de mémoire*, 3 vols. (Paris, 1984–1992; 1997).
5. See Marc Lambron, "Le mythe Cyrano," *Le Point*, no. 916 (9 April 1990): 8–12. See Rostand's speech to the French Academy: *Discours de Réception à l'Académie française, le 4 juin 1903* (Paris, 1904), 22–23.
6. Maurice Rostand, *Confession d'un demi-siècle* (Paris, 1948), 35.
7. Although I am using the terms of fame and celebrity interchangeably here, in the case of Rostand, I am aware that the first rests on the accomplishments of the person considered, whereas the second refers to "a person whose name, once made by the news, now makes the news." Irving Rein, Philip Kottler, and Martin Stoller, *High Visibility* (New York, 1987), 15. See also Leo Braudy, *The Frenzy of Renown: Fame and Its History* (New York, 1986), 14. On female celebrities of the nineteenth century, see Lenard Berlanstein, "Historicizing and Gendering Celebrity Culture: Famous Women in Nineteenth-Century France," *Journal of Women's Studies* 16, no. 4 (2004): 65–91. Berlanstein illustrates that the cult of celebrity in France predated the advent of mass culture.
8. On heroes at this time, see Paul Gerbod, "L'éthique héroïque en France (1870–1914)," *La Revue historique* 268 (1982): 409–429; Christian Amalvi, *Les Héros de l'histoire de France* (Paris, 1979) and Jean-François Chanet, "La Fabrique des héros: Pédagogie républicaine et culte des grands hommes de Sedan à Vichy," *Vingtième Siècle* 65 (January–March 2000): 13–34. See also Edward Berenson on imperial heroes: *Heroes of Empire: Five Charismatic Men and the Conquest of Africa* (Berkeley, 2010) *and* his "Unifying the French Nation: Savornan de Brazza and the Third Republic," in *Music, Culture and National Identity in France 1870–1939*, ed. Barbara Kelly (Rochester, NY, 2008).
9. Robert Nye, *Maculinity and Male Codes of Honor in Modern France* (New York, 1993), 225; Edward Berenson, *The Trial of Madame Caillaux* (Berkeley, 1992), 186–198. See also the important study by Annelise Maugue, *L'Identité masculine en crise au tournant du siècle, 1871–1914* (Paris, 1987).
10. Emile Faguet, *Le Journal des débats*, 3 January 1898.
11. Georges Thiébaud, *Le Journal*, 10 January 1898.
12. Jules Lemaître, "Revue dramatique," originally published in *La Revue des deux mondes*, reproduced in *Impressions de théâtre, 10ème série* (Paris, 1898), 336.
13. See various reviews in *La Fronde* by Jeanne Marnière: "Les Premières: Cyrano de Bergerac," 29 December 1897; Marie-Anne de Bovet, "Les Cadets de Gascogne," 5 January 1898, and Maria Pognon, "Les Femmes et la Paix," 5 January 1898.
14. See the chapter: "The Sword or the Pen?: Competing Visions of the Hero at the Fin de Siècle" in Venita Datta, *Birth of a National Icon: The Literary Avant-Garde and the Origins of the Intellectual in France* (Albany, 1999), 135–182; Christopher Forth, *The Dreyfus Affair and the Crisis of Masculinity* (Baltimore, 2004).
15. I have explored these issues in two different articles: "'L'Appel au Soldat': Visions of the Napoleonic Legend in Popular Culture of the Belle Epoque," *French Historical Studies*, vol. 28, no. 1 (Winter 2005): 1–30; and "Sur les boulevards: les représentations de Jeanne d'Arc dans le théâtre populaire," *CLIO, Histoire, Femmes et Société* 24 (2006): 127–149.
16. Sarah Bernhardt, *Ma double vie* (Paris, 2000 [1907]), 99–100.
17. See Richard Schickel, *Intimate Strangers: The Culture of Celebrity* (New York, 1985).

See also Lenard Berlanstein, *Daughters of Eve: A Cultural History of French Theater Women from the Old Regime to the Fin-de-Siècle* (Cambridge, MA, 2001), 209–236, and Mary Louise Roberts, *Disruptive Acts: The New Woman in Fin-de-Siècle France* (Chicago, 2002), especially, 169–174, both of whom explore this theme. See also Lawrence M. Friedman, *The Horizontal Society* (New Haven, 1999), and the dossier on Coquelin at the Bibliothèque nationale de France (hereafter BNF), Richelieu: Rt6620, as well as articles published at the time of his death: "Grand comédien, grand philanthrope," in *Théâtre* (15 January–15 February 1909); Bibliothèque historique de la ville de Paris (hereafter BHVP); *Dossier d'actualités*. I would like to express my thanks to Mme Geneviève Morlet of the BHVP, who made these *dossiers d'actualités* available to me.

18. Vanessa R. Schwartz, *Spectacular Realities: Early Mass Culture in Fin-de-Siècle Paris* (Berkeley, 1998); Dominique Kalifa, *L'Encre et le sang: Récits de crimes et société à la Belle Epoque* (Paris, 1995); James Lehning, *The Melodramatic Thread: Spectacle and Political Culture in Modern France* (Bloomington, IN, 2007).

19. Indeed, actor André Antoine, in attendance at the Rennes trial, claimed to be able to play Dreyfus better than Dreyfus himself and claimed also to be able to move the public. See Victor Basch quoting Antoine in "Alfred Dreyfus et l'Affaire," *Cahiers des droits de l'homme* (31 July 1935): 503, cited by Françoise Basch, *Victor Basch: De l'Affaire Dreyfus au crime de la Milice* (Paris: 1994), 68–69.

20. Aiglon candies and writing paper were popular at this time, as were Joan of Arc products.

21. Charles Donos, *Les hommes d'aujourd'hui* 9, no. 465, no date, BHVP, ART collection.

22. Emile Faguet, *Le Journal des débats*, 3 January 1898.

23. As occurred with Sarah Bernhardt playing Joan of Arc. See Roberts, *Disruptive Acts*, 217–218, and Berlanstein, *Daughters of Eve*, 235. But Bernhardt too transformed the legendary figure: see my "Sur les boulevards," and Kenneth Silver, "Sarah Bernhardt and the Theatrics of French Nationalism: From Roland's Daughter to Napoleon's Son," in *Sarah Bernhardt: The Art of High Drama*, ed. Carol Ockman and Kenneth E. Silver (New York & New Haven, 2005), 76.

24. Henri de Weindel, *Le Gaulois* of 29 March 1898. When Coquelin died in 1909, most of the articles devoted to him described the actor as a quintessential French hero, who died as he had lived, "in action."

25. "Silhouette parisienne," *Le Gaulois*, 28 December 1897.

26. See Catulle Mendès, *Le Journal*, 29 December 1897 on poets and their "triumphal hour."

27. I am using the Anthony Burgess translation of *Cyrano de Bergerac* (New York, 1985; 1998), act 2 sc. 7, lines 69-71, which although less literally faithful to the original, reproduces the *panache* of Rostand's text.

28. See chapters on the "Aristocrat and Proletarian? Intellectuals and Elites in Fin-de-Siècle France" and "The Jew as Intellectual, the Intellectual as Jew" in Datta, *Birth*, 65–116.

29. Christophe Charle, *La Crise littéraire à l'époque du naturalisme* (Paris, 1979), 169–171.

30. *Cyrano de Bergerac*, act 2, sc. 8.

31. A.F. Herold, *Le Mercure de France*, vol. 25 (February 1898): 594. See also the reviews published in other avant-garde journals: Jacques des Gachons in *L'Ermitage*, vol. 26 (January–June 1898): 236–237, and Alfred Athys, "La Quinzaine dramatique," *La Revue blanche*, vol. 15 (15 January 1898): 150–154.

32. See especially Francisque Sarcey's review in *Le Temps* of 3 January 1898.

33. Lemaître, *Impressions de théâtre*, 344.

34. See, for example, *Le Gaulois* of 5 June 1903.
35. Paul Faure, *Vingt ans d'intimité avec Edmond Rostand* (Paris, 1928), 136–137. See also Maurice Rostand's description of the inauguration ceremony, *Confession*, 85.
36. See de Vogüé's speech in *Discours prononcés dans la Séance publique tenue par l'Académie française* (Paris, 1903), 47. See also the articles published at the time of Rostand's death: Edmond Haracourt, "L'Adieu à Rostand," *Le Figaro*, 21 February 1919; "Souvenirs littéraires: Edmond Rostand," 5 December 1918 by Jean Pschari from Rf 71.533 dossier, no newspaper identification; "L'Adieu au poète" by Gérard Bauer, 5 December 1918, and "La Vie à Paris" by Abel Hermant, 5 December 1918, also from this dossier, no identification.
37. Jean Rostand, "Mon Père Edmond Rostand," BHVP, ART dossier, no date, but most likely from the 1960s.
38. An account confirmed by Paul Faure. On Rostand's refusal to receive journalists at Cambo, see Faure, *Vingt ans*, 65; on Rostand's reaction to Coquelin's visit, *Vingt ans*, 125–126. There is an entire dossier devoted to articles on Cambo in the Rostand file at the BNF Richelieu: Rf 71.534.
39. This description serves a snapshot of the scene, and indeed there is a photo to accompany the text. See also Schickel, *Intimate Strangers*, 14–15. Both Roberts, *Disruptive Acts*, 170–171, and Berlanstein, *Daughters of Eve*, 208–221, speak of these celebrity interviews in actresses' homes. See also Schwartz, *Spectacular Realities*, 40–43. A number of such interviews, accompanied by photos, over the years were conducted with Rostand. See, for example "Edmond Rostand à Saint-Prix" by Saint-Georges de Bouhélier, *Comédia* of 10 March 1901, who describes a "delicious" day spent in the company of the author and his wife. See also Gaston Deschamps, "Coquelin chez Rostand," *Le Figaro*, 10 September 1903; Raoul Aubry, "Un déjeuner chez Edmond Rostand," *Le Temps*, 13 June 1905; Jean Frollo, "Rostand à Paris," *Le Petit parisien*, 30 January 1909. These interviews are collected in a press dossier on Rostand Rf 71.533 at the BNF Richelieu.
40. The interview in the January 1913 issue of *Les Annales* was conducted by André Arnylvelde, BHVP, Rostand Actualités dossier. Other interviews with Rostand over the years confirm this impression.
41. Faure, *Vingt ans*, 172; Raoul Aubry, "Un déjeuner chez Edmond Rostand" (1905).
42. Lambron, "mythe Cyrano," 8.
43. Berlanstein, *Daughters of Eve*, 219.

Conclusion

1. Arnold's distinction first appears in "The Bishop and the Philosopher," an essay written for *Macmillan's Magazine* in 1863, and in the revised essay "Spinoza and the Bible," in *Essays in Criticism* (1865). See Matthew Arnold, *Lectures and Essays in Criticism*, ed. R.H. Super (Ann Arbor, 1962), 215. Also Matthew Arnold, *Selected Poems and Prose*, ed. Miriam Allott (London, 1978). "Solo" as a verb also dates from the same period. "Solo" as a noun goes back to late seventeenth/early eighteenth century.
2. Charles Camic traces the previous appearances of the term in Weber's work and applies earlier nuances to what he argues are later, less complex uses. See "Charisma: Its Variations, Preconditions, and Consequences," *Sociological Inquiry* 50, no. 1 (1980): 5–24.
3. In *The Crowd: A Study of the Popular Mind* (New York, 1960; *La Psychologie des foules*, 1895), Gustave Le Bon elaborates on the idea of prestige, which he associates with

both people and objects. His impressionistic comments intriguingly foreshadow the more elaborate formulations of both Weber's charisma and Benjamin's aura.

4. See Andrew Marvell, *The Complete Poems*, ed. Elizabeth Donno (London, 1976).

5. See Sidney Hook, *The Hero In History* (Boston, 1955 [1943]), perhaps the last gasp in recent times of the Great Man theory of history. Published in 1943, Hook's essay in historiography differentiates between the "eventful man" (e.g., Napoleon), who seizes the historical moment, and the "event-making man" (e.g., Lenin), who creates the historical moment so that he can seize it.

6. "It is recognition on the part of those subject to authority which is decisive for the validity of charisma.... [Its] basis lies ... in the conception that it is the duty of those subject to charismatic authority to recognize its genuineness and act accordingly.... If proof and success elude the leader for long, if he appears deserted by his god or his magical or heroic powers, above all, if his leadership fails to benefit his followers, it is likely that his charismatic authority will disappear." Max Weber, *Economy and Society: an Outline of Interpretive Sociology*, ed. Guenther Roth and Claus Wittich, 2 vols. (Berkeley and Los Angeles, 1978), 1:241–242. The editor of Weber's works on charisma, S.M. Eisenstadt, emphasizes the assumption of audience passivity: "For the most part, [Weber] takes for granted the nature of the appeal of the charismatic." *Max Weber on Charisma and Institution Building* (Chicago, 1968), xxi. In Eisenstadt's version of the passages cited above (48–49), taken from the translation by A.R. Henderson and Talcott Parsons, "duty" is in italics.

7. Walter Benjamin, "The Work of Art in the Age of Mechanical Reproduction," in *Illuminations: Essays and Reflections*, ed. Harry Zohn (New York, 1968).

8. Marvell similarly imagines Cromwell, the non-religious force of nature, to be a potential liberator for other countries as well: "To all states not free/ Shall climacteric be."

9. At Napoleon's insistence, the figure has little resemblance to the real person and is an image of "the hero."

10. With this connection between the public stage and the theater stage in mind, it seems no coincidence that William Hazlitt, the first great drama critic writing in English, spent the late 1820s writing a massive biography of Napoleon.

11. David Lucas, *Various Subjects of Landscape, Characteristic of English Scenery*. Lucas continued to engrave and publish mezzotints based on Constable's paintings even after the artist's death in 1837.

12. Baedeker's guide appears in the wake of Heine's poem on the Lorelei rocks and a decade or two before Wagner sets his Ring cycle in its surroundings.

13. Arnold, "Stanzas from the Grande Chartreuse," in *Lectures and Essays*. Compare this pose of reticence with a phrase often associated with T.E. Lawrence, "backing into the spotlight."

14. Charles Rosen calls the work of Liszt in the 1830s "one of the greatest revolutions of keyboard style in history," *The Romantic Generation* (Cambridge, MA, 1995), 491. In a letter, Mozart had written about his pleasure at coming upon a piano with single escapement. Érard took out a patent in England, where there was a tradition of audience demand for louder instruments.

15. These comments occur at the beginning of Emerson's essay on Shakespeare. *Essays and Lectures*, ed. Joel Porte (New York, 1983), 710, 715.

16. Advertising, journalism's less respectable twin, analogously seeks to create a charisma of objects, products with more charm and allure than usefulness and efficiency. Zola's *Au Bonheur des dames*, his 1883 novel about the creation of a great Paris department store, extends this charisma (or is it aura?) to the store itself, where shoppers are drawn

in by the display and profusion of items that sat so stolidly on the shelves of the mom-and-pop stores it replaced.

17. John Tenniel, who drew the illustrations for *Alice in Wonderland*, worked extensively for *Punch*, while "Spy" and "Ape" were among the prominent illustrators in *Vanity Fair*.

18. In addition to Hogarthian caricature, another eighteenth-century forerunner was the vogue for portraits and busts of opposition political figures, especially after the coming of the Hanoverians and the Whig supremacy presided over by Robert Walpole, the first politician to be called the "prime minister," which was meant as an insult. Such portraits often stressed a need to look to the past for true virtue in the face of the cor-rupt political present. By the end of the century, images in porcelain or the crockery bas reliefs of Josiah Wedgwood canonized a whole array of political worthies for a wide and less wealthy audience.

19. The first halftone from a photograph is published in the *New York Graphic* in 1880, but it is not until 1897 that such images could be used along with full speed print-ing presses and, therefore, had greater reproducibility and dissemination. Wire photos were in use in Europe shortly before the First World War (1910) and were transmitted intercontinentally by 1921.

20. The word caricature itself comes from words meaning to load in, in other words, a supercharging and exaggeration, especially of facial detail.

21. Thomas Richards cites an 1843 article in the *Edinburgh Review* mocking the endorse-ments of some eighty peers of the realm for Mr. Cockle's Antibilious Pills. Thomas Richards, *The Commodity Culture of Victorian England: Advertising and Spectacle, 1851–1914* (Palo Alto, 1990), 84.

22. Richards argues that such advertising created an "acquired charisma" for Victoria that she did not naturally seek to display or even have, in a process by which she became "a semiotic lodestone for events that occurred around her and conferred charisma upon her" (*Commodity Culture*, 77). An intriguing forerunner for this conferral in the realm of caricature is Tenniel's 1876 cartoon of Disraeli, looking much like the Carpenter in *Alice in Wonderland*, offering the crown of India to Victoria. See also Frank Presbrey, *The History and Development of Advertising* (Garden City, 1929); James D. Norris, *Advertising and the Transformation of American Society, 1865–1920* (New York, 1990). Marc Martin notes the greater use of advertising posters in France, especially Paris, along with the interplay between ads for shows and ads for products. *Trois siècles de publicité en France* (Paris, 1992).

23. Benjamin writes of photography, but the most pervasive influence on the loss of aura in his essay is the movies, whose charisma-building potential may have influenced We-ber's thoughts as well. A popular culture analogy to both charisma and aura that was much talked about in the post-World War I period is Elinor Glyn's "It," her euphemism for the sex appeal that she considered to be perfectly embodied by Clara Bow. Since writing this section, I have also been directed to another effort to juxtapose Benjamin with Weber: C. Stephen Jaeger, "Aura and Charisma," *Eadem Utraque Europa* 2, no. 2 (June 2006): 125–154, which particularly focuses on the *Odyssey* and *In Search of Lost Time* as examples of their interplay.

24. Interestingly, as a sales technique, celebrity endorsements for products have dried up as well, with the exception of those made by athletes for specifically athletic products, beautiful actresses for cosmetics, and former public figures for incontinence pills and other supplies purporting to ease the ailments of aging.

∿ NOTES ON CONTRIBUTORS ∾

Edward Berenson is Professor of History and French Studies and Director of the Institute of French Studies at New York University. His numerous publications include *The Trial of Madame Caillaux* and the forthcoming *Heroes of Empire: Charisma and Europe's Quest for Africa*, University of California Press, 2010.

Eva Giloi is Assistant Professor in the History Department at Rutgers University, Newark. Her book *Monarchy, Myth, and Material Culture in Germany 1750–1950* will be forthcoming from Cambridge University Press in 2010.

Martin Kohlrausch is Dilthey Fellow at the Volkswagen Foundation and Lecturer at Ruhr University, Bochum. He has published widely on the German monarchy and mass media, and authored *Der Monarch im Skandal. Die Logik der Massenmedien und die Transformation der wilhelminischen Monarchie.*

Dana Gooley is Associate Professor in the Department of Music at Brown University. A trained musicologist and performing jazz pianist, his research focuses on Liszt and the cult of the virtuoso, as highlighted in his books *The Virtuoso Liszt* and *Franz Liszt and His World.*

Emily Apter is Professor in the Department of French and the Department of Comparative Literature at New York University. Her recent works on French literature, feminism, and critical theory include *The Translation Zone: A New Comparative Literature, Continental Drift: From National Characters to Virtual Subjects*, and *Feminizing the Fetish: Psychoanalysis and Narrative Obsession in Turn-of-the Century France.*

Mary Louise Roberts is Professor in the Department of History at the University of Wisconsin-Madison. She has written on the history of France, women, and gender across two centuries, most prominently in *Disruptive Acts: The New Woman in Fin-de-Siècle France*, in *Civilization without Sexes: Reconstructing Gender in Post-war France*, and in recent articles on sexual relations between US G.I.s and French women, 1944–1946.

Stephen Minta is Professor in the Department of English and Related Literature at the University of York. Trained as a linguist, he has written extensively on the French, Spanish, Italian, and Greek literary traditions, including *On a Voiceless Shore: Byron in Greece*.

Peter Fritzsche is Professor in the Department of History at the University of Illinois at Urbana-Champaign. A prolific cultural historian, he has written on memory and identity; media; fascism, Nazism, and war. His recent publications include *Life and Death in the Third Reich* and *Stranded in the Present: Modern Time and the Melancholy of History*.

Kenneth Silver is Professor of Modern Art in the department of Art History at New York University. A specialist in French and US twentieth-century art, he co-created, with Carol Ockman, the first major museum show on Sarah Bernhardt, installed at New York's Jewish Museum in 2005, and co-authored its exhibition catalogue, *Sarah Bernhardt: The Art of High Drama*.

Venita Datta is Professor in the French Department at Wellesley College. Interested in the relationship of politics, culture, and national identity, her recent projects include *Birth of a National Icon: The Literary Avant-Garde and the Origins of the Intellectual in France* and a work-in-progress, *Legends, Heroes, and Superwomen: Causes Célèbres and National Identity in Belle-Époque France*.

Leo Braudy is University Professor, Leo S. Bing Chair in English and American Literature, and Professor of English at the University of Southern California. A distinguished scholar of English literature, US culture, and the histories of film, fame, and gender, his book *The Frenzy of Renown* is a classic in the field of fame studies.

❧ SELECTED BIBLIOGRAPHY ❧

A Practical Guide to a Journey from London to Paris. London, 1803.

Adams, Robert M. *Stendhal: Notes on a Novelist.* New York, 1959.

Altenburg, Detlef. "Franz Liszt and the legacy of the classical era." *19th Century Music* 18, no. 1 (1994).

Amalvi, Christian. *Les héros de l'histoire de France.* Paris, 1979.

Andres, Jan, Alexa Geisthövel, and Matthias Schwengelbeck, eds. *Die Sinnlichkeit der Macht. Herrschaft und Repräsentation seit der Frühen Neuzeit.* Frankfurt a.M., 2005.

Apostolidès, Jean-Marie. *Cyrano: Qui fut tout et qui ne fut rien.* Paris, 2006.

Apter, Emily. *Continental Drift: From National Characters to Virtual Subjects.* Chicago, 1999.

Arnold, Matthew. *Lectures and Essays in Criticism.* Edited by R.H. Super. Ann Arbor, 1962.

———. *Selected Poems and Prose.* Edited by Miriam Allott. London, 1978.

Bagehot, Walter. *The English Constitution.* Ithaca, 1966 [1867].

Balzac, Honoré de. *Gallery of Antiquities.* Translated by Katherine Prescott Wormeley. Boston, 1901.

———. *The Lily of the Valley.* Translated by Katherine Prescott Wormeley. Boston, 1901.

Baring, Maurice. *Sarah Bernhardt.* NY and London, 1940.

Barthes, Roland. "The Death of the Author." In *The Rustle of Language,* translated by Richard Howard. Berkeley and Los Angeles, 1989.

———. *Mythologies.* Paris, 1957.

Becker, Ernst Wolfgang. *Zeit der Revolution!—Revolution der Zeit? Zeiterfahrungen in Deutschland in der Ära der Revolutionen 1789–1848/49.* Göttingen, 1999.

Bell, David. *The First Total War: Napoleon's Europe and the Birth of Warfare as We Know It.* Boston, 2007.

Bellas, J.and S. Gut, eds. *Correspondence Franz Liszt/Marie d'Agoult.* Paris, 2001.

Benjamin, Walter. "The Work of Art in the Age of Mechanical Reproduction." In *Iluminations: Essays and Reflections,* edited by Harry Zohn. New York, 1968.

Berenson, Edward. *Heroes of Empire: Charisma and Europe's Conquest of Africa, 1870–1914.* Berkeley, 2010.

———. *The Trial of Madam Caillaux.* Berkeley, 1992.

———. "Unifying the French Nation: Savornan de Brazza and the Third Republic." In *Music, Culture and National Identity in France 1870–1939,* edited by Barbara Kelly. Rochester, NY, 2008.

Berlanstein, Lenard. "Breeches and Breaches: Cross-Dress Theater and the Culture of Gender Ambiguity in Modern France." *Comparative Studies in Society and History* 38 (1996): 338–369.

———. *Daughters of Eve: A Cultural History of French Theater Women from the Old Regime to the Fin-de-Siècle.* Cambridge, MA, 2001.

———. "Historicizing and Gendering Celebrity Culture: Famous Women in Nineteenth-Century France." *Journal of Women's History* 16, no. 4 (2004): 65–91.

Berlin und die Berliner: Leute, Dinge, Sitten, Winke. Karlsruhe, 1905.

Bernhardt, Sarah. *My Double Life: The Memoirs of Sarah Bernhardt*. Translated by Victoria Tietze Larson. Albany, 1999. In French as *Ma double vie: Mémoires de Sarah Bernhardt* (Paris, 1907).

Bersani, Leo. *The Death of Stéphane Mallarmé*. Cambridge, 1982.

Bonnet, Jean-Claude. *Naissance du Panthéon: essai sur le culte des grands homes*. Paris, 1998.

Boorstein, Daniel J. *The Image. A Guide to Pseudo-Events in America*. New York, 1961.

Botstein, Leon. "Reflections on Franz Liszt: Mirror to the Nineteenth Century." In *Franz Liszt and his World*, edited by Christopher H. Gibbs and Dana Gooley. Princeton, 2006.

Boyle, Nicolas. *Goethe: The Poet and the Age, Volume II*. New York, 2000.

Boym, Svetlana. *Death in Quotation Marks: Cultural Myths of the Modern Poet*. Cambridge, 1991.

Braudy, Leo. *From Chivalry to Terrorism. War and the Changing Nature of Masculinity*. New York, 2003.

———. *The Frenzy of Renown: Fame and Its History*. New York, 1986.

———. *The World in a Frame: What We See in Films*. Garden City, NY, 1976.

Burger, Ernst, ed. *Franz Liszt: A Life in Pictures and Documents*. Princeton, 1989.

Burns, Michael. *Dreyfus: A Family Affair*. New York 1991.

Burt, E.S. *Poetry's Appeal: Nineteenth-Century Lyric and the Political Space*. Stanford, CA, 1999.

Byron. *Selected Poems*. Edited by S.J. Wolfson and P.J. Manning. London, 1996.

Camic, Charles. "Charisma: Its Variations, Preconditions, and Consequences." *Sociological Inquiry* 50, no. 1 (1980): 5–24.

Cannadine, David. "The Context, Performance and Meaning of Ritual: The British Monarchy and the 'Invention of Tradition,' c. 1820–1977." In *The Invention of Tradition*, edited by Eric Hobsbawm and Terence Ranger. Cambridge, 1983.

Carlyle, Thomas. *On Heroes, Hero-Worship, and the Heroic in History*. Edited by Michael K. Goldberg. Berkeley, 1993.

Catani, Damian. *The Poet in Society: Art, Consumerism and Politics in Stéphane Mallarmé*. New York, 2002.

Caws, Mary Ann. *Surprised in Translation*. Chicago, 2006.

Chadwick, Whitney. "'The Fine Art of Gentling': Horses, Women and Rosa Bonheur in Victorian England." In *The Body Imaged: The Human Form and Visual Culture since the Renaissance*, edited by Kathleen Adler and Marcia Pointon. Cambridge, 1993.

Chandler, James. *England in 1819: The Politics of Literary Culture and the Case of Romantic Historicism*. Chicago, 1998.

Chanet, Jean-François. "La Fabrique des héros: Pédagogie républicaine et culte des grands hommes de Sedan à Vichy." *Vingtième Siècle* 65 (January–March 2000): 13–34.

Chaplin, Tamara. *Turning on the Mind: French Philosophers on Television*. Chicago, 2007.

Charle, Christophe. *La Crise littéraire à l'époque du naturalisme*. Paris, 1979.

Christensen, Jerome. *Romanticism and the End of History*. Baltimore, 2000.

Clark, T.J. *The Absolute Bourgeois: Artists and Politics in France 1848–1851*. London, 1973.

Cornwall, James E. "Die Geschichte der Photographie in Berlin." *Mitteilungen des Vereins für die Geschichte Berlins* 72. Berlin, 1976.

Darrah, William C. *Cartes de Visite in Nineteenth Century Photography*. Gettysburg, 1981.

Datta, Venita. "'L'appel au soldat': Visions of the Napoleonic Legend in Popular Culture of the Belle Epoque." *French Historical Studies* 28, no. 1 (Winter 2005): 1–30.

———. *Birth of a National Icon: The Literary Avant-Garde and the Origins of the Intellectual in France*. Albany, 1999.

———. "Sur les boulevards: les représentations de Jeanne d'Arc dans le théâtre populaire." *CLIO, Histoire, Femmes et Société* 24 (2006): 127–149.

Deane, Seamus. *The French Revolution and Enlightenment in England, 1789–1832*. Cambridge, 1988.

Dion, Isabelle. *Pierre Savorgnan de Brazza. Au Coeur du Congo*. Aix-en-Provence, 2007.

Dizikes, John. *Opera in America: a Cultural History*. New Haven, 1993.

Dohme, Robert. *Unter fünf preussischen Königen: Lebenserinnerungen*. Edited by Paul Lindenberg. Berlin, 1901.

Dyer, Richard. *Heavenly Bodies: Film Stars and Society*. New York, 2004 [1986].

———. *Stars*. London, 1998.

Eisenstadt, S.N, ed. *Max Weber on Charisma and Institution Building*. Chicago, 1968.

Eley, Geoff and James Retallack, eds. *Wilhelminism and Its Legacies: German Modernities, Imperialism and the Meanings of Reform, 1890–1930*. New York, 2003.

Elias, Norbert. *The Court Society*. Translated by Edmund Jephcott. Oxford, 1983.

Emerson, Ralph Waldo. *Representative Men*. Boston, 1850.

———. *Essays and Lectures*. Edited by Joel Porte. New York, 1983.

Emsley, Clive. *British Society and the French Wars, 1793–1815*. London, 1979.

Engels, Jens Ivo. *Königsbilder. Sprechen, Singen und Schreiben über den französischen König in der ersten Hälfte des 18. Jahrhunderts*. Bonn, 2000.

Esterhammer, Angela. "The Cosmopolitan *improvvisatore*: Spontaneity and Performance in Romantic Aesthetics." *European Romantic Review* 16, no. 2 (2005): 153–165.

Feldman, Martha. *Opera and Sovereignty: Transforming Myths in Eighteenth-Century Italy*. Chicago, 2007.

Forth, Christopher. *The Dreyfus Affair and the Crisis of Masculinity*. Baltimore, 2004.

Freund, Gisèle. *Photographie und Gesellschaft*. München, 1974.

Fritzsche, Peter. *Stranded in the Present: Modern Time and the Melancholy of History*. Cambridge, 2004.

Gamson, Joshua. *Claims to Fame. Celebrity in Contemporary America*. Berkeley and Los Angeles, 1994.

Garb, Tamar. *Sisters of the Brush: Women's Artistic Culture in Late Nineteenth-Century Paris*. New Haven, 1994.

Gardner, Viv and Susan Rutherford, eds. *The New Woman and Her Sisters: Feminism and Theatre, 1850–1914*. New York, 1992.

Gay, Peter. *The Bourgeois Experience: Victoria to Freud*. 5 vols. New York, 1984-98.

———. *The Naked Heart*. New York, 1995.

Geisthövel, Alexa. "Den Monarchen im Blick: Wilhelm I. in der illustrierten Familienpresse." In *Kommunikation als Beobachtung. Medienwandel und Gesellschaftsbilder 1880–1960*, edited by Habbo Knoch and Daniel Morat. München, 2003.

Gerbod, Paul. "L'éthique héroïque en France, 1870–1914." *La Revue historique* 268 (1982): 409–429.

Gernsheim, Helmut and Alison Gernsheim. *The History of Photography: from the Camera Obscura to the beginning of the modern era*. New York, 1969.

Gestrich, Andreas. *Absolutismus und Öffentlichkeit. Politische Kommunikation in Deutschland zu Beginn des 18. Jahrhunderts*. Göttingen, 1994.

Glenn, Susan A. *Female Spectacle: The Theatrical Roots of Modern Feminism*. Cambridge, MA and London, 2000.

Gluck, Mary. *Popular Bohemia: Modernism and Urban Culture in Nineteenth-Century Paris.* Cambridge, 2005.

Gold, Arthur and Robert Fizdale. *The Divine Sarah: A Life of Sarah Bernhardt.* New York, 1991.

Gooley, Dana. *The Virtuoso Liszt.* Cambridge, UK, 2004.

Habermas, Jürgen. *The Structural Transformation of the Public Sphere.* Translated by Thomas Burger. Cambridge, MA, 1991.

Hanson, Thomas. "Mallarmé's Hat." *Yale French Studies* 54 (1977): 215–227.

Harvey, David. *A Brief History of Neoliberalism.* Oxford, 2005.

Hazareesingh, Sudhir. "Memory and Political Imagination: The Legend of Napoleon Revisited." *French History* 18 (2004): 463–483.

Hochschild, Adam. *King Leopold's Ghost.* New York, 1998.

Hocke, Gustav René. *Das europäische Tagebuch.* Wiesbaden, 1963.

Hook, Sidney. *The Hero In History.* Boston, 1955 [1943].

Horowitz, Joseph. *Understanding Toscanini.* New York, 1987.

Jaeger, C. Stephen. "Aura and Charisma." *Eadem Utraque Europa* 2, no. 2 (June 2006): 125–154.

Jameson, Fredric. "Mallarmé Materialist." In *The Modernist Papers.* London, 2007.

Jeal, Tim. *Stanley. The Impossible Life of Africa's Greatest Explorer.* New Haven, 2007.

Johnson, Barbara. *A World of Difference.* Baltimore, 1987.

Kalifa, Dominique. *L'Encre et le sang: Récits de crimes et société à la Belle Epoque.* Paris, 1995.

Kohlrausch, Martin. *Der Monarch im Skandal. Die Logik der Massenmedien und die Transformation der wilhelminischen Monarchie.* Berlin, 2005.

Kohut, Thomas A. *Wilhelm II and the Germans: A Study in Leadership.* New York, 1991.

Koselleck, Reinhart. *Futures Past: On the Semantics of Historical Time.* Cambridge, 1985.

Kramer, Lawrence. *Musical Meaning: Toward a Critical History.* Berkeley and Los Angeles, 2002.

Laforgue, Jules. *Berlin: the City and the Court.* Translated by William Jay Smith. New York, 1996.

Laqueur, Thomas W. "Bodies, Details, and the Humanitarian Narrative." In *The New Cultural History,* edited by Lynn Hunt. Berkeley, 1989.

Le Bon, Gustave. *The Crowd: A Study of the Popular Mind.* New York, 1960 [1895].

Lehning, James. *The Melodramatic Thread: Spectacle and Political Culture in Modern France.* Bloomington, IN, 2007.

Leppert, Richard. "Cultural Contradiction, Idolatry, and the Piano Virtuoso: Franz Liszt." In *Piano Roles: Three Hundred Years of Life with the Piano,* edited by J. Parakilas. New Haven, 1999.

Lindenberg, Paul. *Berlin.* 5 vols. Leipzig, 1886.

Lloyd, Sue. *The Man who was Cyrano.* Bloomington, 2002.

Lorcey, Jacques. *Edmond Rostand.* 3 vols. Paris, 2004.

Maas, Ellen. *Die goldenen Jahre der Photoalben: Fundgrube und Spiegel von gestern.* Köln, 1977.

MacCarthy, F. *Byron: Life and Legend.* London, 2002.

MacKenzie, John M. "Heroic Myths of Empire." In *Popular Imperialism and the Military,* edited by John M. MacKenzie. Manchester, 1992.

Mallarmé, Stéphane. *Oeuvres complètes.* 2 vols. Edited by Bertrand Marchal. Paris, 1998–2003.

Mann, Golo. *Secretary of Europe: The Life of Friedrich Gentz, Enemy of Napoleon*. Translated by William H. Woglom. New Haven, 1946.

Mansel, Philip. *Dressed to Rule: Royal and Court Costume from Louis XIV to Elisabeth II*. New Haven, 2005.

Manuel, Jean-Baptiste. *Edmond Rostand, écrivain imaginaire*. Paris, 2003.

Marchand, L.A. *Byron: A Biography*. 3 vols. London, 1957.

———, ed. *Byron's Letters and Journals*. 13 vols. London, 1973–1994.

Marschall, Birgit. *Reisen und Regieren. Die Nordlandfahrten Kaiser Wilhelms II*. Hamburg, 1991.

Martin-Fugier, Anne. *Les Romantiques: Figures de l'artiste, 1820–1848*. Paris, 1998.

———. *La vie élégante, ou la formation du Tout-Paris, 1815–1848*. Paris, 1990.

Martin, Jean. *Savorgnan de Brazza, 1852–1905. Une épopée aux rives du Congo*. Paris, 2005.

Martin, Marc. *Trois Siècles de Publicité en France*. Paris, 1992.

Marvell, Andrew. *The Complete Poems*. Edited by Elizabeth Donno. London, 1976.

Maugue, Annelise. *L'Identité masculine en crise au tournant du siècle, 1871–1914*. Paris, 1987.

McGann, J. "Milton and Byron." In *Byron and Romanticism*. Edited by James Soderholm. Cambridge, 2002.

McLuhan, Marshall. *The Interior Landscape: The Literary Criticism of Marshall McLuhan 1943–1962*. Edited by Eugene McNamara. New York, 1969.

———. *Understanding Media: The Extensions of Man*. New York, 1964.

McVeigh, Simon. *Concert Life in London from Mozart to Haydn*. Cambridge, 1993.

Mecklenburg, Günther. *Vom Autographensammeln. Versuch einer Darstellung seines Wesens und seiner Geschichte im deutschen Sprachgebiet*. Marburg, 1963.

Mehlman, Jeffrey. "Ad Centrum?" In *Literary Debate: Texts and Contexts: Postwar French Thought. Vol. II*. Edited by Jeffrey Mehlman and Denis Hollier. New York, 1999.

Meisel, Joseph S. *Public Speech and the Culture of Public Life in the Age of Gladstone*. New York, 2001.

Meyer, David S. and Joshua Gamson. "The Challenge of Cultural Elites: Celebrities and Social Movements." *Sociological Inquiry* 65, no. 2 (May 1995): 181–206.

Minta, Stephen. "Byron and Mesolongi." *Literature Compass* 4, no. 4 (July 2007).

———. "Letters to Lord Byron." *Romanticism on the Net* 45 (February 2007).

———. "Lord Byron and Mavrokordatos." *Romanticism* 12, no. 2 (December, 2006): 126–142.

Mommsen, Wolfgang. "Max Weber's 'Grand Sociology.' The Origins and Composition of *Wirtschaft und Gesellschaft Soziologie*." In *Max Weber's Economy and Society: A Critical Companion*, edited by Charles Camic, Philip S. Gorski, and David M Trubek. Stanford, CA, 2005.

———. *Max Weber und die deutsche Politik. 1890–1920*. Tübingen, 1959.

Mosse, George L. *The Image of Man: The Creation of Modern Masculinity*. New York, 1996.

Musset Alfred de. *A Modern Man's Confession*. Translated by G.F. Monkshood. London, 1908.

Nickson, M.A.E. *Early Autograph Albums in the British Museum*. London, 1970.

Nora, Pierre, ed. *Les Lieux de mémoire*. 3 vols. Paris, 1984–1992, 1997.

Nora, Tia di. *Beethoven and the Construction of Genius: Music and Politics in Vienna, 1792–1803*. Berkeley and Los Angeles, 1995.

Norris, James D. *Advertising and the Transformation of American Society, 1865–1920.* New York, 1990.

Nye, Robert. *Maculinity and Male Codes of Honor in Modern France.* New York, 1993.

Ockman, Carol and Kenneth E. Silver. *Sarah Bernhardt: The Art of High Drama.* New York & New Haven, 2005.

Orr, Linda. *Headless History: Nineteenth-Century French Historiography of the Revolution.* Ithaca, 1990.

Panksepp, Jaak. *Affective Neuroscience: The Foundations of Human and Animal Emotions.* New York, 2004.

Paulmann, Johannes. *Pomp und Politik. Monarchenbegegnungen in Europa zwischen Ancien Régime und Erstem Weltkrieg.* Paderborn, 2000.

Paxman, Jeremy. *On Royalty.* London, 2006.

Pearson, Roger Ansell. *Mallarmé and Circumstance: The Translation of Silence.* Oxford, 2004.

———. *Unfolding Mallarmé: The Development of a Poetic Art.* Oxford, 1996.

Peters, Ursula. *Stilgeschichte der Fotografie in Deutschland 1839–1900.* Köln, 1979.

Pilbeam, Pamela. *Madame Tussaud and the History of Waxworks.* London, 2003.

Platt, Len. *Aristocracies of Fiction: The Idea of Aristocracy in Late-Nineteenth-Century and Early-Twentieth-Century Literary Culture.* Westport, CT, 2001.

Plumpe, Gerhard. *Der tote Blick. Zum Diskurs der Photographie in der Zeit des Realismus.* München, 1990.

Plunkett, John. *Queen Victoria: First Media Monarch.* Oxford, 2003.

Pohl, Klaus-D. "Der Kaiser im Zeitalter seiner technischen Reproduzierbarkeit: Wilhelm II. in Fotographie und Film." In *Der Letzte Kaiser: Wilhelm II im Exil,* edited by Hans Wilderotter and Klaus-D. Pohl. Gütersloh/Munich, 1991.

Post, J.M. "Narcissism and the Charismatic Leader-Follower Relationship." *Political Psychology* 7 (1986): 675–688.

Presbrey, Frank. *The History and Development of Advertising.* Garden City, 1929.

Rathenau, Walther. *Der Kaiser. Eine Betrachtung.* Berlin, 1919.

Rebentisch, Jost. *Die vielen Gesichter des Kaisers. Wilhelm II. in der deutschen und britischen Karikatur.* Berlin, 2000.

Reiff, Philip. *Charisma: The Gift of Grace and How It has Been Taken Away from Us.* New York, 2007.

Reinermann, Lothar. *Der Kaiser in England. Wilhelm II. und die britische Öffentlichkeit.* London, 2000.

Reinhardt, Dirk. *Von der Reklame zum Marketing: Geschichte der Wirtschaftswerbung in Deutschland.* Berlin, 1993.

Renan, Ernest. *Recollections of My Youth.* Translated by C.B. Pitman. London, 1883.

Richards, Thomas. *The Commodity Culture of Victorian England: Advertising and Spectacle, 1851–1914.* Palo Alto, 1990.

Rioux, Jean-Pierre and Jean-François Sirinelli. *La culture de masse en France de la Belle Epoque à aujourd'hui.* Paris, 2002.

Roberts, Mary Louise. *Disruptive Acts: The New Woman in Fin-de-Siècle France.* Chicago, 2002.

Röhl, John C.G. *Wilhelm II. Der Aufbau der persönlichen Monarchie.* Munich, 2001.

Rosen, Charles. *The Romantic Generation.* Cambridge, MA, 1995.

Rosen, F. *Bentham, Byron, and Greece: Constitutionalism, Nationalism, and Early Liberal Political Thought.* Oxford, 1992.

Rostand, Maurice. *Confession d'un demi-siècle.* Paris, 1948.

Rostand, Rosemonde. *Edmond Rostand*. Paris, 1935.

Rüger, Jan. *The Great Naval Game: Britain and Germany in the Age of Empire*. Oxford, 2007.

Samuels, Maurice. *The Spectacular Past: Popular History and the Novel in Nineteenth-Century France*. Ithaca, 2004.

Schickel, Richard. *Intimate Strangers: The Culture of Celebrity*. New York, 1985.

Schneider, Louis. *Aus meinem Leben*. 3 vols. Berlin, 1879–1880.

Schoch, Rainer. *Das Herrscherbild in der Malerei des 19. Jahrhunderts*. München, 1975.

Schwartz, Vanessa. *Spectacular Realities: Early Mass Culture in Fin-de-Siècle Paris*. Berkeley, 1998.

Seigel, Jerrold. *Bohemian Paris: Culture, Politics and the Boundaries of Bourgeois Life, 1830–1930*. New York, 1986.

Sennett, Richard. *The Fall of Public Man*. New York, 1974.

Shaw, Philip. *Waterloo and the Romantic Imagination*. London, 2002.

Shils, Edward. "Charisma, Order, and Status." *American Sociological Review* 30, no. 2 (April 1965): 199–213.

Showalter, Elaine. *Sexual Anarchy. Gender and Culture at the Fin-de-Siècle*. New York, 1990.

Simmel, Georg. "The Secret in Secret Society." In *The Sociology of Georg Simmel*, edited by Kurt H. Wolff. New York, 1950 [1908–1917].

Skinner, Cornelia Otis. *Madame Sarah*. Cambridge, MA, 1967.

Starl, Timm. "'Mosaik,' Stereo und Serienbild: Anmerkungen zur Vorgeschichte des Films." *Fotogeschichte* 2, no. 3 (1982): 43–52.

Steinmetz, Jean-Luc. *Mallarmé: L'absolu au jour le jour*. Paris, 1998.

Strecker, R., ed. *Franz Liszt: artiste et société*. Paris, 1995.

Streckfuß, Adolf. *Berlin im 19. Jahrhundert*. 3 vols. Berlin, 1868.

Taylor, Antony. *'Down with the Crown:' British Anti-monarchism and Debates about Royalty since 1790*. London, 1999.

Thompson, John B. *Political Scandal. Power and Visibility in the Media Age*. Cambridge, 2000.

———. *The Media and Modernity. A Social Theory of the Media*. Stanford, 1995.

Tosh, John. *Manliness and Masculinities in Nineteenth-Century Britain. Essays on gender, family and empire*. London, 2005.

Turner, Stephen. "Charisma and Obedience: A Risk Cognition Approach." *Leadership Quarterly* 4/3–4 (1993): 237–240.

Vicinus, Martha. "Fin-de-siècle Theatrics: Male Impersonation and Lesbian Desire." In *Borderlines: Genders and Identities in War and Peace, 1870–1930*, edited by Billie Melman. New York, 1998.

Vogel, Juliane. *Elisabeth von Österreich. Momente aus dem Leben einer Kunstfigur*. Frankfurt a.M., 1998.

Wachenhusen, Hans. *Berliner Photographien*. 2 vols. Berlin, 1867.

Walker, Alan. *Franz Liszt: the Virtuoso Years 1811–1847*. New York, 1983.

Watson, J.R. *Romanticism and War: A Study of British Romantic Period Writers and the Napoleonic Wars*. London, 2003.

Weber, Max. *Economy and Society. An Outline of Interpretive Sociology*. Edited by G. Roth and C. Wittich. 2 vols. Berkeley and Los Angeles, 1978.

Weise, Bernd. "Pressefotografie II. Fortschritte der Fotografie- und Drucktechnik und Veränderungen des Pressemarktes im Deutschen Kaiserreich." *Fotogeschichte* 9, no. 33 (1989): 27–62.

————. "Pressefotografie III. Das Geschäft mit dem aktuellen Foto: Fotografen, Bildagenturen, Interessenverbände, Arbeitstechnik. Die Entwicklung in Deutschland bis zum Ersten Weltkrieg." *Fotogeschichte* 10, no. 37 (1990): 13–36.

Wienfort, Monika. *Monarchie in der bürgerlichen Gesellschaft. Deutschland und England von 1640 bis 1848.* Göttingen, 1993.

Wieviorka, Annette. *The Era of the Witness.* Ithaca, 2006.

Williams, Adrian. *Portrait of Liszt: By Himself and his Contemporaries.* Oxford, 1990.

Williams, Richard. *The Contentious Crown: Public Discussion of the British Monarchy in the Reign of Queen Victoria.* Aldershot, 1997.

Windt, Franziska. "Majestätische Bilderflut. Die Kaiser in der Photographie." In *Die Kaiser und die Macht der Medien,* edited by Generaldirektion der Stiftung Preussischer Schlösser and Gärten Berlin-Brandenburg. Berlin, 2005.

Winzen, Peter. *Das Kaiserreich am Abgrund. Die Daily-Telegraph-Affäre und das Hale-Interview von 1908.* Stuttgart, 2002.

Wortman, Richard S. *Scenarios of Power: Myth and Ceremony in Russian Monarchy II: From Alexander II to the Abdication of Nicholas II.* Princeton, 1995.

Yalom, Marilyn. *Blood Sisters: The French Revolution in Women's Memory.* New York, 1995.

❧ INDEX ☙

Winfrey, Oprah, 182
witchcraft, 112
World War I, 6, 22, 145, 148, 164, 169
World War II, 127, 137

Zapatero, José Luis Rodríguez, 3
Zola, Emile, 7, 88–91, 108, 137, 150–51,
155, 186n16, 213–14n16